TRAUMA

Essays on Art & Mental Health

Dodo Ink, an imprint of Dodo Publishing Co Ltd
30 Hollinwood Road,
Disley,
Stockport,
SK12 2EB,
England.

www.dodoink.com

Cover artwork: Christiana Spens
Cover design: Andy Soameson
Editing: Sam Mills and Thom Cuell
Copyediting: Sam Mills, Seraphina Madsen, Venetia Welby
Proofreading: Dan Coxon
Typography and typesetting: Ben Ottridge

ISBN: 978-0993575877

TRAUMA

Essays on Art & Mental Health

Edited by Sam Mills and Thom Cuell

For Tony Herbert

CONTENTS

INTRODUCTION

Jenn Ashworth

The morning I sat down to read these essays, I had spent an hour or so tidying my kitchen and attempting to restore it to some kind of order after the rigours of a week at home with my children, who were not at school. I found myself crushing up the cans for recycling more carefully than usual by putting on my hiking boots and taking the empty tins outside so I could stamp them flat. I folded cardboard into tiny pieces, shoved egg boxes inside cereal packets, and stamped those flat too. I wanted everything to fit inside the recycling box I was about to drag to the kerb, with lots of room to spare.

I am not – I hope it goes without saying – usually so careful and fastidious a housekeeper. It was only after I'd wiped the surfaces and sat down with these essays and a coffee that I became curious about what I'd been up to. What had possessed me? *The bin men might not come*, a voice floated up from deep inside and gave the answer to a question I'd been too anaesthetised by the addictive pleasures of work to ask earlier.

TRAUMA

It is hard to imagine a more appropriate time for an anthology like this, when even those of us cushioned from illness, bereavement and financial disaster are learning the hard lessons of impermanence and dependence. Of having the truth of our precarity revealed to us suddenly, harshly and relentlessly. That morning I met a part of me in shaking fear – even in the midst of the dull, unremarkable preparation for a working day. Fear for the loss of routine, for the loss of the people I rely on for comfort. I want to be clear: this is not suffering. It is nowhere near suffering. But it is the mood in which I read these essays. I read them, of course, during the first lockdown of 2020 when we were all, through losses large and small, life-changing and merely irritating, dislodged from the dream of certainty and forced to attend to our own – and others' – vulnerability. I struggle also to imagine the shape of the world that you – we all – will exist in when you read them for yourself. So I write into a gap, a space, a kind of fertile *nothing*.

The recycling epiphany is nothing to write home about. It is good news, isn't it, that the supports I have greedily taken for granted have been exposed (a minor *apocalypse* – the word means 'a sudden revelation') in the truth of their contingency? It should be embarrassing to remark on this, given what else is happening in the world. But to speak or write about trauma often involves a kind of weighing: a reckoning. Is this – this fear about the bins – bad enough to count? In her short essay collection *Intimations*, written in the time after 'the global shit hit the fan', Zadie Smith performs a similar calculation. 'Privilege and suffering have a lot in common. They both manifest as bubbles, containing a person and distorting their vision. But it is possible to penetrate the bubble of privilege and even pop it – whereas the suffering bubble is impermeable.'

These essays remind us how difficult it is to attend to ordinary personal traumas and fearlessly articulate them. Saskia Vogel, in 'Nacre', faces the problem head-on: 'I never think the legacy of abuse in my life is worth talking or writing about because it's run-of-the-mill suburban nuclear family stuff. It's not the trauma of war. I should just soldier on. Who am I to describe what I carry with me as trauma?' Sometimes bravery is enacted in a refusal to 'soldier on'. Some essayists allow us into the privacy of personal traumas – Neil Griffiths' powerful dispatches from the front of depression in 'Madness as Such' or Rhiannon L. Cosslett's vivid articulations of post-traumatic nightmares in 'Sleep No More' or the unravelling of the intricacies of care, loss and grief that Tomoé Hill explores in 'Inheritance is Silence'.

This 'run-of-the-mill' stuff (which is anything but) is laid against explorations of the systemic traumas inflicted by a sickened society. Thom Cuell remarks on the Black Lives Matter movement and the UK's necessary confrontation with its own racism in the context of a denial that is both a symptom and a cause of damage. Most women have a story of 'ordinary sexual trauma' like the one Monique Roffey relates in 'The Fishbowl' and Emma Jane Unsworth's rage-filled explication of post-natal injury in 'Halleluiah' is more than an account of personal pain, but acts as a necessary corrective to the 'PR sheen-y bullshit' that controls the stories women are supposed to tell about childbirth.

Similarly, the account Naomi Frisby gives of coercion and deceit in intimate relationships in 'Recipe for Madness' is both a personal story, and a systemic one about power. These private stories benefit us all.

The strength of this collection is that the essays which comprise it take a satisfyingly and democratically wide-ranging view of exactly what it is that causes the trauma. We co-experience a relapse into addiction in Azad Ashim Sharma's 'Narcopoetics', or understand the after-the-fact horror of finally acknowledging the scale of its damage in 'Pornography and Me' by Tamim Sadikali. A single tweet by Donald Trump brings into focus the terror of a world careering towards catastrophe in 'The Madness of the Real', a striking essay and a call to action by James Miller. Other writers take a more oblique view, addressing the trauma by glimpses and side-swipes, from childhood memories of disaster movies in 'In the Mean Time' by Catherine Taylor or the implosion of an abandoned hospital in Juliet Jacques' confronting tale of disaster tourism in 'What Are We Looking For Here?' The nature of intergenerational and second-hand trauma is also acknowledged, from Tom Tomaszewski's examination of a difficult relationship with a complex father in 'Landing In Poland' to Christiana Spens' essay 'Inheritance', which uses art to bring unspoken shames and traumas of relatives that died before she was born into the present. Alex Pheby acknowledges that sometimes – often – the thing itself just cannot be spoken, only written around, in his startling essay 'How to Write About Things That You Can't Think About.'

INTRODUCTION

These essays demonstrate that it is through these glimpses into individual lives and experiences that we have a hope of understanding the inevitability of our common human vulnerability. We learn, for example, just what trauma does to time. The 'present-tenseness' of the traumatic aftermath is a recurring theme, as is the fragility of life lived alongside disaster. 'We know it is temporary, the summer will be a mere caesura,' Catherine Taylor reminds us, and captures the breath-held anxiety of life lived after the shock.

Trauma inspires, and sometimes requires, a retracing of one's footsteps – a return to childhood events and experiences in therapy, as Jude Cook explores in 'Thanks, I'll Take the Chair' or even, as Marina Benjamin says in 'Soma', to previous writings, previous writing styles and voices – in order to find the gaps, the elisions, the places where the work, as well as the life, might have been done differently. In 'Unravelling the Self' Joseph Schreiber provocatively returns to previous diagnoses and the gender assigned to him at birth in an attempt to construct a present free from the constructions of others. 'Do we ever know who we really are? What does a diagnosis truly hold? How much does it form your identity, become something to cling to, define and explain the strange and uneven way your life has unfolded?'

Even the idea of 'after' is carefully interrogated. We might be tempted to think of it as some kind of post-explosion heaven, where we'll look back at the horror that kicked us out of innocence from a place of safety and wisdom. After the bang, after the shock, after things get back to normal. But none of these essays – even the ones interested in hope, in healing and recovery – deliver a sentimental view of trauma's aftermath or feed us undercooked platitudes about hard won wisdom, post-traumatic growth, characters formed in adversity or similar nonsense. Venetia Welby addresses this directly in the opening of her essay on insomnia, 'The Art of Lost Sleep': 'I was an interdimensional being, exempt from the normal rhythms of humans. You might think that the upside of this is that it leads to some sort of unearthly wisdom. You would be wrong.'

The reality, as dramatized in this collection, is that the traumatised live a double life: they do carry on, or parts of them do. They return home from hospital, they are patched up, they attend their NA meetings and arrive at their psychotherapy appointments. They go to work and the cinema and have sex and Sunday dinner and meet their deadlines and laugh with their friends at the pub, on the street, at parties. They are out and about, in the world, functioning well. And they are also flies, trapped in the long-set amber of their disaster, compelled through flashback, nightmares, compulsive rumination, acting out, remembering or even some kinds of therapy, 'to return to the moment, to fix it, to survive it.'

In 'As Deep as the Atlantic: On Grief and Writing', Kirsty Logan and Paul McQuade, through a wide-ranging conversation that the essay form makes possible (and more on the essays' varieties of forms in a bit) address this doubleness of existence – the way the traumatised person both gazes helplessly over their shoulder at the wreckage while also preparing themselves for the blast – with arresting clarity: 'It is too late to get ready and that is all we do.'

And yet, life does go on. This is both its inevitable joy and its obscenity.

Perhaps trauma does not only require us to go on in different ways – to find, to use a recently overused phrase, 'a new normal' – but to acknowledge something other than the here and now without obliterating it. The expansion is spatial but not linear – we might have our feet rooted on the scorch-marked ground of our injury, but we're able to see a little further than we once did. Some of these essays use trauma as a way of thinking about either the necessity or painful absence of that something bigger or beyond. *Is there nothing,* one or two of the writers seem to ask, *that is unbreakable*? At the end of 'Blank Spaces', a sensitive and precisely shocking essay about suicide, Yvonne Conza intends to 'say a prayer for the fallen flock'. On reading this we wonder – I wondered – if it isn't only the addicts who may need to rely on, as Azad Ashim Sharma puts it, 'all this god stuff'.

Others find their way through less numinously. Several of these writers ask the question: can art help us with the faltering process of living in the aftermath? Can a story or a poem, a film or piece of art or music help us, and if so, how? In her essay 'The Clown', about clowning and clown therapy's ability to reach the most traumatised of children, Susanna Crossman argues that this type of drama – the serious business of clowning – might provide 'the right material to straddle a river's flow'.

Any mosaic finds its pattern in the spaces between its not-quite-fitting parts. An anthology gives us room for alternatives, for *yes, but what about this* – for *and* rather than *or*. So there is disagreement here – as there is in any healthy system. On the one hand, reading's power to remove us from immediate horror – especially when, as children, we cannot remove ourselves – to comfort and console us, to provide both refuge and succour, are passionately explicated by Anna Vaught's 'In Order to Live'. Momina Masood writes about the ability of cinema to respond to the wounds caused by state oppression. No mere distraction or escapism, the darkened, private yet communal space of the cinema is the place where 'we heal, we find kinder ways back to our bodies, to our mothers, to our collective and historical pasts.'

Additionally (not alternatively), writing (the doing of it and the reading it), slippery and double-dealing as it is, can also provide the necessary disaster to shake us out of a safe, busy life, blanketed in denial and ignorance. Good writing can provide the urgently necessary 'ethical shock', as James Miller argues, that will wake us up as certainly as a bomb or a fall or a pandemic could – and indeed, as many of these essays do. And David Lynch, in his essay 'On Creativity and Meditation', reminds us how deep the creative unconscious runs, and how necessary it is to a life fully lived.

As a parting shot, it is no coincidence that many of the traumatic metaphors these essayists deploy – the earthquake, the flood, the volcanic eruption – remind us of how out of our control the process and sudden movements of the natural world are. Even something as innocuous as a cloud can become a portent of trauma, can remind us of the persistence of shock and the way it lingers, ricocheting down the generations: 'Sometimes I've seen clouds holding onto shapes for so long after the storms in which they've swirled and rolled from one moment to the next have ended.' (Tom Tomaszewski, 'Landing in Poland'.)

We are all held in the hand of the world, a world that is in a crisis of its own. Climate disaster and the threat of mass extinction is the terrible secret that lies between the lines of many of these essays and is addressed directly by Thom Cuell in 'Denial and Difficult Knowledge', where they explore what we do with the things we don't want to know.

As I finish the draft of this introduction my friend is in London, attending the Extinction Rebellion protest. He takes films and pictures and uploads them to Instagram, and vicariously, from my safe and comfy settee in Lancaster, I observe the spectacle, answering my guilt for not being there with a bouquet of excuses about the children, the deadlines speeding past me. None of this matters of course – not the school run (lockdown is over – for now), nor school full stop, nor deadlines, nor the cat food tins I am still carefully flattening before recycling – not when we're already on the edge of the precipice and reaping the rewards of our willful ignorance of our interconnectedness. Death is everywhere: from coral reefs to care homes. It is too much to imagine.

Refusing to imagine it ('it'? – whisper it, then – *death*) is part of the 'great derangement' that Amitav Ghosh has noted in fiction's response to the ecological disaster unfolding around us. An omission that speaks to a great cowardly madness – both a systemic symptom of mass trauma and a cause of it.

I'm not sure that novelists as a breed are an irredeemably short-sighted or cowardly bunch, though I am convinced that the essay rather than the novel is disaster's home form. Anna Maconochie's cartoons, too, are able to hold the moment, to gesture towards the unspeakable while at the same time raising a smile. In this anthology these writers take advantage of the essay's capaciousness: the way this form can hold both the imagined event, and the refusal or inability to countenance it. The essay's freedom from plot and therefore time, its ambiguous relationship with modes of argument and persuasion, its incursions into the lyrical and poetic utterances, the malignant poetry of the repeated image – (Rachel Genn's 'Stingray' being a fine example), its ability to hold image, as Christiana Spens' essay does, to represent silence and ellipses, as Alex Pheby and Neil Griffiths' essays do, to take off from the personal into the political, the biographical and the historical – as Seraphina Madsen does, to contain humour, self-deprecation and the anecdote, as Ian Boulton does, to utilise space, shape and typography to demonstrate the simultaneous contradictions between inner and outer worlds, as Rowena MacDonald does... I could go on. The essay's indeterminacy as a form gives it a near unique ability to show hospitality to suffering, to feel it and think it, to show it and tell it, to speak it and gesture at the unspeakable all at the same time.

INTRODUCTION

We talk about this for a while, me and my friend at the
Extinction Rebellion protest in London – or rather, we type
to each other in Microsoft Teams, which is what suffices
for talking these days. We talk about mourning and hope.
I think it's too late, I tell him. I really do. I don't think it
matters if I do my recycling or not. I don't think we can
stop what is coming. There is no more certainty – or there
never was, we just know it more keenly now. There will be
more floods, more fires, more pandemics and all the rest of
it. And in the face of disaster big and small, systemic and
personal, and the inevitable, criminally unfair unevenness of
suffering caused by them, we will need to find a way to live
with each other more kindly.

Perhaps Extinction Rebellion, through its imperfect
cacophony of small groups, the commitment to non-
violence and inclusion (artlessly and incompletely achieved),
is offering us a model whereby anger and mourning and
love can exist together. For what else is mourning other than
allowing yourself to get painfully acquainted with loss, with
taking the absence – the lack – right inside yourself? Perhaps
these groups and others like them show us a different way
of *going on* together while the world that holds us lets us
go. Or maybe I am just dreaming, here on my settee, coffee
in hand. I think of the conclusion that Monique Roffey
comes to after the new experience of hearing men – so
often turning up in her life as perpetrators – talk about
their pain in another one of these groups – the blame-free
circle of listening of the therapeutic 'fish bowl'. I think of
the way that Sam Mills, in 'The Shattering', writes about her
father's schizophrenia – of the loss, the confusion, the grief

– but also, movingly, of the love that exists between them: sometimes clear, sometimes obscured, but always there.

At the end of her essay on suffering, Zadie Smith reminds us of the ethical worth of attending to our own bad days. This ability to acknowledge our own sufferings is not a luxury – a mental spa-day for the spiritually inclined – but an essential component of compassionate relation with the other. Admitting the reality of our sufferings – puny as they may be – is a preparation for 'that next painful bout of video conferencing, so that you don't roll your eyes or laugh or puke while listening to what some other person seems to think is pain.' The essays in this collection invite us to look but not judge, to hold accountable but not to blame, so let's not get into weighing whose pain counts, and whose can be dismissed, ignored, swept away.

Instead, reading these essays requires us to become what Saskia Vogel calls a 'suitable listener' – or, in these times, a suitable face on the other end of Zoom, or a suitable three-dots coming and going at the end of a weeks-long Microsoft Teams chat. This suitable listener is neither priest nor therapist, but fellow-sufferer – alive to both the experience of others, *and* to the disowned, suppressed or abandoned pockets of his or her own suffering. We meet them in the form of two policemen walking coast-to-coast to raise money for charity in Georgie Codd's essay 'Hazelnuts'. They walk alongside her, sharing jokes and energy gels as she completes her own journey. Is 'friend' the right word for this relation? Reading these essays requires us to be willing to befriend our own sorrow and turn up to the page with all our vulnerability acknowledged. The idea (recklessly innocent, but what else do we have?) is that this model of friendly attention – a kind of open-heartedness, or shared-heartedness – will inspire the compassionate action we are so badly, urgently in need of, or at least provide a hopeful space (that fertile *nothing* I write into when I imagine where you might be when you pick up this book) where it may appear.

NACRE
Saskia Vogel

The traffic slowed on the 101. It was late at night, and I must have been on my way home from a party at a friend's house in the Valley, almost certainly a kinky one, where I'd have been a bit shy but enjoyed the freedom the atmosphere afforded me. I'd probably have been thinking about how I loved my friends, enjoyed my sex life, but just wasn't finding that spark with anyone. My friend and her house were the reason I was so often on that freeway in those years, zipping past Universal City through Hollywood on my way home to my sublet room in an old apartment in Echo Park, where the founders of Spaceland used to host gigs before there was a Spaceland and before I moved in, or so I heard, and that would catch fire soon after I moved out, most likely faulty wiring, but that's a different story, easier to tell. So many parties and late nights, so little romance back then. All I wanted was to fall in love.

The lanes were bright with red brake lights, the hills around me dark. It could have been a concert letting out, nightclub traffic, something to do with the movies. Across the lane, I saw a car parked, driver's door open. An accident? That's when I saw them: the couple standing in the middle of the freeway, wrapped tight in each other's arms. It was as if their eyes had met across the lanes, a flicker of recognition passed between them, and they had to stop right there in the middle of this flow. *I've crossed oceans of time to find you,* that aching line from *Bram Stoker's Dracula.* A split second later I passed the second parked car, and they were out of view. The river rolling me along, the couple embracing like it was the beginning and end of the world.

'Crazy love,' he'd say. Crazy, crazy love. And it was. Will you take my word for it? I've told that story so many times, and every time I tell it, it wears me out and I feel shaky again. I talk about him like he's the worst thing that ever happened to me, and in some ways he was. My body bruised. My trust broken. I no longer recognised myself. If a person who said he loved me so deeply could harm me, then anyone could. Love was no guarantee. I felt ashamed because I should have known better, should have heeded the warning signs that were there from the start. I should have been better than this. Had I let myself slip just because he liked *Bram Stoker's Dracula* too? Its logline: Love never dies. I felt ashamed because physical violence, emotional violence, and lying constituted a hard limit for me in theory, but in practice, I wanted to stick it out. I had hoped that what had once been good could be good again. I chalked lots of things up to confusion and things not being what they seemed. Did I have no self-respect? I wanted so much to believe in this crazy love, the look in his eyes when he said it, the way it made our love feel special, like something no one else could have. Two bodies in the second lane of the Hollywood freeway, locked in an embrace. Of course it didn't start there.

At a family funeral this summer, we were all crying around a table in a bar in Stockholm. One child was sharing the complicated feelings he had about this loss. My mother said: we're always sitting with three generations of pain. I thought about the hole she once told me she has in her heart, and what put it there.

I remember the mood in my grandmother's house. Tense. It was a terraced house in the suburbs of Vienna, shaded by a tree my mother had dug up as a sapling in the Vienna Woods and replanted in her garden. My grandmother was a jolly woman who would make sure there were mini-yoghurts and plastic pots of chocolate pudding topped with industrial whipped cream for me in the fridge. She'd make gulasch because it was my favourite. When I think about the way my mother was with her, all of this stops. I remember us upstairs in my mother's old bedroom, sitting on the bed, my mother whispering instructions to me, codes of conduct, afraid that we'd put a foot wrong.

There was the ghost of a dead man on the stairs – my grandfather, who'd died of a heart attack, young, when my mother had already left Vienna for Stockholm, long before I was born. The dead man on the stairs and a devil at the door, threatening to steal my grandmother away. Nothing

unusual about a devil at the door, not on St Nicholas' Day
when a half-goat half-demon appears to punish children for
their misdeeds. It was just the neighbour in costume, who
thought it funny to play a little joke, above and beyond the
script that comes with this tradition. It took me a long time
to connect the twitch of horror with which my mother tells
this story from her childhood with everything else I know
about her. I'm only really starting to make this connection
now. Why am I so slow?

I wrote 'grandmother,' but I'm not sure which one. There
was her stepmother, the woman with the mini-yoghurts,
chocolate pudding and gulasch, the only grandmother
I knew. My mother would later tell me when I was old
enough to understand: *She beat me.* And then there was my
biological grandmother. She abandoned her young family,
then pretended to her new husband that she'd never had a
child. My grandfather? Kind, generous. He'd tried to make
the best of things, the story goes, but was unaware of what
was going on between his second wife and his daughter.

I related to these stories with a certain factual distance,
never quite understanding what they meant until one night,
during a poisonous argument, my mother, exhausted,
conceded that she had a hole in her heart. *The love pours
in, but I can't feel it.* Until that moment, I'd thought of her as
endlessly strong, the two of us battle-ready, only ever steps
away from entering the ring. My sister has a much easier
relationship with her. To me, my sister says: *You and mom,
you just rub each other the wrong way.* She makes it sound
so simple. I'd always felt that if I bit my tongue, if I didn't

stand my ground, something in me would be annihilated, falling through the hole in her heart, never touching its sides. (There are other stories I can tell you about her, her acts of love, support, and patience, especially when I needed care. My mother gave me my love of books and writing, but those are different stories, aren't they?)

What is trauma, and how am I supposed to write about it? I never think the legacy of abuse in my life is worth talking or writing about because it's run-of-the-mill suburban nuclear family stuff. It's not the trauma of war. I should just soldier on. *Who am I to describe what I carry with me as trauma?* I ask my therapist. She tells me that the big traumas I'm referring to, like the traumas of war, and the ones I'm talking about can express themselves in the body in the same way: fight or flight responses, the release of cortisol, adrenaline. The events might be different in intensity and scale, but they can have the same physiological effect. For some reason, when she brings some science into it, I'm receptive. Maybe it's okay for me to write about this. I still don't understand that not all families have these stories in their past, not all mothers have holes in their hearts, not all families have poisonous arguments. Not all children are cowed and waiting, tense, for their parents to snap and fly into a rage. Not all children have such a shaky sense of self, walking through the world believing everyone else to be more of an authority on life and living than they are. Not all children have such a shaky sense of self that all they see when they see a couple hugging in the middle of a busy freeway, all they can think of is: them, they've got love down.

Never mind what led them there. My Crazy Love drove me to strange places, too, moments so surreal they don't make sense anymore, more like bad dreams than anything else, the way his lies stalked us through the city and appeared like ghosts in our everyday. The lurch of cortisol and nausea when certain names appear in my inbox, still. My therapist and I talk about this distance I have to the stories I tell about the things that hurt, and I keep trying to bridge it, to 'sit with the feeling,' and although I want to, although I try, I don't think I know how. Of course, you feel this distance here. You've noticed my elisions.

A friend in my writing group tells me that of course this essay is full of elisions. It's in the nature of trauma to elide a coherent narrative. The internal consistency of what I'm writing is likely to be sound, she says, but when it comes to talking about what has traumatised me, I'm likely to use a different language for the telling of those things compared to how I narrate the rest of my life. I describe trauma to my therapist as an event that is out of joint. I draw a line in the air, beginning to end, then wrench a chunk out of it and set it at an angle.

My mother, a therapist, tells me about the success she's having applying a technique called Narrative Exposure Therapy, in which she helps her clients suffering from PTSD establish a coherent narrative about their lives in which they contextualise their trauma. I've experienced PTSD. It was my diagnosis, which I treated with the same distance as everything else. I'd tell people I had PTSD like I'd tell them about tickets I had to a concert. It gave me a framework that helped me make sense of myself, but mostly it felt incidental, like a virus dormant in the blood. My mother's clients tell her about their trauma, and she asks them for all the details, and asks them to tell her their story again and again. The story of the trauma, but also how hot it was that day, what they were dreaming about, what else was going on in their lives. I wonder if this is what she's always done: *She beat me* is less clear to me than the image of her cat Mautzi lazing in the cool garden, teasing the sparrows with one outstretched paw, or the nylon stockings her father presented to her biological mother soon after the end of the Second World War, and the game my mother would play with the milk can, swinging it in fast circles so the milk would not spill, not even when it was overhead.

When I talk about my Crazy Love, the crazy love is all I talk about: our arguments, his violence, the lies. And then I marvel that 'it' was happening in the same period as I was actively trying to make a different life for myself. I was applying to grad school and moving back to London, where it took longer than expected for my boxes to arrive, so I had to make do with a summer wardrobe in an autumn that was, at least to me, exceptionally wet and cold. I mostly had pencil skirts and blouses of a certain kind, which I'd packed because I also had a job that required me to go into an office once in a while, and the old friend who I was to live with in London insisted I had the same vibe as Sherilyn Fenn in *Twin Peaks*. My hair was shorter then. Her hair made her look like Françoise Hardy. Are these the details that are supposed to help? Does it help that I'm telling you?

NACRE

I'm trying to put the pieces together, trying to find that bridge, trying to defuse the trauma, trying to master it. I'm committing an act of memory. Philosopher Susan J. Brison, in her essay 'Trauma Narratives and the Remaking of the Self', writes that this act will only work if I have a suitable listener, a trustworthy community. Am I right in thinking it might be you?

There was a time when my mother and I were having a fresh spell of arguments after a period of calm, and I was together with my Crazy Love. I remember thinking: my arguments with him and her, they're no different, except for the violence, which was unique to him. I remember noticing that these arguments had a similar flow, a similar arc. We'd speed to the edge of a cliff and rev the engine, but at the last minute, we'd reverse, four wheels on solid ground. But it's not 'reverse', really. When you argue like we did, there's something that gets broken down. It's not resolution so much as capitulation. The arguments ended with me making promises, atoning for my behaviour, accepting my blame. They were always in the right. The script of the arguments with her, the arguments with him, it was an uncomfortable echo, to say the least. But maybe it was also the sand in the oyster, layer upon layer of nacre, that meant eventually I could roll right out of there.

I was an echo for a while, a liminal being, a ghost. I put an ocean between my Crazy Love and me because I knew he wouldn't follow. I moved in with my old friend. She was about the only person I trusted enough to spend time with.

We wore leather jackets, smoked Parliaments or menthols, and always drank rye. At university, I could just about stretch to tea with my classmates, but I was afraid of everybody and tried to keep things superficial. I was boring. As soon as I opened up to anyone, I'd tell them about him, and when I did I'd feel it all again and all I wanted was to not be carrying this with me and by sharing it, I was making them a part of it too, so I tried to keep my mouth shut. I acquired a minor eating disorder.

I wondered if I really was a worthless slut who would never be loved by anyone but him, he who so kindly overlooked my faults. The funny thing is, once away from him I really started to feel like all the terrible things he'd said I was. In his presence, I felt defiant. I was battle-ready, standing my ground. In his absence, defiance was replaced by dread: could it be true? Had I deserved this crazy love? Was crazy love all the love I would know? When I tried to be more like a 'normal person' and started going out into the world, I was afraid of what people would see. I no longer knew how I could expect myself to behave. I wasn't sure of who I was anymore. I decided to gather data about myself. I set some ground rules, limits that would help me understand how I felt by keeping me from losing myself in something else. I wouldn't go home with anyone or bring anyone home, but if I wanted to I could flirt. I'm embarrassed by how square that sounds. 'Flirt.'

'Flirt' had become such a dirty word. I was lugging around a strange set of morals, his. I'll put it flat and plain: he wanted a heteronormative relationship, where he could be the patriarch and fill me up with kids. He drew me a picture of it once, literally. Me in a long skirt with three kids admiring a milestone in his career, the year specified. It was on a yellow Post-it. I was horrified. To have three kids that old by then, we would have to start now. I couldn't imagine wearing that skirt; mine were mini or midi-length at most. He didn't know me at all. Another grain of sand. Until death do us part, he asked me to promise, under threat of rage. Anything else was a betrayal.

Brison might say that by going out and trying to be social, I was putting myself in relation to others to see what 'self' was there. If, as per Judith Herman's book *Trauma and Recovery: The Aftermath of Violence from Domestic Abuse to Political Terror*, 'the traumatic event destroys the belief that one can *be oneself* in relation to others,' then, as Brison adds, 'without this belief one can no longer *be oneself* even to oneself, since the self exists fundamentally in relation to others.' I wanted to see what was there. I didn't want to be a ghost anymore.

I cried every day on the bus to uni, right when it reached the end of Fortess Road and I could see the sun glinting on the train tracks at Kentish Town, the beauty of it and the far away of it all, me on the top of a double decker bus, it was so picturesque, until I think about what led me there. I couldn't sleep, so I streamed TV shows until my eyes closed for me. Why didn't I read books? The only thing I was good at was staring. And hot yoga. I did a lot of hot yoga. I'd cry there, too, in camel pose.

There was one other person who I felt safe with. At first we never talked about our love lives, but later we'd tell each other that we'd both applied to grad school because we were looking for transformation. Hilarious really, that we both thought an MA in Comparative Literature was the answer to a life that wasn't rolling in the right direction. We'd have dinner once a week, usually. It was my big meal. I'd eat so much I'd feel full, stuffed. I'd eat meat and cheese and bread and fries. I remember a revelatory puttanesca. And we'd talk about everything but this. That's all we'd do: eat and talk. I couldn't tell if I wanted to love him or if I just wanted the satisfaction of knowing he wanted me, and I wasn't sure that he did. The fact that he never made a move was confounding. What did he want with me if he didn't want sex? I resigned myself to us being buddies, and remember thinking that if this is all we'd ever be, at least I'd know that a person like him existed. Someone kind. Someone who allowed me to believe that I could trust again, and that I was a person worthy of a gentle, honest love.

Two people meet and promise they will never do harm to the other in the way that harm was done to them. They embrace, clinging to each other like two people stranded in the second lane of a midnight freeway. First flush of love, all is well. One day they will have their first fight. A proper fight, a big one, and they will realise they are not fighting with each other, but they are fighting with ghosts. But unlike in the past arguments they've known, something compels them to stop, pause, not react for once but witness. The one says to the other: I don't know who you're fighting with, but the argument you're making, it doesn't relate to me. And the argument I'm making, it's not for you. They sit down on the bed in silence, the four of them, the twelve of them. My mother has a hole in her heart, one of them begins. The other looks at her, not just looks, but really tries to see. When it's his turn, she does the same for him. They do this again and again. It is the beginning, and it is the end.

SOMA
Marina Benjamin

Last spring, as leaves unrolled to catch the light and flowers nosed their way out of bushes and plant pots, the American writer Melissa Febos took to social media vowing to drop the word 'seminal' from her lexicon of praise: because 'why should formative, ground-breaking things evoke semen?' The post caught my eye, since in conversation with writer friends I'd recently taken to excoriating my younger self for having considered Gore Vidal king in all matters of style, as if he were the acknowledged fount of literary and linguistic innovation. After Febos put out a playful call for female-centred alternatives to 'seminal', sourced in women's pleasure zones, I joined the gaggle of respondents who offered a string of high-spirited replies. Because it made me laugh and picture cartoonish ideas budding, ballooning out, then floating off like soap bubbles, I suggested *boobissimo*. But the coinages that really sang to me announced themselves with more poetry: clitoral, oveal, vulvate, luteal, lacteal, hysteral, gyntastic. Here were terms that evoked dark and brooding spaces – undergrowth, caverns, grottos, hidden streams, the richly symbolic unconscious: places where things might be synthesised from organic mulch and unusual elements combine, becoming impressed with secret shapes before oozing forth from the gloaming. There was something messy and uncontainable about these words, so unlike the clean linearity we associate with sprouting seeds.

Febos clearly had politics on her mind. She wanted to kvetch about the way maleness is always and everywhere universalised, not least when encoding creative achievement. It is the seed not the egg that implants ideas in our heads and suggests vistas pregnant with possibility; and the seed (or inspiration) that counts, even when the most promising ideas need to gestate before they can bloom, or incubate, or marinade: that is, sit for a time in a stew of nutrient-rich fluids. Her post made me think of the way maleness aggrandises itself, arrogates territory to itself, then 'others' the things it discards. It made me think of those early modern theories of reproduction that imagined microscopic homunculi folded up inside every spermatozoa, the egg conscripted only to provide food and shelter.

Although the alt.generative terms Febos crowdsourced were contrived to make a point, the same way 'herstory' makes a point, they hit my ears just so, setting off a chain of satisfying little tingles all along the neural axis that links visceral sensations to head and heart. I have been thinking a lot lately, you see, about the co-dependence of language, body and self, the way each constitutes the other and the inescapable sense it makes to acknowledge that where we speak *from* and who we speak *for* is bound up with our experience – not just as historical beings but as material beings. I have been thinking about this, and in ways that run explicitly counter to all my old commitments, ever since having my uterus and ovaries removed six years ago. At the time, I hoped the surgery would free me, and it did, from the daily drag generated by my fibroid-mangled organs, which had a way of stopping me in my tracks, paralysed with pain, and from the different kind of drag that came from living with the bleak spectre of ovarian cancer. With my organs gone I moved more lightly through the world.

But I was unprepared for the toxic shock of sudden menopause that caused my body to snag up like a choked machine, gears rattling, rivets loosening and popping off, red lights flashing at the controls. It was as if one set of problems (compromising, but nevertheless known) had been elbowed aside only to make room for a new and entirely foreign set, more onerous than the ones they had replaced. Instantly I swung into fire-fighting mode, determined to combat the rage, tearfulness, severe depression, insomnia, night sweats, fatigue and memory loss that arrived out of nowhere to assail me, failing to see that all the while I was so intent on putting out the flames the ground was giving way elsewhere. Something more nebulous was happening to me. My centre of gravity was shifting, or migrating, my sense of self, dissolving: the person I'd always been was morphing into who knows what.

Displaced from any sure-footed terrain, I wandered about the world queasily off balance. Out and about on basic errands in my neighbourhood, I'd be so high on a sense of unreality as to be practically levitating; and because language is expressive of our material natures, not just the seemingly free-floating thoughts 'inside' our heads, my command of that suffered too. In the weeks after my surgery, when I'd turned bodily from a linguistic modality that felt compromised, I may as well have been a hologram. I'd speak to people in the course of everyday encounters only to be looked through and unheard.

A range of interesting speech impediments took hold. Where once I communicated fluently, without giving the mechanism a second thought, I now kept stalling, lapsed and confused. Words flew from my brain and dissipated upwards on the breeze like a flock of summer-seeking birds. Nouns, in particular, kept disappearing. To this day I have no idea what was happening in cognitive terms, since there was never a time I did not recognise objects or grasp what they were about, it was just that I couldn't name them.

This broken link between word and object matters. When you name things you acquaint yourself with the world, reinscribing it daily via a ritual 'hello again'. More importantly, you constitute who you are to yourself. You affirm that you're the kind of person who notices this or appreciates that, has an affinity for this and an aversion to that, who arrives at an understanding of their particular interiority through calibrating the temperature between inside and out. Noun-mute, I had a hangdog feeling of being locked out of my own mind. The place I was speaking *from* was the void.

Now and again, I surprised myself with what did come out of my mouth. I'd say 'pencils' instead of 'flowers', substitute 'wallet' for 'fridge'. If my husband shot me a look of concern I'd brush it off, joking that my brain appeared to be hung up on morphological resemblances. Yet too often sentences that began well, with clear intention, would lose direction and peter out or else freeze abruptly, midway between the starting line and the finish. Too many times, talking to someone at home, at work, socially, my mouth would open and nothing at all come out. Perpetually I strained for language without finding it, dredging and trawling my brain only to surface dumbfounded. People looked at me expectantly and in apology I'd shrug. I figured this was what dementia must feel like from the inside. But given that trauma is by definition unspeakable, I can't help but wonder now if my problems with language weren't masking something else.

***

In all its varied symptomology, menopause put me on intimate terms with what Virginia Woolf, writing about the perspective-shifting properties of illness, called 'the daily drama of the body'. Its histrionics demanded notice.

Menopause asked that I pay closer attention to bodily experience almost minute by minute, because with each bodily dip and lurch, each hormonal spike and roundabout, every shiver and sweat that wrenched my guts, a new filter was placed between my reality and that of the larger world. As Woolf described the push and pull of it in regard to illness: 'meaning comes to us sensually first, by way of the palate and the nostrils, like some queer odour,' but because this proximal knowing – raw, experiential, strangely insistent – so fully absorbs us as it twists our existence around new co-ordinates, 'the whole landscape of life lies remote and fair, like the shore seen from a ship far out at sea.'

'Landscape of life' is just right. Its connotation of painterly remove perfectly captures how, when ill (or menopausal), we're estranged from the world beyond our sickbed. Turned inwards, we have to contend with an immediate reality prone to kaleidoscopic collapse, or sudden reconfiguring: once familiar, its shapes, textures and smells (that 'queer odour') grow alien. No wonder Woolf called for a new language – 'more primitive, more sensual, more obscene' – for describing where we speak from when we find ourselves in this altered state. We need, she insisted, to 'speculate carnally'.

Woolf's endless struggles with nervous fatigue and what we might now call manic-depression are well known. She suffered multiple breakdowns, often following the completion of a book, as if the process of writing it was what kept her sane. The year before she wrote her short essay *On Being Ill*, she'd fallen down in a faint at her sister's house in Charleston. She'd been over-working, as usual, and though she couldn't admit it to herself, she was 'a little used up & riding on a flat tire'. The faint led to many months of illness, debilitating headaches and rest cures. She felt weak, then melancholy. She wanted to begin *To the Lighthouse*, said she had 'a whole novel in my head', but she was forbidden by her doctors from writing. Then T.S. Eliot commissioned her to write an essay for the *New Criterion* and *On Being Ill* (1926) was the piece she submitted. He was less than enthusiastic about it, which naturally sent Woolf into fresh spasms of anxious self-doubt. She worried about her 'wordiness' and the 'feebleness' of her writing.

Woolf's essay bears all the hallmarks of having been written in the heat of the lived moment and with all the feverish urgency of a patient wanting the particulars of their condition to be better understood. There is constant reference to the body throughout, to its intrusiveness, its insistence on being heard, its animal wants. In illness, the body dominates our existence: it is at once tuning fork and transmitter, the principal medium through which experience resonates through us. Perhaps this explains why, for Woolf, the ill are so lawless – unlike 'the army of the upright'. Subject to the wiles of a body that ails, and yet wants, the ill become rash, wilful and contrary; they spurn sympathy, wallow in sensation. Their critical faculties, responsibilities and good sense desert them, and into the vacuum 'other tastes assert themselves: sudden, fitful, intense.'

I am ashamed to say that I came late to Woolf's fiery essay, after having given a book-length account of my own menopause as an embodied experience, raw and visceral as anything I'd encountered, either in the tumult of puberty or childbirth and early motherhood, or in the shuddering grief of losing a loved one. I wrote it as I lived it – as an embodied woman, come into the inheritance of ageing. It was a passion project, something I had to write, and full of carnal speculation, and it was turned down by every major publishing house: when my proposal was doing the rounds back in 2014, none seemed able to muster an appetite for such corporeal reckoning with womanhood. Then again, before crashing headlong into menopause, neither could I. Looking back over my earliest efforts in non-fiction, I see only cerebral books that wilfully trespassed into areas that bore a distinct masculinist pedigree. They concerned end-time religious cults, the space age and Middle Eastern geo-politics. The minded body – my minded body – didn't get a look in.

I do not subscribe to simple binaries that insist 'this is female' and 'this is male'. Never have. But every feminist knows that male cultures and male hegemonies are not in the habit of announcing themselves as male. They just are. They are what we have and what we are asked to accept is the way the world is. If you put your neck out as a woman and give voice to female experience, or travel against the grain of patriarchal norms, you risk marginalising yourself. But I wish to do something a little different here. I wish to denounce my own former (and, at the time, unconscious) collusion.

This is my affidavit. My first book about millennial end-timers was an act of ventriloquism. The words I mouthed in it were not mine, the posturing borrowed. In scope and tone, the book was crafted to engage a critical-professional class of reader largely made up of men, the assumption being that if you write like a man then maybe men will read you. But I wasn't really writing at all. I was channelling. Much of the time I worked on the project various 'style bibles' sat on my desk, beside my computer, most of them by Gore Vidal, whose orotund, word-clever sentences I sought to emulate, and when it wasn't Vidal, I modelled my thinking on Frank Kermode, Oliver Sacks or Richard Holmes, men with evident status and to whose authority I deferred, every one of them now a Dead White Man.

Deferring, demurring, apologising, explaining themselves: this is what women do when they intrude on male territory. Did I think these 'intellectual giants', or their successors, would beckon me into the fold of their unremarked privilege? Offer me a matey pat on the back as they pressed forward to open doors? Did I think they might review me, or use my book in the classroom? I did not. Yet at some fundamental level I believed that if I cloaked myself in a masculine aura I might somehow pass for the real thing.

Proof of concept aside (after all, I'd produced 80,000 words and arranged them into some kind of coherence) there's practically nothing about that book I'd defend as authentic. I wish to be precise here, because the very qualities it aspires to are those I now repudiate in my work. Where to begin? The book pretends to expertise – and not in a humble way that acknowledges due diligence by the research, but with a brash swagger that today makes me cringe. It aspires to comprehensiveness, that is, to a lofty generality and off-handed sweep. It is too loud (in places), at times pompous, and it wears its puffed-up learning like chest-borne medals. It is a piece of performance art, a strut in literary drag. In projecting a persona that bears no resemblance to my own, I seem to have pulled off with that book a smoke-and-mirrors extravaganza worthy of Oz-style wizardry. Except that where the wizard booms and declaims, the persona I cranked into being is more portly, bookish and self-satisfied, more patrician, entitled and unquestioning. If I listen in close enough, trying to catch what lives between the lines of my book, all I can hear is the wind blowing through empty space – a howl of under-confidence.

I know now – indeed, I knew then – how to think differently. I knew that *the master's tools will never dismantle the master's house*. I'd travelled back and forth pondering the merits and demerits of an *écriture féminine*. I was all too aware of the feminist thought police, who, if you didn't renounce the patriarchy at every turn, accused you of being 'self-hating'. I even had role models to look towards: Janet Malcolm, Joan Didion, Julia Blackburn, women writers who managed to 'pass' without compromising themselves. And still I wrote like a man. It is not that second-wave feminism offered no alternative ways to be and write and dream, but the options available did not come made-to-measure for every feminist fit. The politics of difference, in particular, hinged on a relentless separatism that forever dragged women back to the body, enchained them to it, and in ways that were the opposite of liberating, at least for me.

It is difficult for me to recapture now, as a woman who has always gravitated towards cerebral things, my horror of biological essentialism. When politicised at university in the mid-1980s, it was Wollstonecraft's rights-based politics that I clutched to my chest, not rediscovered ancient goddesses, fertility cults and white witches – those shades of old female power from which I instinctively recoiled for bringing back to me my ancestral Baghdadi bubbas whose bony grip I imagined extending from beyond the grave to claim me. I found 'wimmin' whimsical, while the righteous feminism, symbolised by the buzz-cut, bulldozing lesbians who strode across campus striking terror and guilt into my very soul (ostensibly about shaving my legs, but really about being heteronormative), felt needlessly tyrannical. I joined a consciousness-raising group where I cried each week and railed against my disciplinarian father, but there I was made to feel bad for being femme and for sleeping with men. Also for using tampons – slated as just more evidence of self-hate since they mimicked the penetrative prerogative of the penis (others, clearly more self-aware than I, preferred moon cups, or so they said).

Mostly, I resented the way any kind of 'feminine' logic was anchored in women's flesh, which became the groundsoil for flourishing dualisms: women were 'naturally' more peaceful, men aggressive; women listened, men opined; and while men gazed, women submitted to being seen then shaped themselves into what men wanted to see. *If women ruled the world, they wouldn't have made such a hash of things.* This was the anti-war cry of the day, heard everywhere. And so it went. I can't have been the only feminist in my generation concealing a knee-jerk repugnance towards everything Greenham Common.

Or indeed, a distaste for the high-flown French feminist philosophy that situated female subjectivity in the groin. With my troublesome gynaecology, problematic even in youth, I sought escape into the pain-free and unbloodied immateriality of pure (and as it turned out, male-colonised)

Mind. I had no time for theorists such as Luce Irigary, who seemed to think it was a good thing if a woman's voice, her thinking, her female jouissance, was essentially vaginal: 'in her end is her beginning', wrote Irigary in *This Sex Which is Not One* (1977), picturing a female subjectivity that perpetually revolves around itself, its edges never-ending, lips always touching, and at its centre, a nothing.

It is not uncommon these days to hear women castigate themselves for internalising male judgement, even personifying it, and granting a miniature judge and jury or god-like father and white-haired lawgiver the right to enthrone themselves inside their heads.* But whether or not as a legacy of my struggles with second-wave feminism, I have also got a righteous second-waver kicking ass inside my head, perpetually telling me how to be a better feminist. She doesn't shave, or even wash much: she's not a pleaser. She slobs around the house in her dressing gown for much of the day, grazes at the fridge door, neglects her family's needs, her mothering duties and her daughterly duties, and justifies all of it in the cause of furthering women's interests. This is the feminist who wins the day when I am writing and I don't always like her. But she has earned the platform because for a long time she put up and shut up while the miniature judges strutted about, tut-tutting at my failings.

Looking back now, I can't quite believe she wasn't more vocal back in the days when I was man-aping. Especially since I

---

* See Claire Vaye Watkins's essay, 'On Pandering', published in *Tin House*, 23 November, 2015, and Olivia Sudjic, *Exposure*, Peninsula Press, 2018.

never stopped identifying as a feminist. And especially since feminism itself was widely regarded at the new century's dawn as an artefact of the 1970s, quaint as hotpants or glitter-framed specs, while the girl power of the 1990s looked like little more than a marketing ploy. Still, my sweaty, snarly, stompy avatar was ready to bring me back to myself when I was lost. Emptied out by menopause, my sentences thwarted, she reminded me that I could not, after all, escape biology. Even if it was not exactly a female biology I was now reckoning with, but a non-biology or mirror-image biology: one that substituted a set of curious absences for the politically (oftentimes physically) bothersome presence of femaleness.

It bears repeating that if ageing brought with it an unexpected inheritance of undreamed of and unwanted experiences – which, with only the old repertoire to hand, I had no language to frame – it also placed me beyond reproductive life, if not in fact beyond the body. I was now on nodding terms with the barren woman, the bitter woman, the empty vessel, the widow and the crone, all of them singular types but converging upon an archetype almost as repugnant to feminists as to anyone else: the spent woman, the woman whose purpose is no longer evident, whose use value has expired – the woman whose very existence requires justifying. It represents (I represent...) the stony ground on which nothing ever seeds. In fact, you can scatter any amount of seed upon this ground and nothing seminal will ever take root. What kind of subjectivity dwells in this desert terrain?

I hadn't a clue. But I hadn't a choice either. If I was going to give adequate testimony of menopause then I would have to write from inside of this altered state, re-routing my thinking via a body-consciousness that had broken free of rules and rhythms and gone rogue. Instead of pretending that there was no crisis of the self, I would write directly into the crisis, attending closely to my anomalous symptomology and sticking fast with that feeling of being unmoored. Here was a manner of self-witnessing that, oddly enough, already had correlates in other guises. The outsider looking in, the ingénue delivering dispatches from the frontline, the anthropological participant-observer, the existential voyager: all of these tropes fit with my field-noting agenda.

But there were still things I had to learn. In venturing forth like a querent, I'd would come to cherish not knowing over knowing, to value answering every question with another question. I wanted to 'live the questions', just as Rilke instructed the young poet who sought his advice on writing to do: 'perhaps one day', wrote Rilke, you might 'live your way into the answers'.

One thing was clear: the male voice I had earlier ventriloquised, with its unitary, forward-pointing, linear intent, wasn't going to cut it when it came to exploring my traumatised state of lack (hormonal lack, the absence of a reproductive identity, the profoundly alienating experience of sleep deprivation). It was too assertive to dwell inside the gaps of broken language and explore the silences therein, or brave the void and bring absence into presence.

Just as you can feel enlarged by giving things away, you can build confidence, in writerly terms, by being humble. I don't mean posing as humble, hedging everything you say with 'possiblys' and 'perhapses'. I mean actually revelling in not knowing. I mean interrupting yourself and entertaining contrariness, letting your thoughts wander then circle back upon themselves, trail off and fragment. For me, it was a liberation to let it all hang out, put it all on the page. And that went for the body, too, in all its menopausal, ageing complexity.

Like Woolf, I had been forced to acknowledge that at every turn 'the body intervenes' but does not define us. It opportunes us, blindsides us, pleads with us, pleasures, pains, arouses and depresses us, sways our judgement and shapes our sense of self. Which is to say our bodily self-consciousness has a hand in forming our subjectivity. Writers can heed it or not, though I find I'm increasingly drawn to those who do – Adrienne Rich, Maggie Nelson, Carmen Maria Machado and many others. The point is that in pain or grief, love, rage or illness, in hormonal extremes or sleepless desperation, the body gifts us a window onto the world that changes what we see by virtue of shifting how we see it.

Audre Lorde, so passionate about and precise in using language, so committed to its world-creating potential, celebrated the notion of *feeling* our way into knowledge rather than thinking ourselves into it. She understood that the body knows, and that this knowing, calling on skin and gut and nerves, ears, eyes and tongue, is individual and particular, not categorically gendered. I like to think of this knowing as a 'somatic sensibility', and these days I actively cultivate it. Not just because it gifts us a sensory idiom ('more primitive, more sensual, more obscene,' just as Woolf envisaged) but because it carves out a place for writing that jars, disrupts and disorientates, just like the experiences it inscribes. I can't think of anything more radically feminist than to return to the body – not as an acted upon thing, or a passively gendered substrate, but as an agent – and cross-question what it is to be female.

THE MADNESS OF THE REAL
James Miller

Seven a.m. and as usual I'm awake shortly before my wife's alarm goes off. I lie in bed, listening to the traffic outside, resisting the urge to check my phone.

What has happened what has happened what has happened?

Okay. I give in and check my phone.

BBC News. *The Guardian.* Twitter. Overnight, the algorithms have prepared a selection of 'highlights' for me. They're all hellish.

The day has hardly started, I'm still half asleep, but already the dread has escalated. There's no point pretending I can escape the crisis: it leaks out of my phone, continuously, and by the end of the day – even though I don't watch a single news bulletin – I'm exhausted, sickened, drained by what's happening, worn out by the gloomy certainty that although it has been going on for years this nightmarish turn to world historical events is just getting started.

Among the manifold horrors delivered to me through my phone is the fact that Trump has tweeted again.

Of course, he's always tweeting.

I don't want to look at it.

I certainly don't want to write about it – but I am. I'm going to write about it. Briefly.

I'm sorry.

For a start, what can we say? Each Trump tweet is an act of violence against language, truth, decency, tolerance and democratic values. The world's biggest troll playing the world's biggest victim, gaslighting supporters and enemies alike. Each tweet a violation of so many 'norms', so many conventions, so many...

Oh fuck it.

Look, I'm sorry. This is the tweet I'm going to talk about:

Donald J. Trump ✓
@realDonaldTrump

(Follow) ⌄

HAPPY NEW YEAR TO EVERYONE, INCLUDING THE HATERS AND THE FAKE NEWS MEDIA! 2019 WILL BE A FANTASTIC YEAR FOR THOSE NOT SUFFERING FROM TRUMP DERANGEMENT SYNDROME. JUST CALM DOWN AND ENJOY THE RIDE, GREAT THINGS ARE HAPPENING FOR OUR COUNTRY!

5:08 AM - 1 Jan 2019

Now, as a 'Presidential' New Year's message it is unusual, to say the least. But as a Trump tweet it is mild, compared to many – the attacks on Congresswomen, American footballers, Hollywood celebs, the mayor of London, the quote tweeting of racists, the endless defensive whining... I mean, to attempt to itemise Trump tweets, to list them, to attempt to understand or engage – well, this way lies madness. A creation far stranger than any fiction, far less plausible than any fiction. And yet, here we are...

As we all knuckle down to endure a President who resembles a left-wing satire of a megalomaniac right-wing President, what struck me about this particular demented tweet was his reference to what he calls 'Trump derangement syndrome.' Because, if nothing else, Trump – his Presidency, his tweets, the whole shebang – is one of the clearest signs that 'reality' is broken. Or if not broken, then certainly deranged. And I'm using the word in the fullest sense, not just in the common meaning of 'insane' but literally dis-arranged – out of order, disturbed. We see the mad king, delighting in his misrule. The performance of Trump's Presidency is underpinned by a sort of wild nihilistic joy, one that says: it's all a lie, it's all a joke. And it has released a troubling libidinal energy; the sexual-energies of fascism as noted by Wilhelm Reich are fully on display at every Trump rally as the mob brays 'lock her up' or 'build the wall' or 'send them home.' Everywhere, violence. The horrible ecstasy in the faces of his supporters: it's like a religious service – after all, America has perfected the fusion of entertainment with religious and political performance until the three are pretty much indistinguishable – but for all their appeals to Jesus and the Bible, their real God is Moloch and Trump's congregation cathect their frustrations and resentments in a frenzy of performative hatred. Trump licences their emotion, gives them permission to speak their unspeakable desires: his Presidency, his authority, the final 'proof' that the Law is obscene, the Law is a joke, that everything is a sham: the state has no truth, no ethics, no restraint, as if Trump is the real spirit of the Law, the obscene Father – a rapist, an abuser, a fraud – look at me, he says, here I am with my dick out, masturbating in your face. Suck it up.

Over there we have Trump. Over here we have Brexit. And now, Boris Johnson. A mini Trump. Another self-invention, another confection for the media... another celebrity buffoon fronting a criminal government of hard-right extremists.

Time for some deep breaths. Maybe a walk around the park. It's very confusing, really, to ponder how all this has come about. Was I really so out of touch?

Since World War Two the Anglo-American world – cultural, social, political, economic – was predicated around a spectrum of assumptions. Assumptions which the majority of people internalised and accepted, even if they were outwardly critical.

The idea, for example, that the Anglo-American world was at the vanguard of progress.

The idea that the rest of the world – whether post-Communist, post-colonial or the global South – would gradually become more like 'us' and move away from totalitarianism, religious extremism and sectarianism towards a form of liberal democracy.

The idea that our elected representatives had some share in a common good, that they were rational actors, reasonably sane, and even if they were tainted by special interests or a degree of corruption we still felt as if these failings could be checked by robust legal and political structures.

The idea that pragmatic, technocratic government is more effective than one oriented by ideology – by which I mean fantasy, delusion, nonsense, idiocy. Fact-based government, evidence-based government, grounded in a pragmatic tradition and compromise, one that respects its own rules, mandates and mechanisms (the independence of the judiciary, the impartiality of the civil service, for example).

Time for another walk around the park (yes, already). Or perhaps just scream into your pillow. Whatever helps.

Back in the 1990s, I read a lot of postmodern theory.

I considered myself a postmodernist.

I still consider myself a postmodernist. Sort of.

Back in the 1990s some of these ideas were very exciting, but also quite abstract and hard to connect with the lived experience of reality. Baudrillard's hyperreal, for example: an image of reality that's more real than reality itself. Wow! I mean, I sort of got it – like video games or drone footage from the first Gulf War – but at the same time, I didn't. Things were still basically analogue. We still had landlines. I wrote letters to friends abroad. We left one another notes on the doors to our rooms. Techno-Capitalism had not yet learnt to monitor, analyse and monetise our movements. No one could have imagined than in a few short years we'd be arguing about politics with Russian trolls masquerading as patriotic Englishmen in just 280 characters. The distinctions between celebrity and politics, entertainment and news were slipping (remember Ronald Reagan? Good times) but they were still there, just about.

I remember reading Jean-Francois Lyotard, *The Postmodern Condition*, in which he writes about the end of metanarratives. Metanarratives were clunky old-fashioned things like the Bible, nationalism or Communism. They clearly didn't work, they were done, the vector of world historical progress showed as much and it was exciting to think of the multiple, fragmentary, personal narratives that would replace these lumpy old dogmas. As Lyotard puts it: 'Postmodern knowledge is not simply a tool of the authorities; it refines our sensitivity to differences and reinforces our ability to tolerate the incommensurable.' Yay! We would be liberated from totalising Truth, free to explore our own partial, contingent truths – a bit of this, a bit of that, fashioning versions of ourselves like a groovy remix album.

The trouble is – as Lyotard's quote acknowledges – 'postmodern knowledge' was also 'a tool of the authorities.'

There was another metanarrative, one we couldn't quite see because it was so inconspicuously all-consuming: neo-liberalism, an ideology disguised as a pragmatics (an economics) that also promised an end to ideology. But in 2008 it was undone as real debts were called in on inflated values. Reality bit hard.

Ouch.

Perhaps it's possible that things could have been done differently. But then came... nothing... except more neo-liberalism, a zombie neo-liberalism, a neo-liberalism of last resorts and elite interests, accelerating the transfer of wealth from the majority to a new transnational aristocracy of finance bros, tech bros and oligarchs. They got much, much richer and the rest of us got poorer, working hard for less in a desperate scramble to the bottom. As Timothy Snyder notes: 'For many Americans, oligarchy meant the warping of time, the loss of a sense of the future, the experience of every day as repetitive stress. When economic inequality suppresses social advance, it is hard to imagine a better future, or indeed any future.'

Pragmatics led to a different sort of ideology, in which money and monetisation became the chief source of value, an instrumentalised force to eclipse all others. And capitalism is nothing if not expansive, a rapacious, invasive force, relentlessly short term, a force that engulfs time, that works to reduce the experience of time and reality into totalised moments of intensity; a force that respects no boundaries, no orders, no hierarchies, no traditions or sanctuaries. There were still a few redoubts – education, the arts, healthcare, journalism, law – places that claimed to exist for something more than or other than the profit motive. But like virgin rainforest before the developers plough, they too would be opened up, levelled, all possible profits extracted. This is the end game we're dealing with. But hey, back in 2008 we had Facebook and then Twitter and Instagram, virtual worlds where we could fashion versions of ourselves and where – without us really knowing – the algorithms would mediate our experience of reality to suit our prejudices and then sell those prejudices as data, extracting surplus value from every little click and like. The super-rich tech bros and their backers got richer and more powerful. The rest of us didn't, drifting ever more into a perpetual present alternating continually between tranquilised distraction and anxiety triggers (usually via the same device – our true friend, our most constant lover – the ubiquitous smartphone).

Indeed, something else started to happen. Via devices dependent on GPS systems people began to think that the world was flat, that vaccines could kill you, that Trump was a credible Presidential candidate, that refugees were a menace, that leaving the EU was a good idea.

With this transition, other counter-narratives began to creep back, filling the void left as the general population fell out of love with neo-liberal globalised capitalism and began, instead, to understand their experience of the world as cyclical, repetitive and hopeless. No longer the progressive narrative where everything was supposed to get better. No one can really imagine the future anymore. Snyder calls this the shift from a politics of inevitability – where 'no one is responsible because we all know the details will sort them out for the better' to one of 'eternity' where 'no one is responsible because we all know the enemy is coming no matter what we do.' He argues that under the politics of eternity a nation is placed 'at the centre of a cyclical story of victimhood' and eternity politicians 'instruct their citizens to experience elation and outrage at short intervals, drowning the future in the present... eternity politicians deny truth and seek to reduce life to spectacle and feeling.'

Sound familiar?

It's no wonder everyone is so stressed and anxious and depressed and angry.

I'm so stressed and angry I'm writing an entire essay about a Trump tweet!

Fuck me...

It's hard, as a writer, to know how to respond to all this. Is there a way in which writing can disrupt or disturb such an experience of time or the appearance of the everyday? Jolts of perception, juxtapositions that might lead to awakening? Intervals in the cycle of outrage, moments of pause, brief resistances to the endless shitstorms of idiocy... is it too much to hope for? Literature as a critical-utopian construct? It wasn't so long ago people believed art had a value that had nothing to do with money.

Just look at me harking on with my quaint ideals.

No, let's just click on a mindfulness app and enjoy five minutes by ourselves. 'Re-connecting.' Focus on the sensations in the body (perspiration, racing thoughts, pounding heart, a bad taste in the mouth, lack of concentration, lack of appetite, diminished desire) try not to think about the news.

The phone that leaks the crisis is also the phone that has the mindfulness app...

There is a tacit connection between literary form and political ideology. Since the mid-nineteenth century the dominant literary mode – for the novel at least – has been realism of one sort or another. The *Oxford English Dictionary* gives these relevant definitions of the adjective *real*: having an objective existence, a foundation in fact; actually occurring or present; natural; genuine, true, honest, sincere. Realism implies fidelity to nature or to real life, to accurate representation without idealisation and the exploration of mundane, sordid or trivial incidents or 'ordinary people' that once upon a time would have been deemed unfit or unsuited to literature.

In the nineteenth century, with Balzac, Zola and Dickens, realism was a radical mode for all these reasons, because as it shed light on the lives of the poor, it humanised the working class and enabled the middle class to experience moments of sentimental outrage when faced with sympathetic, humanised representations of the terrible consequences of industrialisation. As Ian Watt and subsequent scholars have shown, realism as a literary mode is inseparable from the rise of the middle class and the concept of the private individual. The realist novel also shares foundational reciprocities with courts of law, its rules of logic and evidence, witness and proof. The idea that there is a tangible, common reality we can all agree on: that events have definitely happened and these events mean something. Time and history are subject to narrative time and via this mediation and the organising structures of the realist novel, historical events and the lives of historical figures become legible. From this, the Anglo-American worldview expands to embrace human rights and democratic franchise (first for men, then everybody*), private property, a private life, the rule of Law and capitalist free enterprise.

But wait, wait, wait – what, I hear you say, has any of this got to do with mental health? I thought this is what this anthology was about – depression, anxiety, insomnia, abuse – what on earth does any of that have to do with realist modes of fiction, the rise of the novel, blah, blah, blah.

* well, sort of

Well.

My thesis is this: slowly, but surely and for reasons outlined above and others too complex and occult to discuss here, the Anglo-American world has, for want of a better word, gone mad. 'Trump derangement syndrome' is part of it. Brexit another. The fragmentation, compartmentalisation and intensification of lived experience via social media would be another; both an inciting factor and the determinant field where much of this conflict is performed. Then there are other meta-contexts. Paramount, the crisis of global warming and the collapse of planetary ecosystems – a problem so vast and so totalising it eclipses everything and yet is still ignored by President and Prime Minister alike. And by saying 'it' has gone 'mad' I mean that a huge chunk of political-media discourse has divorced itself from reality, which is another way of saying it has lost touch with the truth. To quote Ihab Hassan: 'the perpetually moot issue of realism is, at bottom, one of truth, but that truth is not transcendental or foundational: it is a matter of trust... I mean personal, social and epistemological trust.'

And as we've seen, as we now know, there's no trust anymore. Writers of fiction have an unusual relationship to the truth. On the one hand, we're all liars. We make shit up. But this shit has to be credible, it must have some basis in 'the truth' otherwise no one will 'believe it'. Which is to say, they'll stop reading and turn their attention to some other made up shit on Netflix, Twitter or whatever garbage Trump is saying. (Who am I kidding, no one who votes for Trump ever reads an actual book. Fuck me.) The complex relationship between fiction and the truth also has its corollary with the rise of auto-fiction, where much of the pleasure of the text emerges from the implicit speculation that what is recounted did/did not happen, foregrounding both the authenticity of the narrator/speaker and the relativity of all experience and perception. It represents, too, a withdrawal from the sort of grand social fictions of the nineteenth century: the writer no longer presumes to speak for or understand the whole of society or the world-historical moment, the writer can merely explore their own contingent truths and experiences grounded in their subjective identity.

Let's face it – if a writer wrote about a President like Trump, no one would believe it either. 'That's funny,' they'd say, 'but it's a little far-fetched, don't you think?'

So, can we, as concerned writers who still harbour naïve hopes that we might leave the world in a better place than we found it, can we restore some meaningful truth to fiction, to the novel – is there a way to bridge the disparate and broken realities of the present, to cut through the bullshit and generate an ethical shock strong enough to bring the world (or at least the reader) back to their senses?

Because, actually, the end of truth, this loss of trust, isn't quite as fun as we thought it would be. It's not liberating, it's enslaving and terrifying. Ihab Hassan again:

> Pragmatic or 'soft' universals... enable both individual and collective judgements. Without them, the UN Declaration

of Human Rights would vaporise; without them, Amnesty International would whistle in the wind; without them, jurists at The Hague would sit in an empty court; without them, Greenpeace or the Kyoto Protocols would founder in the Pacific. In short, without qualified generalisations, no appeal to reason, freedom or justice can stand.

Perhaps we need to remember something. What is happening, here and now, is not particularly new. Or rather, it's new for us, isolated as we are in our Anglo-American exceptionalist bubble. But ask the Argentinian or Brazilian intellectual, the secular scholar in India, Pakistan or Bangladesh, the activist who lived through Apartheid, the ordinary citizen of a post-Soviet state – what's reality been like for them?

Perhaps, if we seek a literature of sanity that is also able to reflect the derangement of present-day reality, a literature that can stand as a site of resistance to the spectacle, that can remind us that our experience of reality is, in part, a fabrication designed to serve the interests of the rich and powerful, then perhaps we need to look towards the literature(s) of these nations, these people, these experiences. Writers like (to take some contemporary examples) Roberto Bolano, Annie Ernaux, Svetlana Alexivich, Adania Shibli, Olga Tokarczuk, Fernanda Melchor, Mathias Enard, Agustin Fernandez Mallo, Amitav Ghosh, Percival Everett, Irenosen Okojie and Camilla Grudova to touch on just a few. In them we may see, reflected back, a dim outline of what it is we are going through. And, perhaps, we can find inspiration, strength and solidarity. Old tools to build new weapons, elixirs to cultivate forbidden dreams.

Who knows? Maybe, by the time you actually read this, things will be different.

Perhaps they'll be better?*.

---

* Some good news. In between writing and publishing this essay Trump lost the Presidential election to Joe Biden. Fuck Trump! Let us hope that by the time you're reading this, the Anglo-American world is finding its way back to semblance of sanity, valuing compassion and kindness over division, disorder and dishonesty.

IN THE MEAN TIME

Catherine Taylor

Three months ago, on a cold, sunny day in the middle of March, my boyfriend left me.

In his defence, the leaving was not wholly intentional. It is the year 2020: the year of contagion, of pandemic, of panic and denial. When we exchanged our usual rushed goodbyes in the middle of that Tuesday afternoon, we expected to meet again at the end of the week, or the beginning of the following one. The rest is woeful recent history. By the Friday the schools closed; Monday brought the lockdown, its steel shutters slamming down on all our lives.

His domestic arrangements are such that we cannot for the time being, or possibly ever, live together; in addition our houses are miles apart across the city. We had anticipated the separation, but in the end it happened so abruptly, with such swift indecency. Once the death toll started to climb in Italy, the insistence of the myriad autoimmune conditions bequeathed me through genetics, and which are so daily present as to almost make up a second, more rancorous me, took hold. As a result I have, at the time of writing, been alone for three months. Our parting, uncannily, resembled our coming together almost four years before: suddenly, in the middle of a crisis, and without much forethought.

Lying in bed together on that last day, with the trees barely in bud outside, and the warmth and occasional clicks from the boiler reassuring against the hard early spring, I revisited *The Towering Inferno*. I have a morbid passion for the big-budget disaster films of the early 1970s – aged fourteen, I was the only willing watcher of doomed ocean liner movie *The Poseidon Adventure*, shown with some irony on New Year's Eve – the day the film's actions take place – in the cramped cinema room of the cruise ship on which I and my classmates spent the Christmas holidays that year, as part of an educational trip to what was then called 'the Holy Land'. The film is one of my clearest memories of that two-week period, along with the sharp, sweet taste of the oranges we bought on the road to Jericho.

One scene in *The Towering Inferno*, in which a botched development job turns the lavish opening night of the newest, tallest skyscraper in San Francisco into a blazing calamity, continues to stick with me. In two smaller roles, Robert Wagner and Susan Flannery play lovers taking the opportunity to sneak away from the grand party and hole up in an office room on the 65th floor. When the fire takes hold, Wagner's character makes an ill-judged dash into the smoke-filled corridor to seek help; Flannery's is left alone to die as the fumes creep under the door. I recounted this scene to my boyfriend, who looked alarmed; over the weeks

I have had much recourse to mull over it, and to ponder the implicit moral judgements around the fate of those two characters. The one running away to meet his death; the one remaining behind to meet hers. The fact that no one knows they are there at all.

Writing on the Seattle-based film review website *The Parallax View* in 2015, Robert C. Cumbow comments:

'*The Towering Inferno* is a good movie about a fire. That is its strength. Its weakness is that, despite a promising array of characters and several passable actors, it is a very bad movie about people.'

On the evolution of the disaster movie, which reached its heights in the 1970s, and the inevitable squandering of what Cumbow terms 'character studies', he goes on:

'As the disasters got bigger, the people got smaller, and the only kind of response most viewers could give to the people on the screen was to play the guessing game of who's going to live and who's going to die horribly.'

Big disaster, smaller people: wars, famines, genocides, pandemics; like a roaming, endlessly greedy King Kong, they threaten variously to swallow us all up. How can we do more than react; how can we retaliate? My father's favourite film was Michael Curtiz's *Casablanca* (1944). The best scenes in the movie, the shivery, stirring ones, highlight its central triangle – Humphrey Bogart, Ingrid Bergman, and Paul Henreid. 'It doesn't take much to see that the problems of three little people don't amount to a hill of beans in this crazy world,' Bogart's character, Rick, famously says to Bergman's Ilsa. Born in 1928, my father would have been sixteen when Casablanca was released in a world exhausted from five years of war.

Sixteen was also the age when I stopped almost all communication with him; we wouldn't meet again for another fourteen years, by which time I was thirty. Big disaster, small person.

I have always had a strong sense of what psychologists categorise as separation anxiety; and it solidified into intense fear at the age of nine, when my parents split up: another unforeseen, completely unanticipated occurrence. My father had been having a relationship with another woman for about a year: in the spring, just before my birthday, he left our family and did not come back. Before that awful, and still unendurable, point, I was too young and too oblivious to notice what was happening – the parent/child divide was more clearly delineated in the 1970s, and when I questioned my mother about why my father wasn't coming home at night, she would say that he was working in the bookshop that they had set up a few years before. 'Is he sleeping on the shelves?' I remember asking. In fact, my father was sleeping in a house on the same road as my school – situated conveniently on the opposite side of a crescent – so that I was spared the sight of him and his girlfriend there, before they moved away from Sheffield and to another city. After this I did not see him for two years, until a court order enforced the soon-to-be hated regularity of fortnightly access visits, where, on alternate

Saturdays, I would sit, frozen with misery, in my father's car, as he enumerated his dislike of my mother and all the friends who had stood by her, and not him, after the divorce. (We no longer had a car of our own: bailiffs had come to our house and taken it away when my parents' business went bankrupt after the marriage ended.) Looking back now, at a distance of nearly forty years, I can only imagine that these meetings were as desperate and unhappy for my father as they were for me. At the time I could not comprehend what had happened to replace the adored and adoring parent with this weeping, angry stranger.

Once, my father sent me a present of a cuckoo clock: so alarmed were my mother and I at the noise of ticking issuing from the parcel that we fleetingly thought it might contain a bomb. Nevertheless, we opened it, and hung the clock on the wall in the kitchen, where it kept neither the time, nor its temper: I was relieved when it broke a few months later. By this time my relationship with my father was also hopelessly impaired, and despite intermittent attempts to fix it, would remain that way until he died.

To compensate for the small-scale disaster movie in which my early life had a starring role, I have tried to build a good one, but its interiority – already exacerbated by having no actual job, exchanged a few years before for the precariousness of freelancing – only increased with self-isolation during the lockdown. Several commissions, the generosity of friends and neighbours, and emergency grants kept me going, but I also felt trapped in time, similar to the years immediately following my parents' divorce: the contented before, and the alien after. In Meg Wolitzer's 2005 novel *The Position*, this type of non-recovery from the early disappointment of family break-up is beautifully expressed: 'There was closure in every divorce, but a new fissure opened up each time, too, a pit that could never be filled in, for just look at those bitter or mournful faces, years later. Just look at those grown-up children, lumbering around the earth with their freight of sadness and detachment.'

Detachment is essential for writers. While others succumbed to mass readings of Defoe's *A Journal of the Plague Year* or Tolstoy's *War and Peace*, Zoom meetings and bake-offs, I mostly kept away from anything which resembled the simulacrum of a social life. Too distraught and afraid to do very much, I retreated to the sofa, curled up, and waited for it all to pass over me and to end. My throat ached constantly as it had for weeks – did I have it? Had I had it? Would I?

Time passed, and a sort of order formed. The last art exhibition I had attended was in late February, when I had gone with my boyfriend to the Jewish Museum in Camden to catch the final few days of *Life, or Theatre?*, Charlotte Salomon's extraordinary series of gouache paintings depicting her life in Berlin before and after the Nazi rise to power, and her later exile in France until she was transported east and gassed at Auschwitz in October 1942 at the age of twenty-six. Salomon's father and stepmother survived her, as did most of her *Singspiel*: an autobiography and a self-portrait. In *Life, or Theatre?*, which to contemporary audiences most closely resembles a graphic novel, Salomon, born into a cultured, assimilated Jewish family in Berlin, worked through her traumatic past, her terrifying present and her foreshortened future. Her mother had committed suicide when Salomon was eight; in 1933, when she was sixteen, Hitler became Chancellor of Germany. Salomon separated from the rest of the family in late 1938, directly after *Kristallnacht*, by moving to the South of France to look after her maternal grandparents, a transplanting which was to have devastating results. It was there too, in Villefranche, near Nice, that her creativity flourished. An only child, the sole representative of the next generation, she declared her exile – away from parents, lover, friends and the city in which she had been born and had grown up – to be the source of her art: 'I had to go deeper into solitude, then maybe I could find – what I had to find! It is my *self*: a name for myself. And so I began *Life, or Theatre?*'

During that visit to the Jewish Museum I was repeatedly drawn to Salomon's self-portrait of her bedroom the night before she left Berlin. Sitting on her small single bed, the room sparsely furnished with just a bedside table and a lamp, Charlotte is in pyjamas, a suitcase at her slippered feet; next to the suitcase are piles of books and, most poignantly, a tennis racket – an emblem of the freedoms that Jews no longer had access to, and of a life which somehow had to be disassembled and boxed up. The subject of the painting has her hands to her mouth, her eyes unfocused. All the torment and trepidation of Salomon's before and after – along with millions like her – is contained in that image.

The imprint NYRB Classics chose this particular gouache as the cover for its edition of philosopher Gillian Rose's memoir *Love's Work*, originally published in 1995, not long after its author's death from cancer at the age of forty-eight. Like Salomon's *Singspiel*, Rose's brief book arrived fully formed – a life lived, a life cut short, a blossoming of art, a mordant two-fingers-up at death. Early in the book Rose, who was Jewish, recounts a journey to Poland in 1993 for an academic conference: 'In the beech forests outside Tarnów, where 800 children and 1,000 old and infirm Jews were shot, the roughly marked mass graves are surrounded, mid-March, by masses of tiny, white wood anemones, wind-flower and bird-song, and the audibly rising sap of the pearly trees, as if a fairy tale has taken place here.'

The spring weather of 2020 was, similarly, incongruously and outrageously glorious: as the list of casualties rose throughout the remainder of March and all of April like a grisly league table of death, I observed, from the front windows of my first-floor apartment, the silence of the street outside, and from the back, the extravagant blooming of my neglected garden. Opening my front door to the external world, the air that flooded in was pure, piercingly sweet: but also, to my solitary state, heavy with the threat of invisible infection.

Emptiness, and the searching out of emptiness, suited me. Unable to concentrate on reading apart from the required literature for book reviews and features, I looked over well-worn passages or fragmentary works. I watched films in which the catastrophic element is implied, rather than writ large, where the action is subdued, viewed aslant or as if through a veil of gauze, and which takes place in seemingly

depopulated cities: the wartime Paris of Jean Pierre Melville's
Army of Shadows (1969), which features an imperilled
underground Resistance cell; or of Joseph Losey's *Mr Klein*
(1976), in which Alain Delon plays a trader of mostly looted
art who becomes mistaken for a Jewish man of the same
name. The film's disturbingly sudden ending, in which
Klein is swept away in a matter of hours from all he knows,
haunted me for days.

I thought back to the Paris of Patrick Modiano, who, since
his Nobel in Literature win in 2014, has become more
widely translated and therefore more than an acquired taste.
Modiano's novels fixate on the old, forgotten *quartiers* of
Paris during World War Two and the twenty years after,
of seedy cafes, sleazy nightclubs, far-flung Metro stations,
shabby hotels, mildewed telephone directories and dusty
registers, and the lives distorted and disappeared under
German occupation. In *Missing Person*, both a noirish
detective fiction and a quest for the self, a middle-aged
man who has lost his memory tries to retrace his steps back
to the occupied Paris of his younger days and the ever-
growing certainty of his part in a personal betrayal. 'I believe
that the entrance-halls of buildings still retain the echo of
footsteps of those who used to cross them and who have
since vanished,' Modiano writes. 'Something continues to
vibrate after they have gone, fading waves, but which can
still be picked up if one listens carefully.'

Over the years my self-discipline in shutting out and
suppressing any memories of my father grew so successful
that the good ones were inevitably wiped out along with the

bad. It came as a shock, therefore, a few winters ago when, back in Sheffield for the day, I dropped in to the Central Library, an elegant Art Deco-style building, first opened in 1934. The basement, then, and now, holds the Children's Library: descending the stone staircase, I suddenly and violently experienced the distinct sensation of being very small and of holding tightly to my father's hand: an agitation so physically overwhelmingly that I felt faint and had to sit down at the top of those same stairs.

In October 1917, on the outbreak of revolution, the Russian poet Marina Tsvetaeva was visiting a friend in Crimea. Somehow she had to make the long and difficult train journey alone back to Moscow, where her children were. Her husband had been drafted into the Imperial army. In a letter entered into her notebook she wrote: 'If you are alive, if I am to see you again, listen: yesterday, approaching Kharkov, I read *Yuzhny Krai*. 9,000 killed. I cannot tell you about this night because it's not over yet. Grey morning now. I'm in the corridor. Try to understand!'

Later: 'This is all a terrible dream. I try to sleep. I don't know how to write to you... you, you yourself, with your self-destructive instinct. Could you actually stay at home? If everyone stayed home, you would go out alone all the same. Because you are irreproachable. Because you can't stand for others to be killed.'

In another passage Tsvetaeva simply states: 'Everyday life is a sack: with holes. And you carry it anyway.'

A terrible dream... if everyone stayed home... it's not over yet.

At various points during the coronavirus crisis, the public has been encouraged to keep diaries, just as they were during World War Two and more recently with the Mass Observation project, to form a special archive of this period, a shared history of a situation which has affected so many so differently. I have felt no such inclination: this essay will probably be my only record. Now it is midsummer: we have moved to Level 3; the lockdown restrictions are easing. But the virus has not gone away. It remains, invidiously.

Anne Frank, possibly the most famous diarist of the last century, revised her journal's early sections in response to a similar call-out from the Dutch government in exile. On 13 January 1943, concealed in the Secret Annexe in the centre of Amsterdam – the canal-side hiding place above her father's offices in which she, her parents and sister, and four other people lived for nearly two years between July 1942 and August 1944 – the thirteen-year-old Frank wrote: 'Terrible things are happening outside. At any time of night and day, poor helpless people are being dragged out of their homes... Families are torn apart; men, women and children are separated. Children come home from school to find their parents have disappeared. Women return from shopping to find their houses sealed, their families gone.'

I re-read Anne's diary recently, finding it astonishingly different from the heavily censored and sanitised edition which all girls of my age read as teenagers: until 1991, *The*

Diary of a Young Girl had had its more radical contents – negative comments on the Germans, an astute analysis of the progress of the war, Frank's difficult relationship with her mother, her growing awareness of her own physical changes and sexual feelings – expunged by her father, the only former occupant of the Secret Annexe to return from the camps.

I preferred this newer, different version of Anne – bolder, more insightful, more mature, less given to sentiment. Yet her canny editorship of her own juvenilia, her priming for publication, made me aware of the erstwhile unreliable narrator existing inside every writer.

My father's story ended eleven years ago, but the narrative of him and me continues and it probably always will. By the time he died, of cancer, in May 2009, I hadn't seen him for six years. Two hours after his death, my sister and I stood nervously in a small hospice room, regarding his body. It both was, and was not, our father. I saw an old man with the sheets tucked up to his chin, one eye still partially open, looking at nothing. My sister and I sobbed uncontrollably, the only time in thirty years we had been together in the same room as him. Tiptoeing nervously around the bed, I wondered aloud whether we should kiss him goodbye. 'I don't think so,' my sister replied: already his face had taken on a faraway, waxen sheen.

This week, I was reunited with my boyfriend. We know it is temporary; the summer will be a mere caesura; a second wave of plague is predicted for autumn and on into winter: there is no cure, no vaccine. For the time being, giddy with euphoria, we have escaped. We walk under trees bouncing with cooing woodpigeons and through perfumed air turning cloudy with returning pollution, past people wearing masks, or not wearing masks.

We say our goodbyes lightly now; the future is a blank; we are learning to live in the mean time.

June 2020

Sources and further reading:

Robert C. Crumbow, *The Towering Inferno*, from The Parallax View, 29 June 2015. https://parallax-view.org/2015/07/29/review-the-towering-inferno/

Meg Wolitzer, *The Position* (Chatto and Windus, 2005)

Charlotte Salomon, *Life? or Theatre?* quoted in Mary Lowenthal Felstiner, *To Paint Her Life: Charlotte Salomon in the Nazi Era* (University of California Press, 1997)

Gillian Rose, *Love's Work* (Chatto & Windus, 1995)

Patrick Modiano, *Missing Person* (translated by Daniel Weissbort, Jonathan Cape, 1980)

Marina Tsvetaeva, *Earthly Signs: Moscow Diaries 1917–1922* (translated and edited by Jamey Gambrell, New York Review Books Classics, 2002)

TRAUMA

Anne Frank, *The Diary of a Young Girl: the Definitive Edition* (edited by Otto Frank and Mirjam Pressler; translated by Susan Massotty, Penguin Classics, 2000)

DENIAL AND DIFFICULT KNOWLEDGE
Thom Cuell

When coronavirus hit Europe, I was in Lisbon, staying with my wife while she worked in a Portuguese GP's surgery, as part of a European exchange programme. As cases began to mount in the city, the response was swift; within days, the government declared a lockdown, followed by a state of emergency. Shops and restaurants, if they stayed open at all, adopted social distancing, and mask-wearing was ubiquitous. At the surgery, emergency protocols were put in place, and we were advised to stay away. We spent our days in our rented apartment. When we ventured to the local corner shop for supplies, the streets were eerily quiet. While the numbers in England were much lower, my colleagues exchanged panicked WhatsApp messages, wondering when our office was going to close, and we were going to begin working from home.

Within hours of landing at Manchester, we saw that things were different back in the UK. In Arrivals, there was no distancing, no checks. But when we went to the supermarket, the shelves were stunningly bare. If the government was slow in taking action, the people were preparing for something serious. This time, it was my wife's WhatsApp that was full of anxious messages from medics who were being asked to go onto emergency rotas, being reassigned to ICU roles or worrying about being deployed to rumoured super-hospitals.

***

It was three or four weeks into the UK's lockdown period that I first became aware of coronavirus conspiracy theories. In America, the 'empty hospitals' movement saw members of the public filming deserted hospital car parks, as evidence that the pandemic was nothing more than media hysteria (obviously, the lack of cars was down to non-essential procedures being cancelled, and visitors banned). In the UK this gained less traction. Rather than vigilante journalism, British 'truthers' focused on minimising the impact of Covid-19 as 'no worse than the flu', the mounting mortality rate brushed aside with the thought 'they would have died soon anyway'.

These denialists clearly took their lead from the government's daily Bullshit and Equivocation Conferences (BEC). When the Prime Minister of the country with the worst death toll per capita in Europe, who had himself spent several nights in ICU, perhaps as a result of his cavalier behaviour during the early stages of the crisis, could stand in front of the press and declare that 'we have succeeded in avoiding the tragedy we saw in other parts of the world', is it any surprise that private individuals might also downplay the scale of the catastrophe? This process was further enabled by legions of pliant journalists. I'll pick on James O'Brien here, who stated on Twitter that 'we can't even report [on political decisions and incompetence] in the way we would if another country was failing so badly. It would be so unhelpful and frightening.'

However, there is a difference between the official bullshit and the unofficial variety. In the early stages of the crisis, the government clearly decided to adopt a tone of vague optimism in their dealings with the public, tempered with grand empty gestures to boost morale. In the first camp came messages about the number of ventilators and tests soon to be available – the 'jam tomorrow' school of political communication. The latter was exemplified by the empty Nightingale Hospitals dotted around the country. Boris has never met a white elephant he didn't want to ride, so the prospect of converting conference centres into vast pest-houses was an irresistible temptation, regardless of their doubtful efficacy (the government subsequently chose the much tidier method of allowing elderly victims of the pandemic to be sent into care homes, or else die untreated at home, alone and uncounted, rather than clutter up these pristine new facilities, or overwhelm existing ICU capacity).

Despite all this, there was no question of the government entirely denying the existence of the problem. Whilst for a brief moment 'keeping calm and carrying on' may have seemed tempting, events (and public opinion) moved rapidly.

There was, and remained, robust public support for the lockdown, to the point where the only people questioning it appeared to be the frothingly reactionary Tory MPs of the 1922 Committee and the leader of Her Majesty's opposition, Sir Keir Starmer QC. They may have quibbled over details (exact death tallies, provision of PPE), but they remained committed to a policy which placed the threat posed by Covid-19 as a significant and pressing emergency.

This was not true of the Twitter reply guys. Whenever an expert mentioned the death toll, or a medic spoke out against the lack of essential supplies, the responses would read 'this is just the same as seasonal flu', 'how do we know they really died of Covid?' and 'our trust has plenty of PPE'. This was even mirrored by the likes of Sir Alan Sugar, who, in an interview with Jeremy Vine, asked: 'who's dead? I'm not. I'm still alive. So's everybody else I know.' While the UK suffered at least 40,000 deaths, a record drop in GDP and the significant mental health effects of lockdown, a core of the public seemed determined to explain events away as though nothing were happening.

***

In June, three months into the lockdown, Black Lives Matter protests were held across the UK. Prompted by solidarity with American activists, in the wake of the killing of George Floyd, these demonstrations also addressed Britain's own racist history. The protests culminated in the toppling of a statue of the slave trader Edward Colston into Bristol harbour, and the temporary boarding up of a statue of Winston Churchill. These events, once again, were met with a wall of denial, from politicians down, of Britain's role in slavery, imperial crimes and ongoing institutional racism.

Statues, we were told, were designed to educate people about history – despite evidence showing that organisations such as Merchant Ventures in Bristol had long prevented any mention of slavery from being added to the plaque on Edward Colston's statue. Boris Johnson, meanwhile, elided Churchill's historic crimes with 'opinions that were and are unacceptable to us today'. The motley crew of far-right activists and football hooligans who gathered to 'defend' the Cenotaph (and, incongruously, a statue of George Eliot in Nuneaton) were referred to in the weaseliest of terms as 'anti-anti-racists' as media organisations scrambled to preserve the fiction of British tolerance.

***

In his 2018 essay 'Denial: The Unspeakable Truth', the sociologist Keith Kahn-Harris attempted to define the characteristics of denialism. Khan-Harris explains that through his Jewish faith, he developed an interest originally in the psychology of Holocaust deniers, but that this expanded to take in everything from climate change denial to fringe beliefs such as flat Earth theory. He separates the everyday practice of 'being in denial' from the practice of denialism: 'denialism is more than just another manifestation of humdrum deceptions and self-deceptions. It represents the transformation of the everyday practice of denial into a new

way of seeing the world and... a collective accomplishment.'
While denial may be passive, denialism is active, sometimes
aggressively so: 'denial is furtive and routine; denialism is
combative and extraordinary. Denial hides from the truth;
denialism builds a new and better truth.'

The word 'extraordinary' is important here. Denialism exists
because some truths are so shattering that to accept them
would require us to completely re-evaluate our view of the
world. The sociologist Eviatar Zerubavel states that denial
'usually involves refusing to acknowledge the presence
of things that actually beg for attention... Those highly
conspicuous matters we deliberately try to avoid.' It thrives,
says Michael Spector, 'when an entire segment of society,
often struggling with the trauma of change, turns away
from reality in favour of a more comfortable life.'

The present situation in the UK has created a breeding
ground for denialism. The December general election had
been viciously fought, with the Labour leader Jeremy Corbyn
being routinely demonised in the press, and journalists
disseminating false stories about Labour voters attacking
Conservative staffers. Social media was particularly fertile
ground for fostering denialism: a report published the day
after the election found that 88% of social media adverts
paid for by the Conservatives during the first four days of
campaigning featured inaccurate or misleading information.
The ongoing battle over Brexit had become a form of culture
war, with trust in the media and political establishment
diminished on both sides. This exacerbated an emerging
generational divide between boomers (predominantly

Conservative and Leave voting), and overwhelmingly pro-Labour and Remain millennials.

This is not an entirely new development, more an acceleration of an existing trend. A shift in attitudes towards Britishness began around the Golden Jubilee. Britain's imperial and military history began to be viewed with a sort of cloying twee nostalgia encapsulated by the phrase 'Keep Calm and Carry On'. As Owen Hatherley noted in *The Ministry of Nostalgia*, this Blitz-era slogan had actually been rejected in its own time because of its patronising tone, but was embraced in 2008, as austerity began to have its impact on the poor and marginalised within British society. In tandem with this, Union flags became more common sights outside of international football tournaments, and the wearing of poppies became rigorously policed, with news anchors and footballers being shamed for their failure to wear this symbol of British sacrifice.

At the height of the Covid crisis, the government seized on this new ideation of nostalgic patriotism to create a feel-good event around VE Day, complete with nauseating socially distanced conga lines dancing through predominantly white suburbs. At a time when Britain was being criticised for its handling of the crisis by comparison with the rest of Europe, the population could imagine a time when Britain stood alone as a player on the international stage – itself a mythologised view of the past. Predictably, the papers which had previously criticised Londoners for sitting in parks during their allotted daily exercise times were delighted to report on these events.

The idea that people should stop worrying and get on with enjoying themselves is an important element of modern right populist tactics. In *Other People's Politics: Populism to Corbyn* (Zero Books, 2020), the academic J.A. Smith described the appeal of right populism as being libidinal: rather than concerning itself with winning arguments, populist discourse was atavistic, a promise of power without consequences. This lack of consequences was embodied in the figures of Donald Trump and Boris Johnson, privileged white men who got their own way and never apologised. Johnson's vocabulary, including descriptions of Africans as 'piccaninnies' and gay men as 'tank-topped bum boys', gave a jolly, upper-class acceptability to common prejudice.

Thinking too deeply about the details of politics was actively discouraged by the Tories' 2019 election campaign. While Labour's manifesto argued for big structural changes, including nationalisation of utilities, free broadband and a green new deal, Johnson showboated, driving a truck through a wall of polystyrene blocks marked 'get Brexit done'. Their programme was a buffet of contradictory options – as journalist Stephen Bush put it, 'you cannot have a Brexit that unlocks trade deals with India and reduces the uncontrolled flow of people from elsewhere around the world to the UK. You can't have a more generously funded public realm and pursue a Brexit that makes everyone poorer' – and allowed people to pick their favourite bits, helped by highly targeted social media advertising.

In this context, asking a population who had gleefully provided Johnson with a huge majority in December to realise in March that this decision had led to a rapidly increasing death toll was always going to be hard. Is it any surprise that a significant number of people turned away from traumatic reality in favour of a more comfortable life? To face up to the government's failures, and to confront the UK's racism, would be to acknowledge the brief libidinal rush of electing Johnson had a devastating long-term consequence, and that the jolly VE Day Union Jack bunting had a bloody history.

The paradigm-shifting impact of coronavirus challenges beliefs that go beyond one election result, however. As David Rowland writes in his *Tribune* article 'We Need a Public Health Revolution', 'in one short shock, this crisis has overturned the neoliberal notion that individuals are best placed to manage and navigate risk in the modern world, while government is simply there to nudge us, and to steer and shape the market environment to meet our preferences.' Rowland argues that a succession of governments, steered by neo-liberal ideology, have weakened the status, resources and capacity of public health bodies, as collective, top-down solutions to health issues were abandoned in favour of a reliance on 'behavioural economics' and individual 'lifestyle changes'. To acknowledge that this ideological shift has exacerbated the crisis of Covid-19 requires us to ask questions of a system which has dominated British politics for decades, and become entrenched in the national psyche. It requires individuals to reassess their relationships and responsibilities towards others in their community, in all aspects of our lives. No wonder that so many are willing to engage in denialism rather than face up to this reckoning.

TRAUMA

We have already seen that the UK's political system is woefully ill-equipped to deal with denialism. There is no mechanism by which the government can be punished for their refusal to acknowledge the UN special rapporteur's report on the impact of austerity, or for their attempts to sweep the effects of Grenfell and the deportation of members of the Windrush generation under the rug. When government adviser Dominic Cummings was revealed to have broken lockdown rules, the government's response was to organise a mass-gaslighting session in the garden of 10 Downing Street, in which transparently phony explanations were given, to provide talking points for online denialists. The pliant media and opposition played their part, lining up to ask softball questions and then forgetting all about it.

So how do we confront denialism on this scale? In Britain, the default response to catastrophe is to commission an inquiry. Whether this is an effective way of responding to collective trauma is questionable, however. When countries attempt to promote healing through a process of 'truth and reconciliation', there is inevitably a tension between narratives which promote unity and positive outcomes, versus those which remind us of conflict, justice and the experience of victims. So far, research has been inconclusive as to the benefits of either approach. It has been argued that truth and reconciliation commissions put an unfair burden of responsibility on the victims of events, while psychologists now feel that debriefing in the immediate aftermath of trauma can actually increase harm.

DENIAL AND DIFFICULT KNOWLEDGE

Key to understanding this dilemma is the idea of 'difficult knowledge'. This term describes 'knowledge that remains incommensurable and cannot be assimilated into one's world view' and is contrasted with 'lovely knowledge', which reinforces our existing beliefs. In 2003, the psychoanalysts Deborah Britzman and Alice Pitt published a paper examining the use of difficult knowledge in learning. They recognised that there is 'a kernel of trauma in the very capacity to know' – as we have seen, it is this kernel of trauma that often seeds into denialism. Britzman and Pit argue that the pedagogy of difficult knowledge lies in 'provoking, not representing, knowledge'.

One of the most pernicious effects of denialism is that anyone who wants to fight back against it is forced to confront difficult knowledge directly; many Black Lives Matter activists described their exhaustion at having to educate well-meaning white people about damaging incidents their community had experienced. Similarly, combatting Covid denialism meant immersing oneself in mortality rates and harrowing accounts of overwhelmed hospital wards. There was the gaslighting effect of columnists and pundits decrying criticism of the government's approach as 'hipster analysis' one day, and asking why hospital admissions were so high the next.

The language of difficult knowledge is complex: 'though the traumatic event can be felt, it is often untranslatable into meaning, leading to breakages and aporia, moments in which language can no longer create holistic arguments or sustained statements.' In the absence of straightforward narrative, Britzman and Pitt propose the benefits of allegory, which, 'with its lack of totality of meaning and preponderance of fragmentation, can be related to the experience of difficult knowledge'.

Of course, the toppling and immersion of the Colston statue can be read in these terms, as an allegorical act which gives voice to the various demands of protestors whilst also provoking knowledge in the general population, through its unignorable anger.

The use of allegory also encourages a literary approach. While we are seemingly long past the point where a book could be so ubiquitous as to change society, literature is still a driver of culture. One of the immediate reactions to the British Black Lives Matter movement has been the dissemination of anti-racism reading lists, with authors like Eddi Reno-Lodge, Akala and Afua Hirsch topping bestseller lists. Whilst these are predominantly non-fiction, each confronts difficult knowledge about the Black experience in Britain.

There is precedent: in the wake of the right-wing dictatorships which spread across Latin America in the 1960s and 1970s, many writers expressed themselves through allegory. No doubt this was in part as a means of avoiding censorship (or assassination), but there were also literary benefits, as detective fiction and magic realism provided extremely effective means of conveying the menace and paranoia of the society the writers existed in. It is only in recent years that the likes of Alia Trabucco Zeran have been able to confront Chile's past directly. Likewise, in her book *Human*

Acts, the Korean novelist Han Kang directly addressed the difficult knowledge of a government massacre, giving ferociously realistic voice to the victims of brutality. David Peace has used stories of crime and police corruption as allegories for the UK's collective trauma in the early years of Thatcherism. Maybe this is how writers will approach the period of coronavirus, racial inequality and the rising tide of populism in 2020.

***

I write this piece in week fourteen of lockdown. Whilst my situation is privileged, there is a mental shock that comes with the suspension of normal activity, the necessity of distance from family, friends and strangers alike draining to maintain. Sleep and work patterns are disrupted, everyday activities are inaccessible. Since beginning to work remotely, I realise that this period of lockdown is the longest I have gone without physically being in Manchester for fifteen years, and there is a sense of loss that comes with that absence.

For weeks, I struggled to read anything, never mind write. My routines were jumbled, but just as damagingly, I was mentally overwhelmed by the difficult knowledge the pandemic was forcing me to confront. Each news cycle brought stories of mounting death tolls, failures in the supply of PPE and testing kits, and other signs that Britain's neglected infrastructure was straining under the pressure. When I was able to stop myself doomscrolling through Twitter, the first books I managed to read were a series of thrillers and horror stories:

Stephen King, China Miéville, Dan Simmons. The mixture of conspiracy, lurking menace and otherworldly threat was both a form of escapism, and a way to indirectly confront the paranoia, confusion and fear in the outside world. These were the stories which helped me to approach and understand the difficult knowledge of lockdown.

The challenge of coming to terms with the impact of Covid-19 is one that each of us will have to face. Many will have lost relatives or friends, had their lives turned upside down, and experienced a multitude of traumas. They may also look at the government's response to the crisis, the crisis of funding in the public sector, and the possibility of remote working reorganising the way that we structure our lives. Coronavirus has exacerbated existing problems in Britain, from insecure housing and employment to regional inequalities, access to services such as broadband, and the future of the NHS. Concurrently, the Black Lives Matter movement has challenged institutional racism and the ongoing legacy of Britain's imperial past. It is crucial that these issues not be swept under the carpet in our haste to get back to 'normal'. To make a progressive case for change, it is vital that we confront the difficult knowledge surrounding coronavirus and empire. The challenge, as artists, is to find the allegories that will help Britain explore these vital and traumatic issues.

INHERITANCE
Christiana Spens

I.

Tubs of ink are lined up on the shelves, stacked against the wall. A large window looking out onto a car park and then the Tay, with cardboard tubs of transparency sheets on the sill, clear but smeared with the residue of old inks – black, grey, dark blue, partially scratched off, flaking.

Large sinks, where inks dilute and settle in puddles before being washed down the drain. Rags dyed a hundred different colours, lying out to dry on the side. Buckets, sponges, squeegees, plates, cleaned and drying out on the porcelain rack.

Nylon stretched over a wooden frame, taped around the edges so that there is a window the size that the image will be.

I scoop some of the pink onto the bottom of the screen, close it down again. Get the squeegee, draw it up, over the screen. Press it down, the ink passing through the fabric, clean and perfect on the paper beneath.

Another and another. Sheets of pink, some more perfect than others, some not perfect at all. I lay them out on the drying rack: twelve squares of pale, warm pink, drying flesh and shadow and sky.

As the sheets dry, I clean the screen, the pink diluting with water and bubbling at the edge, the rags picking up the inky puddles. I dry the nylon with a hairdryer; it warms in clouds, shrinking smaller as I hold it up.

***

We moved back to Dundee on my mother's birthday, the last Sunday in April. We had been staying with her since the divorce came through exactly four months earlier. Before that, we'd been living between hers and various places in London – sleeping on friends' sofas, single guest beds, sometimes their own beds, when they were away. Caspian, two years old then, snuggled into me in each place, played with the same group of animals and cars on every train journey, every two or three weeks, as we went between Scotland and London. He was still breast-feeding, then. I felt bad stopping, with everything else upended in his life.

Our new flat was opposite a church whose cross – a Celtic one, with a circle behind it – absorbed the evening sun nicely, on a long street off the Perth Road. The sofa took a while to arrive, so we sat on cushions and a mattress that folded into a sort of seat, or at the table by the window. We didn't have a TV but I laid out his various toys – a train set, cars, a doll's house. Everything was new because the setting was new; old things became more precious. Outside the blossom bloomed on the tree across the road, then the bluebells in the short stretch of a garden in front of a window, then the peonies – deep crimson – in the bush by the wall.

I wanted art for the walls; that was the original reason for learning how to screen print. I wanted to choose images and make them bigger, hang family portraits on the walls, or old drawings, or anything else that inspired. But quickly it all became about Susan, about reprinting Susan.

***

At the workshop, we'd been asked to bring in a few photographs to choose from, and that's when I had remembered the album. It had been a year since I had found it, and I had looked at the pictures of Susan last. I had been sitting on a sofa at seven in the morning with a coffee, as my son played with his toys. I was barely awake.

I had been thinking a lot about her recently; she was on my mind again. She would have been born a hundred years ago, perhaps that had something to do with it. I told myself that was the reason, anyway.

When my father had died, three years before, he had left behind diaries and notebooks. One of them contained notes for a novel he wanted to write about his parents. I had never

known much about either of them, because he had never
spoken about them, or really about anything at all. I just
knew that she had died at twenty-six, when he was four
years old, the year before the war ended, of an overdose. 'A
wartime accident,' the death certificate had read. People had
doubted how accidental it was, but he had not.

*She watched as the sun dropped over London with a whiskey
soda and then, much later, took her medication.*

He didn't mention that the medication had been codeine,
that it was her fifth wedding anniversary, a cold night in
December. There had been a song by the Mills Brothers
playing at number one for a few weeks before, called 'Paper
Doll', about a man who wants to have a paper doll instead of
a real-life girlfriend, because he feels so hurt that his own girl,
Sue, has cheated on him. He'd rather have a paper doll, the
song goes, so no one else can steal her. It was number one
the week she died, on her fifth wedding anniversary.

He mentioned the Polish officer, in the two-page sample he
had written. *Since his last leave in September, she had for
consolation taken up with Leczeq – a fling to relieve the
sorrow of absence, just as for so many... Leczeq's life was
not short of tragedy – his family had been eliminated in the
German occupation of Poland.*

The affair had ended, though, and she was distraught.
London had been partially destroyed in the Blitz, and yet
she chose to stay there rather than Caithness, as she had
done before. In his notes, my father wrote that she had been

stressed by the bombs; perhaps that was why she was taking codeine. He didn't say that she was pregnant, that she might have had other reasons to be anxious.

Patrick, who had been an officer and fought at Monte Cassino, a brutal battle that few came back from, had returned to Blitz-torn London to find his wife had died. Not from a bomb but from pills. He had been shot in the lung, but kept smoking. He had been heartbroken, but remarried. He died in his seventies, of cancer in the remaining lung.

In his notes for the novel, my dad imagined the Polish officer meeting his own father in a hospital in Italy, and his father forgiving him. 'Admission and confession,' he had noted down, in the plan. And then: 'Forgiveness and friendship.'

II.

My son was born nine months after my father died, after a long battle with cancer, which had been first diagnosed eighteen years ago. The doctors had said, however, that the tumour had been growing for around a decade before that, before I had even been born. The cancer was older than me.

I had come back from Paris for the funeral, and I was staying at home, when I found out I was pregnant. I was sitting with a Thai green curry (after craving curry all week). I'd been putting off taking a test, and even took it in the evening rather than the morning (when hormones are strongest and you're meant to take it), perhaps to lessen the risk of a positive test. But the evidence was there anyway. Two strong pink lines. I couldn't eat the curry, then. I was beginning to feel nauseous.

I went to the Pavilion – it was really a wooden studio at the end of the garden, at the edge of the woods, but it had originally been a tennis pavilion that had been scheduled for demolition by the council, and my dad had persuaded them he could take it off their hands. So he rebuilt it on the edge of the woods, and it became a studio, and library, and for many years my bedroom. I went there, anyway, as soon as I found out. I sat on the single bed in there, surrounded by canvases and an easel and many books. I couldn't even cry; I was too shocked.

Later on, I called my boyfriend with the news. He had only left a few days ago. He just laughed, though, nervously. And then, 'It'll be okay. Everything will be fine.'

For a while, it was. We moved to Dundee, and I kept writing my PhD from home, so that I could work around the nausea that lasted the entire nine months. He worked in a bookshop and started writing a book about imaginary places, using my dad's library (he had been an architect and writer) for the research.

At nine a.m. on New Year's Day, my waters broke. Twenty-three hours and emergency surgery later, he was born – sucking two thumbs, purple. In the same hospital my dad had died in nine months earlier – sedated, pale as paper.

A huge, formidable, serene baby boy. Blue eyes, dark hair. Wouldn't take his eyes off me. Didn't scream, like the others. Just had a look. Insisted on sleeping on my chest, nuzzled in.

***

When he was five months old, we went back to the country, where my mum was still living. When she went away for a year, we stayed there with the baby, because we couldn't afford rent anywhere else. Things became difficult. In fact, they had been difficult from the beginning, I began to admit to myself. There had been no support – we couldn't afford any childcare, and in the early days, we had no family help at all. There wasn't even a half hour of babysitting until he was eighteen months old. I did everything. My boyfriend started writing a book about his family history, about his inherited wounds and silences, and as he did so, he fell into them, like some modern Orpheus. He turned away, became cut off, closed; he drank. The past seemed to suck him, and then me, into some Underworld – along different rivers, though, away from each other.

As he wrote his book, I went back to the notes my dad had left, too, and the rumours I had heard about Susan. I thought about how alone she had been in the countryside. How her mother had recently died. How she brought up two children without a partner around, until her death. I didn't realise at the time, but I was fascinated by her because I identified with her. The relationship breakdown, the depression, motherhood, isolation.

There were just a few photographs of her that I had seen, then. They were taken in Caithness, which was even more remote and freezing than where we were, in Fife. She was holding her baby son, my father, on a doorstep, miserable. In another, she was laughing as he lay in a white shawl, also laughing.

I wanted to know more – these photographs were not enough. I wanted more of her and more of him. I wanted to see the resemblance between a baby him and my baby son. Between her and me. I wanted to feel as if I had a family around me, us. If only there had been more photographs, I thought. Then it would start to make sense. But I didn't find them.

He kept cutting himself further and further away, and the idea of being physically apart, too, began to play on my mind. If I couldn't have love, at least I could have freedom. This was what I was thinking, anyway, when I sat with my coffee in the morning, as my son played. This was what I was thinking when I noticed the album in the bookshelf.

I thought I might find more baby photos of my father, but there was none of that. Instead, it was Susan before she married, when she was a teenager and in her early twenties. A photo of her skinny-dipping somewhere in the Highlands, laughing; a picture of her handing out sandwiches, also in the Highlands, to her friends, by a grand car. Pictures of her and her sister in bathing suits on the beach. Photos of other children – her cousins – toddling around in 1937. Glamorous headshots, her hair in curls, lips lined, false lashes. Newspaper cuttings about her and her sister snapped at parties in London. Glamorous, beautiful girls.

And then, she and Patrick. She is smiling, in love. He is a little more reserved. She wears trousers in some, skirts in others, as they walk over the cobbled streets of Edinburgh. There are photos in sailing boats: he is rowing, relaxed. Another, where she stands on a beach, boats behind her, serene. Their engagement photos and announcements in the papers. Their wedding day, in December 1938, in London. Their honeymoon, in the Alps, in January 1939. She must have fallen pregnant then, because my father was born nine months later, in September, three weeks after the war started. Patrick would have left by then; he had been an officer before war broke out. He went to Italy. They barely saw each other again.

III.

A year later, when he had gone and the divorce had come through and we'd finally moved into a new flat, I chose a few images from the album: Susan and Patrick together on a mountain. He is dressed for skiing; she is wearing a leopard print coat. In another, Patrick is rowing a boat, somewhere in Scotland. Then Patrick is sitting with the Alps in the background, smoking a pipe and holding his sunglasses. And the last one, a portrait of Susan which was used to announce their engagement. In profile, her dark hair curly, sad eyes, at least it seems so to me.

I took photographs of them, and brought them into the workshop. For the first print, I chose the image of them both together. I printed layers of pale pink, ochre and grey, for the skies, the leopard print coat, their skin. After these layers, the photographic image itself was developed onto the large screen in the darkroom with an emulsion, and then I could print that onto the layers of colour that had dried. They came alive; I made ten prints, but only two really worked. As they dried on the rack, I looked at them both, on their honeymoon.

War had cut everything short. Whatever had happened, this image, together with all the others, showed how their lives – their lives together, which had so much promise – had been destroyed by war and the chaos and separation it had caused.

Their honeymoon, though, their time together before the war, before depression, before death. I wanted to celebrate that time. I wanted to see beyond the legacy, the silence, the shame of her likely suicide. I wanted to see her, and him, as she had presented them in her album. I wanted to bring her own creations into the light, to reprint them, enlarge them, let her tell her own story. And in so doing, though I didn't quite realise it at the time, I told my own story, too, or began to. She had always been part of my story, that was what I realised. She echoed in my voice, was imprinted in the lines of my face. Perhaps even our pain had felt similar, our bodies hurt the same, when the babies fed and grew and needed to be held.

***

I joined the print studio, after that, and I kept going back, printing more of Susan's photographs. It felt like a collaboration: some of the images she had taken herself, so we were both producing this new image together, despite having never met, and eighty years apart. I was, in a way, a reprint of her, at least partially; we shared genes, features, people. She had held my father and fed him in his first few years; I had done the same in his last. He had missed her his entire life, and my entire life; I had felt his loss as if it were my own, thick in the atmosphere, in the silence and invisibility.

Now, printing, I wanted to change that. I wanted to make her visible again. I wanted to relax the repression, the tension. I wanted to show how we printed and reprinted our people in ourselves. I wanted to forgive her, love her. 'Admission and confession,' my dad had written. 'Forgiveness and friendship.' It went for her, too. And him, too. These truths needed to be acknowledged before they could be forgiven and understood.

Susan's death had caused such extensive issues for my father and then, in a way, me too, and the rest of the family. He had barely spoken to us. The only time I remember him speaking about his mother was when I was about eleven years old. 'You're like her,' he had said. It felt, then, like a pressure rather than a compliment, an impossible thing. As time went on, she became ghostly to me, the more I found out. This sacred person who had abandoned him to us, a void we could never fill. But printing these photos – collaborating with her from beyond the grave, in a way – was my way of reconciling with her and with him. Putting her to rest, mourning her, finally. A person I never met but whose ghost – whose image, mainly imagined – had haunted our family for years and years.

***

In our new flat, I hung the images, these family portraits. I took her back in. I was proud of her. I didn't blame her. I loved her. Beyond the shame of an affair, a pregnancy, a likely suicide. I loved her.

I write this now, under those portraits. My son often asks me who they are, and I tell him. 'Susan and Patrick. Your great-grandparents. They were skiing, on their honeymoon.' I let him see them and know them in this moment, and I let myself see them that way, too.

'Can I Facetime Daddy?' he asks, then. I smile. 'Yes.' Had I been Facetiming her? Is that what this has been, too? An image on a screen, or behind a glass window, or pressed into a sheet of thick paper. Trying to reach the absent through reproduction. It is something, though.

***

We settled into the new flat. Into the absence of what I thought of as family, before. Into the presence of future ideas. We started over. And I was grateful for that freedom

– to divorce, to be independent, to have a choice. Some things had changed since 1943. A lot had changed.

When I finished the series of prints based on Susan's photographs, I took drawings from my own sketchbook, and drew new ones, and started using them in my prints. I created collages of drinking men and friends and my son. New faces, tangled up together, tangled up in me. Boundaries hazy, memories present.

Eventually, we left Dundee. I packed up the prints of Susan and Patrick, and put them in a box. We drove over, and unpacked them into a new flat. I joined a new print studio. The prints of Susan and Patrick were not so prominently placed in the new flat; I moved around the order. I put Susan in my bedroom, near postcards from a Mapplethorpe, Arbus and Woodman exhibition I had been to recently.

And then I went back to my father's notes. I had taken photographs of them, too. I read them over again, and started writing about him, as he had once started himself, with his parents. This process of unearthing, rethinking, having conversations, even workshops, with ghosts. And yet they live with us, and their traumas do too. And I cannot write my own stories until I have acknowledged theirs, and how, silently, they have determined my own.

Their faces, their illnesses, their injuries – the blueprint for everything that follows. But in printing and writing, I hope not only to acknowledge them, but to let them fade with reprinting and retelling, to arrange them differently, so that other shapes emerge, other images and stories.

My son plays as I write this. My ex often says that he sees other family in him. He errs on the side of nature in that debate. But I err on the side of nurture, perhaps because I am here, nurturing, my faith so solidly in that. Every day, I see my son's personality develop and change, and I think he is really not very like anyone else at all, not even me. He looks like me, but he is his own person. Entirely his own.

We reprint and retell to free ourselves, I think. We are our own people, but we inherit traumas and stories. We also inherit, hopefully, the creative motivation necessary to move on from them, if they have been left to us unresolved. Or perhaps that is just innately human. One day, perhaps, my son will find these old stories and pictures. How he retells and reprints, if he does, is up to him. Which stories stay with him though, I know, is partly up to me too.

INHERITANCE

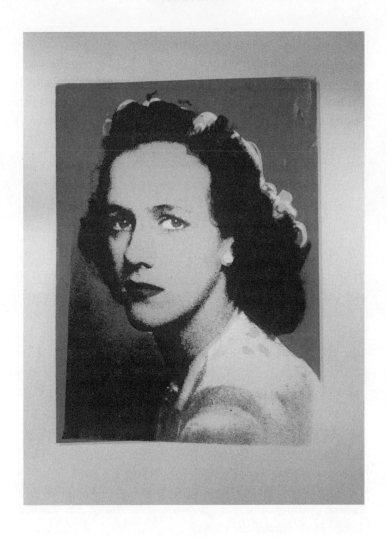

THE CLOWN
Susanna Crossman

Ha. Ha. Ha Ha. Ha. Ha. Hahaha! HA! HA! Ha. Ha. Ha. Ha. Hah. Ho! Ho! Ho! Hee, hee hee! Giggle. You will wriggle on your seat when they enter the ring. Laugh as they stumble. Chortle as they fall. Laughter is involuntary. Open your mouth. Stretch your zygomaticus muscle, draw your lips up. Your body will bend double. Shaking. Vibrating. Face creased. Eyes crinkled. You'll laugh until you cry, eyes moistening. A tear gland reflex. Shout. Scream with laughter. A bellyache. A howl. Laugh to the moon, laugh together. Laughter is shared. Laughter unites. Everyone, everywhere will be laughing now. Schopenhauer says laughter emerges at the tipping point between intuition and reason, between what should happen and what does not. A space is opening before your eyes, a gap, a crack. The music has started. Look! Here comes the clown.

For over a decade, as part of my clinical drama-therapy practice, I work as a clown. In French child psychiatric units, during New York lectures, in Germany, Portugal and Korea, at international academic conferences, I put on a red nose. A mask. I am British, but my clown works in France, and speaks a second language. *Il dit: Voici, le clown.* Here comes the clown.

The clown meets children with diverse diagnostics including Pervasive Development Disorders, Attention Deficit Disorders, terminal diseases and special needs, children with little or no speech, children who cannot stop talking: Pierre, a little boy with a slanted head, deformed from spending every waking hour of the first year of his life in a baby bouncer watching *Spider-Man*. Romain, a sweet six-year-old with a crystalline voice, who tried to strangle his sister. Helene, who uses one finger to scrape holes in her bedroom wall every night. Hole after hole. Kevin, a hyperactive five-year-old, who rocks back and forth with stereotypical movements, tapping his head. Arthur, a teenager, with exceptional story-telling capacities, but whose scenario is always the same. He only comes to the imaginary circus having lain on the floor, imagined falling asleep, imagined waking up to listen to an early morning radio show and being told he's just won a call-in competition. From his imaginary bed, he shouts out: *'J'ai gagné, j'ai gagné.'* 'I've won. I've won.' Then, he stands up and comes to meet the clown. Without this prelude, Arthur will not participate.

In meetings, a multidisciplinary team of psychiatrists, psychologists, speech therapists and nurses prescribe the drama-therapy sessions for the children and young people. Nine months of weekly hour-long sessions. Many patients present symptoms, found in forms of autism, related to the fact that they produce little or no imaginary play, or like Arthur, a play scenario that is repetitive and ritualised. Between two and seven most children develop symbolic play. But these kids cannot pretend a banana is a telephone, cannot play at being happy, sad or angry, or imagine a chair is a train. Everything is real. In consequence, in a drama-therapy session, when one of these children accepts the clown's gift of a mimed, magic, invisible sweet, shaped like a zigzag, produced from a magic bag, and the child giggles as the sweet goes *Dradadradra* in their belly, that is a miracle.

Often during this period, and still today, I think about my work as a way of using art to build bridges, finding the right material to straddle a river's flow, balancing the arch of the construction so that isolated people can meet in the middle. Bodies, sounds and gestures recount. The painful singularity of an existence is both heard and told. I am here, the clown says, and the child responds, I am here too.

In the case of clown and drama-therapy work, the bridge is invisible, theatre being, as Ariane Mouchkine says, 'A monument to ephemerality.' Acting, the magic of illusion, Koestler writes, 'enables the spectator to transcend the narrow confines of his personal identity, and to participate in other forms of existence.' Stepping out of where we are to reach the other side.

Once a week, here comes the clown. He enters, creates a space, a gap.

THE CLOWN

A clown personality has multiple facets, and can give an impression of total incoherence. Therefore, a distinguished clown can, under certain circumstances, reveal a beautiful sense of vulgarity, and a hero clown can expose total cowardice.

During these ten years, on the days when I am not working as an actress, I travel in France and abroad, meeting international academics and students. We gather in lecture theatres, dressed in jackets, shirts and ties. Bold, geometric glasses are balanced on each serious nose. Words are spoken, heads nod. Theoretical wars are lost and won. Ethics, practice, psychiatry, observations, demonstrations, pathology, clinical approaches. Case studies are explored. In Powerpoints, Freud is heralded or reviled. Winnicott's notion of play is upheld. Occasionally, there is a little art, a piano tinkle, a splat of paint, just to remind us who we are.

One wintery November, at the start of my career, I take a train from Paris to Heidelberg, eat my first white egg, and present a talk based on a case study of a special school group, detailing 'A combined aesthetic and neurobiological approach applied to clinical drama-therapy work'. One evening, during this conference, we are invited to see the unique Prinzhorn collection, containing over 5,000 art works, made by patients in European psychiatric institutions from the late nineteenth century. Standing by the glass panes, which encase full-size body sculptures made from stuffed hessian sacks, (the only material available), I want to weep at the resilient human desire to make art under any circumstances. My favourite piece is *Come* (1909), a hand-written letter from a woman to her husband. The German word *'Kumm',* in pencil on paper, is repeated dozens, hundreds of times. A plea for liberation.

The following day, I give my lecture, entitled: *Singing with our toes before meeting the clown.*

The lecture begins:

'Four children with bare feet are sitting on chairs. In front of them are four carers and therapists, holding the childrens' feet and playing with their toes. Slowly and gently they make each toe "sing", producing a note to accompany a squeeze. Feet touch feet. Sounds are improvised. The children smile, squeal and giggle. Few words are exchanged.

'Next, the drama-therapist begins to bang a drum and leads the group, stamping their feet and singing, to a circle of mats. Once seated, there is an opening ritual involving a movement and sound sequence associated with the first name of each person. After, the group splits off into twos and works on communication and expression using a series of pushing and pulling movements, involving arms, feet, hands and fingers, once again associated with sound. This sequence finishes with a collective movement.

'Suddenly a clown appears from nowhere.'

Clown experts say a clown has no function, no status, no engagement, no job and no responsibility. In this sense, the clown can become anybody, is a screen upon which anything and everything can be projected. Yet, the clown cannot be heavy, even when the clown weeps. The clown is like a flower, or a star, immutable. The clown is always light.

My lecture progresses, and I put on a red nose. I think of a quote by Terry Eagleton, who writes, 'Theatre and theory make uneasy allies. Theory is a cerebral affair, whilst theatre is among the most fleshy of art forms.' In Heidelberg, the academic audience breathes in, giggles as I speak:

'Forestier says that if we consider that all art is expression, *"toute expression n'est pas l'art"* means that all expression is not art. One fundamental defining factor is the aesthetic intention involved in any artistic process. The Chambers Dictionary defines "aesthetic" as "relating to a sense of beauty... to perception by the senses. Beauty is the quality that gives pleasure to the sight". The etymological origin of the word aesthete is the Greek word *aisthanesthai*, which means "to feel or perceive". The aesthetic process is a response to sensory gratification, involving an initial archaic and sensory interpretation and a second neuro-psycho-physiological interpretation, an alternating movement between instinct and reason.

'The Art 1 / Art 2 model developed at the Faculty of Medicine at the University of Tours integrates this physiological aspect into its analysis of the artistic activity. The initial phase Art 1 is of a sensory and archaic nature, a passage between an instinctual and a voluntary action, with an aesthetic orientation, using the body as its primary mediator. The second phase, Art 2, relates to specific artistic techniques. A pendulum movement between these two phases accentuates the coherence and profundity in the artistic oeuvre.

'Taking into account this physiological approach to art allows us to simplify this practice to its most easily accessible form, for want of a better term, democratising the artistic process, and opening it up to, for example, the child with severe learning disabilities and no or little speech. Highlighting the importance of the physical aspects of the artistic process allows us to underline the importance of the non-verbal side of art...

'In a creative activity, imagination also plays an important role in giving meaning to our action. Yet, once again, we can reduce imagination to its essential part. Bachelard claims that instead of considering imagination to be our ability to form images, we should rather accept that our imagination allows us to deform the images provided by our perception, that our imagination liberates us from our initial response to a physical stimulus and allows us to change these images. Perrière describes this in her clown / art-therapy workshops as the possibility to leave behind the "real" and the "everyday" perception using the emotion of surprise to move towards that that is "*Merveilleux*" – marvellous.'

A clown can be old, young, sick and healthy, a lady and a tramp, scientific and primary, selfish and generous. The clown lives in the here and now. Yet, historically, women have been denied the role of the clown. In French they say: Une femme qui rit c'est une femme dans son lit. A woman who laughs is a woman in bed. The insinuation being that the laughing woman is a whore. As I work as a clown, I begin to research female clowns. Yet, I feel my clown has no sex, no gender. My clown is simply part of me. My clown emerges in the hospital.

My clown goes most frequently to a French child psychiatric day-care centre attached to a psychiatric hospital. At this point in my career, I work freelance, am contracted by state institutions and organisations to provide arts-therapy clinical care. Mornings and afternoons, I drive from city to countryside, hospital to special school, often working in four different places each day, seeing over twenty clients. Being a clown requires a concentrated presence, and in these workshops I dart between roles and identities: I am myself, an arts-therapist, I am a clown. By the evening, I am exhausted. My car becomes my second home. Inside are my case files, a peanut butter sandwich for my lunch, and my collection of red noses in a small white drawstring bag.

On arrival, before each session, I set up my working space. In different institutions, inside various empty rooms (stripped of any distracting stimulus), I place eight mats in a circle, four chairs, a drum, and hide a secret red nose.

The clown comes from nowhere, elsewhere, arrives from the periphery, and plunges, naively, into the eye of the cyclone. The clown creates a space, is an aperture, an approachable other.

In Heidelberg, the lecture continues: 'Depending on the group, the general content of each drama-therapy session is divided into seven ritualised sequences, each sequence symbolised by either a sound or movement and situated in a specific part of the room. This theatrical ritualised time-space organisation is found throughout history, from the Greek amphitheatre to the Japanese Noh theatre. In each theatrical form certain things happen in certain places at certain times, influencing the role of the spectators, the performers and the play. In Greek amphitheatres, for example, spatial organisation attempted to be democratic, theatres designed so that 14,000 audience members could see and hear a play "equally" without having the "bad seats" which exist in a proscenium arch theatre (spatially designed hierarchically in the seventeenth century to please the king's eye). In Noh theatre, the "shite" – the main characters – use a linear bridgeway, leading from the stage, the *hashigakari,* for parts of the narrative where actors express deep feelings. Visual depth provides a space for mental depth. In French classic theatre, a stick is banged three times on the floor – *les trois coups* – indicating to spectators that the play is about to start. In Greek theatre, plays opened with trumpets and priests bearing olive branches. All of these devices are culturally specific, but share a framing of the theatrical performance. They allow us to separate the pretend from the real, cross over a liminal space.

THE CLOWN

'In our clown workshop, we have:

1. A "welcoming" time in which the group removes socks and shoes and "we sing with our toes".
2. A collective movement using a drum and song and dance to reach the circle of mats.
3. A ritual opening to the session to greet each person in the group using sound and movement, marking the beginning of the workshop.
4. A sensory touch, movement and sound sequence, beginning with a one-to-one period focusing on pushing and pulling, and finishing with a collective movement.
5. The meeting with the clown.
6. A ritual sound and movement closure to the session to say "goodbye" to each person in the group.
7. A "leaving" time, where we put on our socks and shoes.'

In Heidelberg, I describe the workshop's sequences, explain why toes must sing before meeting the clown:

'Within Sequence 1, the "singing with our toes" allowed the participants to tune-up or warm-up the sense organs. This sequence consciously used the idea of surprise, taking our everyday perception of our feet into Perrière's "marvellous" aesthetic state where toes can sing, referring again to Bachelard's notion of imagination relating to our ability to deform perception. The sequence was also gentle and non-threatening in order to develop a sense of trust, allowing the participants to gradually prepare and awaken the senses, progressively entering an aesthetic and creative environment...

'We can identify a movement in the workshop content between Art 1 and Art 2. A general shift occurred from the instinctual to the intentional (meaning was added to action), from the sensory to the imaginary and from the individual to the group. We can see a movement from the archaic, sensory work (the first four sequences) towards a process that is more artistically specific and technical (in Sequence 5). The early sensory work in the sessions can be characterised as Art 1 in its sensory, global and archaic nature (in the sense that no technical artistic skill is required). In contrast, the clown work used a clearly defined theatrical framework. For example, the audience members (the children and care staff) watched while the clown (the drama-therapist) performed. This involved potentially difficult constraints for the children such as adherence to a role, taking turns to speak to the clown, respecting "the other", imagined play. Yet, their interest and involvement in the scene was intense, joyful and shared. The majority was able to acknowledge that the clown was "acted", laughing as he cried, taking the mimed sweets and "eating" them (even in the case of one child with an eating disorder).

'Nevertheless, a pendulum movement between the two phases was necessary. The collective movement, sound and touch sequence led to a group dynamic, meaning it was possible to share the experience of being a member of an audience watching a clown. The gradual waking-up of the senses was an integral part of the process. Singing with our toes was necessary before meeting the clown.'

In Heidelberg, I develop Maclean's triune brain theory, and conclude my speech to scattered applause. A man tells me crossly that I will remove the soul from art-therapy work if I insist on speaking about neurobiology. The conference organiser tells me she loved my talk, and that she selected my lecture because of the intriguing title. For the following years, I toy with the idea of becoming an academic; I lecture, write papers, and am published constantly. But the constraints, and my gnawing hunger to make my own art, keep me on the outside.

The clown comes and goes as s/he pleases. The clown is not linked to an institution.

For ten years, in the middle of each drama-therapy session, the clown appears. Wherever I am working, the story of this clown is always the same. There is a beginning, middle, and an end.

In an empty room, having driven to a circus in a mimed magic bus, four children sit in a row next to a psychiatric nurse, waiting for the show. On the stage, the clown begins singing circus music. Back to the audience, s/he bellows: 'DA da dadadada DA da da da...' The children stop wriggling, and start listening. Suddenly, my clown turns and proclaims,

'Ladies and gentlemen, boys and girls, welcome to the circus. I am pleased to introduce myself: I am the clown.'

My clown bows dramatically, lurches back and forth. The audience claps. My clown says, 'As you can see, I have a red nose. All clowns wear red noses.'

My clown is proud of this knowledge, of his/her professional attitude. My clown points to his/her nose. The children start giggling. The clown insists, pointing at her/his face, says, 'Look, here is my red nose.' The children laugh louder, and my clown repeats, 'I am wearing a red nose.' Then, the children interrupt the clown, and they speak as one: 'But you haven't got a red nose.'

At this point, my clown touches her/his nose and realises it is bare. The clown is naked. There is no nose. No nose! My clown is shocked, mortified, panicked. S/he begins searching frantically for the red nose, lifting theatre mats, patting walls, and seeking out hiding places in corners, behind doors. All the while, the children are laughing louder and louder. The clown begins to weep theatrically, stating, 'I cannot find my nose. I can't be a real clown. How can I be a clown without a nose?'

My clown sits on the stage, wipes imaginary tears from his/her cheeks, and faces the children. The clown says, 'Could you help me find my nose? I need my nose to be a clown, all real clowns wear red noses.'

The children nod; they always help my clown. The children may have autism, bite their siblings, be non-verbal, rip bedsheets, be victims of sexual abuse, have alcoholic fetal syndrome or Angel disease, suffer from childhood depression or school phobia. They always help the clown. A girl (the twelfth child born to an alcoholic mother) comes and strokes the clown's arm. A boy with ADD offers my clown a pill. Another boy tries to convince my clown, saying, 'We will find your nose.'

An actor puts on a mask to bring a character to life, whereas a clown takes off a mask to reveal her inner fool. In a 1905 text, Freud states that the unconscious processes involved in the development of jokes are nearly the same as those involved in dreaming. Jokes come to their creator complete in a momentary period of blankness, signalling their emergence from the unconscious mind.

Every week the audience comes to rescue my clown from this moment of loss, this question of identity, of un-doing, of not being.

My clown and the audience search for the red nose together.

Finally, miraculously, the clown looks inside a little girl's red sock and by some amazing turn of magic finds the nose. My clown yells, 'It is here. We have found the nose.' Everyone is happy. My clown is joyful, relieved, feels utterly stupendous and eternally grateful.

Clown theory states that everyone can find his or her clown. A clown is a doppelgänger, an alter ego, a reflection, and an echo.

Who is this clown inhabiting me, constantly losing, seeking and finding their identity?

Finally, at last, the clown says, 'Now, the show can begin...'

My red nose. My clown story is imagined one day and for years, I use it every week. My clown loses his/her mask, fears humiliation, extradition, rejection, and not-being.

The red nose is the smallest mask in the world.

It doesn't hide us.

Instead, it reveals.

Every week, at the end of the show, my clown stands with his/her back to the audience and removes the red nose. When I turn, I say, 'The show is over. The clown has gone home.' A cheeky little boy says to me, 'But you are the clown.' I say, 'Oh no. But the clown is my friend.'

After a lapse of silence, the little boy and I agree this is a possibility.

We found the red nose together. We exist. In this parallel world, we crossed a bridge, laughed and cried. We have been heard, seen, recognised.

HAZELNUTS
Georgie Codd

I was in the back of a taxi on my way to a very long walk. Sitting still and going nowhere would have been dangerous. At that time, when I was still, I could not cope.

I was planning to cover the breadth of the Hadrian's Wall path during a bank holiday weekend, 83 miles between a Saturday afternoon and Monday evening, finishing east of Newcastle, in Wallsend. That gave me less than three days for a distance I had never attempted before – a challenge no one had asked me to take on.

Before this, the closest I'd come to walking so far was 45 miles over three days (and that with a twenty-four-hour break in the middle). As I sat in the taxi, I promised myself that the same length of time for 83 miles was feasible. I had no idea if that was true. Or how badly I would react if I found out it wasn't.

I stared gratefully at the scenery on the way to Bowness-on-Solway, relieved to have motion and purpose. The taxi driver told me about her uncle: a heroin addict, homeless then dead, long before his time. Minutes later she confessed to drinking twenty-six cans of Red Bull to get through each day. I imagine this is why we took one too many turns around the roundabout. And possibly why she asked me, with no preamble, 'Is it true, do you think, that Prince Charles murdered Diana?'

In another country, a time zone away, my boyfriend was on an extended weekend with his family, touring mountains and bright blue bodies of water; sending heart-pricking pictures to my phone. Because he was gone, so was I. Being in my small bedroom, alone, hadn't felt safe.

He wants to leave you.

I pasted my eyes to the horizon.

Not this time. This time I'm the one who leaves.

I was dropped outside a whitewashed pub, where I waved goodbye to the driver. Adjusting my backpack – bags of snacks rustled – I turned down a footpath to the starting point: a simple wooden structure by an empty Solway beach.

Between that beach and the trail's other end, in that 83 miles of path, I hoped my mood would be lulled into settling; take on an equal rhythm with my boot steps. Perhaps, at points, it would rise with control, curving up the grassy slopes of Cumbria and Northumberland. I wanted a rising slope. I wanted to walk and keep going.

Clutched tight in my hand was a Dictaphone, my ally for the route: a small plastic friend there to listen, and keep me company. I set the box up to receive my revelations; the stuck feelings I hoped might come loose during three days of exercise.

I stood by the hut for a minute, watching the waves without seeing them, then ordered myself to get going. I needed to walk 18 miles by dusk or I wouldn't reach the bed I had booked for Night One. My carrot for the day – the first of three – was a comfortable B & B. The second, for Sunday – a bunkhouse – was 34 miles further on. The last carrot lay at the path's very end, to be reached after 32 more miles of solo trekking.

If make it through to then, I thought, *I will show that successful version of me to my boyfriend. 'This is what you missed,' I'll say.* In the interim, the more that I moved, the further I walked, and the more time I could spend with my better kind of self. The one who could take on long distances, fuelled by a water pouch and dried mango strips. The one that would not cry her eyes purple, in her small room, on the bed.

Mere metres on, I was caught by a trap, a signpost with wooden arms pointing in every direction. Bootle: 44 miles to the left; Burnley: 149 to the right. 'Stand underneath it,' said the man who owned it. 'Tell me where you're from, I'll work out the distance and take a nice pic.'

I told him not to worry about the miles – I was a woman who didn't have time, that day; the distance between the guest house and me was pressing. 'Then just the picture,' he said. 'I'm raising money for cancer relief. Actually, I'm in remission.'

I released myself with a ten-pound note, knowing I ought to stay and listen to what this man had been through. But I couldn't face that cancerous zone.

I can't stay, I can't, I must walk.

***

The skies were warm and overcast as I followed the line of a tarmacked Roman road. The birds around me were vocal. I missed the chat of the taxi driver, and began my own conversation, chirping into the Dictaphone as I went.

There is something snorting in the next field. I hope it's a horse, not a person.

...

This is what my backpack sounds like.

It was all so easy to say. Quick and smooth and undemanding. My mind was clearing its throat.

Suddenly, I then told the Dictaphone my name and age. I explained where I was born and used to live. I gave it my mother's phone number, giddy, laughing.

HAZELNUTS

I realised that I've used the pronoun 'you' a few times, like I'm addressing this recording to somebody. And I was wondering who I would address it to. And then I realised that I'm actually addressing it to the person who finds my body on this path.

It took five hours and 14.5 miles for me to break back into Carlisle, where the London train had left me that late morning. Under the vapours of a biscuit factory, a group of kids was trying to sell their Akita puppy for seventeen quid. When I said no they grew cross. I reported the event to Dictaphone before lapsing into doggerel. Then: how much I hated hard pavements. Then: how much I preferred no roads. Then: how tired I was. Horribly tired.

I moaned that my feet felt swampy; that my blood was *squish-squashing* inside my walking boots.

At least I have the B & B, I said – except maybe I didn't. On arrival, watching guests pad across the lounge in their bare feet, I was informed there had been a mix-up, then driven apologetically to a nearby motorway truck stop with cheap beds: 'We're so sorry. We double-booked. And everywhere else is full.'

They didn't want you.

I talked and talked into the Dictaphone's mic; confessions without direction or substance. I relayed the wording of signs that warned not to use deep fat fryers inside the rooms. When I took a bath, the glue from my first blister plaster floated up to my head. There was no way to get rid of it without cutting off some hair. I unfolded my scissors.

Several times, I ran out of things to say. The babble eased, I paused, and then I was confronted with:

The end.

The end.

The end.

End.

End.

En—

I stopped recording. Life felt momentarily simpler listening to trucks arrive, the crackle of my papery mattress protector, than engaging in that conversation.

***

My mind cracked open further the following day, somewhere between Steel Rigg and Crosby-on-Eden.

Your boyfriend is kayaking round a lake.

...

HAZELNUTS

You haven't even found the sodding wall yet.

As I lumbered through grass, over fences, round mud, my words took on the sound and shape of white noise.

Talking's a bad idea. I feel like it wastes energy.

...

Just said hi to a sheep.

...

I'm taking a picture. I'm at the top of a hill.

When other hikers passed me by, I saw myself reflected, sustained, in their faces. Not long after the emperor's wall appeared – 'What's it like being Hadrian's Wall?' I asked – I enjoyed swapping smiles with a woman who was heading west, leading a man who appeared to be her husband. I was out of breath from walking and talking – too many one-sided interviews. White tides encircled my armpits. My red face. My bloodshot eyes. 'At least we're not building a wall on this,' I puffed, pointing up at the ridge.

She laughed while our paths were crossing. Then it was done and we grew further apart.

***

Craving a sense of structure – whether illusory or not – every other hour I played music. For forty-five-minute sessions, I plugged into my earphones – *maybe this'll help pass the miles* – and blocked out what I had travelled there to confront: a tumour of loss and sadness, dark and deep. In a lull between crags, Cat Power began to lecture me. 'What are we doing?' I echoed.

'Sitting on a ruin,' she sang. 'Bitching. Complaining.'

At the base of another hill, Pharoahe Monch yelled: 'Simon says GET THE FUCK UP.'

Miles passed. I made no progress. The path went on. The hills went on. For a while, clean hikers appeared in clusters. Hikers who wouldn't share smiles with someone like me, not while they were having fun smiling together. I tramped the fringes of scenic car parks and pull-ins, with salt-puckered lips and a T-shirt that reeked.

Permitting myself a sit-down and tortilla chips, I made the mistake of checking the map. That morning had felt like a whole month of life. Why were there still 8.5 miles left until the bunkhouse?

I haven't even walked a marathon. Paula Radcliffe could have jogged this in under three hours.

My heart muscles tensed. Ouch. It was too much. I pulled myself up, lightly shaking, and set off again. The sun was low. The hikers were dispersing. I couldn't tell if the creaking I heard was my bag or my legs. Something nasty was happening with my right ankle.

HAZELNUTS

You did this to yourself, Georgie.

Then: *No. My boyfriend made this happen.*

Retrieving my phone from my pocket, I dialled his number ready to confront him.

He answered breezily. 'How's it going?'

I tried to keep the panic from my voice. 'Why aren't you here?'

He almost laughed. 'Because I'm in France?'

'I need you,' I shouted.

I could hear his frown when he told me I didn't. 'You can do this, mate,' he said. 'You're strong.'

'No, I'm not.' I started to cry. Then: 'Are you jealous?' I asked.

Silence.

'Well?'

'Er...'

'You should be.' I sobbed out a bubble of snot. 'The walk is very scenic. And for the record, you didn't just leave me, I left you too.'

'What do you mean? Who's leaving?'

He tried to talk me back to normality. He might as well have been reasoning with an earthquake. A persistent voice said, *maybe this is it: the rupture you wanted.* But it wasn't a release.

After fifteen minutes of sympathy, my boyfriend had to go. 'I'll talk to you later,' he promised. 'I'm sorry. I love you. I'm not sure what's happening. Keep up your blood sugar levels.'

Once the call was done I stopped trembling. *Blood sugar.* Could it be that this breakdown was simply a lack of glucose? Maybe all my seismic reactions were diet-related.

Inside my nearest zip pocket was a bag of mixed nuts. I pulled out a flaking hazelnut and put it between my teeth, applying a firm amount of pressure. I was too sick to crunch and swallow. Instead, I held it there, where it easily stayed.

In agony, I crossed the next stile, retrieving a second hazelnut. This one sat inside my lip, and bulged under the skin.

Their sturdiness felt sublime.

I scurried away from the path to pee, and watched an elderly couple amble past. I was hidden in a ditch, and masked by foliage. *I don't need people now I have my nuts.*

HAZELNUTS

The hills were starting to flatten out, but were still too intense for me. More shout-singing. Frequent wails. Loud demands directed to my ankle.

I urged myself to keep walking, to keep myself in the world with that solid sensation of a nut. At the same time, I pictured simple things: snacks, sunlight, shoes. For a few nanoseconds, in between these pictures, I succeeded in existing without thoughts. Neither the quiet, ugly ones, nor the rattling ones that concealed them. I was too tired. I was nutting.

Being thoughtless felt sublime. Until, when I glugged more liquid, I heard a gurgle. The sound of a near-empty water pouch. Both hazelnuts fell down my gullet.

'I'm losing it, people,' I cried. I double-checked my surroundings – so empty – and opened my throat with a howl. Without breaking stride I decided I had three options: call a taxi, lie down until somebody found me, or continue to walk on.

I summited the brow of a hill and was granted the sight of two figures, far away. Were the people heading towards me? It was hard to make out. Switching Dictaphone back on, I began to file verbal reports.

There are two walkers.

...

They're both wearing blue.

After minutes of surveillance, it became clear that we were all three heading east. I plucked out a new hazelnut and secured it with my teeth.

They're going slower... than me.

These were not normal humans. They were Frodo and Samwise. I, meanwhile, was Gollum, warily scurrying. I ran through things to say if I should catch up, if I ever caught up. I dreamt they were also heading to my bunkhouse. That we three would walk there together.

After an age, the gap between us was closing. I heard voices. Two men, a unit, walking in the dusk. It occurred to me that it might not be safe to befriend them. But my ankle. My lack of water.

I cleared my throat. Two faces turned my way.

***

That night, in a dorm room shared between seven, I was in no state to sleep; onto my last set of blister plasters; socks tacky with goo.

I relived my meeting with Frodo and Samwise, policemen walking the wall to fundraise for cancer relief, over the same three days as I had picked. There was cancer everywhere. The men had a support car, weren't carrying heavy bags, and still they suffered.

HAZELNUTS

'This fucking wall,' said Frodo.

'All these *fucking hills*,' said Sam.

'YES,' I said. 'Fuck the hills.'

I recalled how they were supposed to be camping, but that Samwise had packed a windbreaker instead of a one-person tent. 'No roof on the thing!' said Frodo. 'HA.'

I laughed and laughed.

We parted ways at the road where their car was parked. The policemen would maybe see me the following day. Ten minutes later, my water ran totally dry, then a woman walking the opposite way shared the last dregs of her energy drink with me.

In the barn of the bunkhouse, I tossed between dread and wild elation. Thirty-four miles completed today. Thirty-two miles left.

I was the only person alone in the room: the others were in twos or threes. An Irishman discussing the movement of custard for his degree; a small group of Polish men spilling jokes and beer.

My breasts were sore. My ankle: possessed. The tumour in my core was knotty and gasping.

Too scared I might sleep past my alarm, I barely slept at all.

***

When the third day arrived, I stumbled out, imagining I could somehow outpace my own limp. The hills were beautiful to my eyes. A chocolate bar was beautiful in my mouth. I drank from a tap jutting out of somebody's house. Winced down into a valley, then grumbled slowly out the other side. 'Good morning,' I said, to a dog-walker. She greeted me as if I was well and functioning.

My boyfriend sent encouraging texts. His parents and brother too. *They're thinking of me. They're rooting for me. They're sure I can make it all the way.*

By mid-morning I was criss-crossing roads like a drunk, shouting at every gate and wall in my way. *Who put these here, and why do they want to hurt me?*

Why am I trying to follow a dead man's fence?

Why do stones get to outlast me?

Why am I not as important as a wall?

I ran out of water by lunchtime, and staggered towards a tea room. It claimed to be shut, but one of the women inside could see me waving. I rapped on the window, and mimed desperation. 'There's a tap round the side,' she shouted, keeping the window closed.

I drank my fill and looked at the road I had come from. My knees quivered. My back and shoulders curved.

I have broken the walk, broken the weekend, probably broken my ankle.

I let myself drop to the grass. In a while I would decide what I was going to do next. Call my boyfriend and apologise. Admit that this hadn't worked. Display myself appropriately as someone who has rotted and cannot be fixed.

The end.

The end.

End.

End.

Except, before I reached that point, a runner would donate me blister plasters.

The policemen would arrive with their energy gels.

Frodo would pull me to my feet, inviting me to join them for that final 20 miles.

I would snigger about drugs raids beside the Tyne. I would trip past a pair of black knickers, on fire in the street. I would give Samwise my scissors when the seams of his boxers chafed, and he would stop to slice them off, yanking the fabric free from inside his trousers.

TRAUMA

I would curse all the bridges, circle a dog shit, thank these men repeatedly for absorbing me into their pack.

Meanwhile my ankle would bulge and contort. And that night I would remove my sock to find fluid, rawness, pink.

BLANK SPACES

Yvonne Conza

Tick tock of the clock and I'm still in pajamas. To complete an assignment before its noon deadline, I've been up since predawn corralled at my desk. Precious morning hours, a treasured time of satiny silence, grants me greater access to interior thoughts, and provides a false sense of freedom from a racing stopwatch. The temptation to step out onto our 40th floor balcony for fresh air tugs at me, even on a dreary day with a slate grey sky patched with pouty, potbellied rain clouds. From this height, I enjoy looking over the edge at our building's newly renovated pool area. It reminds me of a David Hockney painting where he brings complexity to the surface by collapsing the vision-field of an image, leaving vivid details in the foreground.

Today my husband plans to take me to lunch. He is a punctual man; *we can't be late* pecks at me as I hit the 'send' key to my editor. His annoyance at my dawdling means there is no time to bask on the balcony. I dash to dress, and we snag an elevator and exit into the lobby. His attention is fixated on filling in the location and destination blanks on the Uber app. I am drawn to a larger screen and spot a Miami Beach Crime Scene Unit van and several black-and-white patrol cars lined up around the circular driveway of our condo building.

The atmosphere in the lobby is jittery and jolted. Approaching the front desk to ask about the commotion, I'm steered to a discrete location and whisper-informed that an owner's guest plunged from the 31st floor of her balcony. *No – ooo.* Nearby, with her arms roped around a tween son, the jumper's wife huddles in a corner, both heads hanging heavy, toppling over their knees. Someone mentions that only yesterday he'd lunched by the pool. *Not far from where he landed?* Plainly wondered, not asked.

The blank spaces of suicide startle me. I discovered that a 300-foot vertical deceleration can reach speeds of 75–80mph, jumpers tend to scout out the place where they will leap, and while falling is not generally a popular method of lethal self-harm, in Hong Kong it accounted for over half of all suicides in 2006. The decision to plunge from a tall building is made only by those who are determined to die.

Life and death are in a non-stop spiral all around us in a discomforting way. Throughout our building many stories exist, including mine. In 1979, when I was fifteen, Nick, my oldest brother, was found badly decomposed with a self-inflicted bullet wound in his gut. Suicide's subtle silence is a subtitle in my life. Routinely witnessed by me were family squabbles and a menacing time when Dad lit his undershirt on fire and threatened to jump off the one-storey roof of our outdoor patio. When I was seven, something incensed my unsound brother and, on a scorching July day, he snapped, grabbed me like a rag doll and locked me in a car trunk. By then I knew how to surrender into the stillness of a corpse. Trauma heightens certain effects and dulls others. I cope by acting as though I'm a confident spelling bee contestant given a strange word like 'petrichor'. Without knowing what it means, I roar out each letter like a cheerleader.

My earliest survival tactic came from idolising and imitating ponytailed Nadia Comăneci. At twelve, I wanted to be her. On the first night of the 1976 Montreal Olympics, her coiled steel composure enthralled me as she neared the uneven bars. In a stark white leotard with blue, yellow and red thin side-piping stripes, the colours of the Romanian flag, her eighty-six-pound doll body, muscled with determination, stood less than five feet tall. With the competitor number 73 – seven plus three equals ten – she'd be the first athlete to ever score a ten at the Olympics. Prior to mounting the uneven bars, Nadia lowered her head in concentration. Champions visualise their required skills and routine over and over, for hours and hours, perfecting them with mental precision. As she rubbed her chalked hands together, floral-white dust puffed out. Then she guzzled air, lifted onto the balls of her feet, sprinted towards the springboard, pushed off and straddled-sailed over the low bar. When she reached up to grab a hold of the high bar, my hands also soared skyscraper high.

That summer of 1976, I changed my diet to tuna, rice and Grape-Nuts and began to write stories on cornflower blue-lined loose-leaf paper. New York City was a-calling, my ambition, and a decision that required me to hunker down and demand more of myself. Nadia was six years old when she began training. I was already twelve and needed to catch up, study more and get out of bed early to jot down ideas for plots and characters. To write without a wobble was my goal. Achieving perfection would take me places.

Nadia's coach was a man called Bela Karolyi, a former Olympic discus and hammer thrower who said that she was the only gymnast that he could never break.

Other kids had more talent, but I was more focused. When he asked me to do twenty-five push-ups, I'd do fifty. I wanted to be better than anyone else, and to be extraordinary. I don't know why. It's the way I am. – Nadia Comăneci

My trauma, my uneven bars, was channelled into an active sixth sense that influenced my vision, hearing, taste, smell, touch and detection of movement, and I used it to warn me of danger. It's like being able to smell the distinctive atmospheric odour of an oncoming storm that fills your nostrils, or the earthy-musty wet tang in the air after a hard rain. Scientists call the damp smell after rainfall 'petrichor'. I found the word while doing research on trauma. I also learned that during a thunderstorm, lightning can split oxygen and nitrogen molecules, leaving behind a sharp chlorine-like scent. When I was locked in the car truck, or witnessed family fighting, fear's stench was metallic like rust.

BLANK SPACES

Suicide is the tenth leading cause of death in the United States. Alaska, Montana, New Mexico, Wyoming, Nevada and Utah have the highest suicide rates. Global statistics show a high rate of suicide in the countries of Lithuania, Russia and Guyana. In Afghanistan, Iraq and Syria, places of war-torn conflict, the numbers were comparatively lower, without explanation. The lowest suicide rates were found in the Caribbean Islands of the Bahamas, Jamaica, Grenada, Barbados and Antigua. Suicidal warning signs vary and include hopelessness, withdrawal from friends and social activities, changes in personality and appearance, self-harm behaviour (increased use of drugs and/or alcohol, unsafe sex, reckless driving) and threatening to kill oneself. They might be caused by recent trauma or life crisis, such as the death of a spouse or pet, divorce, break-up, diagnosis of major illness, loss of job, or a financial problem.

Animals are not immune to despondency or self-harm. Werner Herzog's Antarctica documentary features a penguin retreating from its colony and waddling towards a mountain, seeking certain death. His film captures a wide lens, ice-glazed, rocky outcropping of brutal barrenness, and the breeding area for the Adélie penguins. Herzog suggests it's the *closest to what a future space settlement would look like.* A penguin expert, described as taciturn, tells the filmmaker that returning the wayward bird to the tuxedoed rookery would do no good. The camera tracks the black and white, donkey-braying bird, wings adapted to flippers, heading towards the bleak ridge.

Sheep are another example of animals with a possible disposition towards suicidal melancholia. In 2005, stunned Turkish shepherds watched more than 1,500 sheep jump off a 15-metre cliff. More than 400 died, the survivors cushioned by the fallen flock. Then there are dolphins. Kathy, who played Flipper on TV in the 1960s, is said to have taken her own life. She swam into the arms of Ric O'Barry, her trainer, before ceasing to breathe as she sank to the bottom of her tank.

She was really depressed, explains O'Barry. You have to understand dolphins and whales are not air breathers like we are. Every breath they take is a conscious effort. They can end their life whenever. She looked him right in the eye, took a breath and didn't take another one. *I let her go and she sank straight down on her belly to the bottom of the tank.*

Referenced as 'failure to thrive', dolphin suicide occurs when they fade away from not eating or socialising. I understand the slow fading out, the inability to desire a future. Sleep is how I first started to shrink and sink into depression. Underneath sheets, with eyes closed, stillness and silence were a relief.

During my senior graduating class picnic, I swam in shorts and a T-shirt in Lake Erie, drunk on rum. Classmates were exchanging names of colleges that they would attend in the fall: Buffalo State, Fredonia, Geneseo, Potsdam and a few small universities in Virginia and Pennsylvania. I hadn't applied to a single school.

BLANK SPACES

As I distanced myself from the shore, my classmates were reduced to tiny splotches swatting a motion-blurred volleyball over a net. The sun was setting and my arms were tired from paddling. Nobody could see me struggling. Bewildered by all that had happened to me and afraid of the future, I was a penguin wandering away from the colony, a flightless bird no longer content in the world. Bobbing and starting to black out, I recalled the question I was asked at my brother's wake: *How are you feeling?* Without giving me the opportunity to answer, they continued: *He's in a better place. I know how you feel. Be strong. Would you like a 7-Up? Have something to eat. You must eat.* They'd repeat themselves as if I couldn't hear. I was handed Kleenexes that I crumpled and balled in my hands. *You look so grown up in that dress.* My sorrow was suppressed in bereavement's etiquette, seated and sutured all in black. Sadness is a sandalwood scented funeral parlor, a *Beloved Brother* sympathy sash strung across a lily floral arrangement, a graveyard landscaped with neat rows of hardwood folding chairs, and a family transformed into statues.

At fifteen, I was confused, scared, filled with blank spaces – shushed, silenced from asking a single question – *What comes after ending a life?*

In 1977, Nadia Comăneci drank bleach but claimed it wasn't true, just a rumour. Fifteen years old and unstoppable, at the peak of her sport and fame, it did seem improbable, and for years afterwards she denied it. Then in 1990, she admitted to *Life Magazine* that it was true, saying she was *glad because I didn't have to go to the gym.*

As a kid, in our bathtub and heated pool, I held my breath as long as I could. The cavernous, soft echoing beneath the water's surface was seductive, but my resilient heartbeat pleaded to be heard. I visualised Nadia's fluid flyaway dismount off the uneven bars, cited as *swimming in an ocean of air.* That day in 1982 in Lake Erie, tugged by undertow and near drowning, I gasped for air and fought for each stroke back to the shore. The next day, still buzzed from alcohol and the thought of a near watery grave, I received my high school diploma without having a clue about my future.

Jumping from heights has been facilitated by the high-rise culture of our cities. In our 250-unit building, days before the plunge, an elevator broke down and remained out of commission for days, challenging owners and their guests, creating queues to go up and down, halting construction projects and suspending deliveries. People were grumpy about what amounted to a small inconvenience. The replacement part arrived and the repair was completed the same day as the jump.

As a child I was afraid of heights. I had no problem climbing up trees, ladders and play structures, but getting down was a terrifying dilemma. In 2015, I decided to confront my anxiety. Trapeze. The azure blue sky with its soft, billowing clouds was the perfect backdrop. In fear, beauty still exists.

BLANK SPACES

At the trapeze rig I felt uneasy. Two men and a tiny, muscular-shouldered woman were using the swings, each of them taking turns diving off the platform and flying with their legs pitched forward in solid 'L' and 'V' shapes. Their swift back-and-forth pendulum motions, acrobatic somersaults and theatrical mid-air free fall landings on the spongy safety net were pulled off with a childlike ease.

I signed the release form and was put through a series of on-the-ground warm-ups. Before climbing the ladder to the perch platform, the instructor asked if I had any questions. *Is it okay to text up there?* While ascending the rope ladder, I slowed to a snail's pace, then froze. A foot away from the modest perch was an impossible distance. *Keep coming.* Spider was a foreigner who didn't speak much English. The inflection of his consonants was melodic and his vowels echoed joy. He'd seen many come to trapeze to break through personal obstacles, to face risk and live on the edge, to leap towards something that they had yet to understand.

Vanity pushed me upward. I climbed each rung with a yo-yoing *yes-no-yes-no-yes-no-yes-no-YES!* Trembling and sweating, I made it to the trapeze platform, crawling onto it with rigged, stop-start motions like a frazzled toddler.

Spider hooked a double-belay onto my harness, but the extra buckling-up did nothing to make me feel safe. *I can't-I can't-can't-can't. It's okay.* I think that's what Spider said. *Okay* feels like the right word. Nothing feels okay.

I desperately wanted down, but the only way to get down, agreed prior to my ascent, was to snatch the fly bar and jump. Reaching it meant grabbing the bar and having to let go. I became rattled, paralysed.

Atop the platform, I viewed the fly bar dangling in the distance. Spider took this as a sign to reach for it and snag it with a long pole called a noodle.

You can do this, shouted someone safely on the ground.

In a way that no person has ever held me, Spider gripped me tightly around my tiny waist. His arms were equipment, stronger than any rope, harness or anchoring device. As I reached out for the fly bar with my right hand, the left one froze and I let go and huddled back into the crevice of Spider's chest.

I can't do this. I'm so sorry. I was falling apart – losing control.

No words were exchanged between Spider and me as I stretched my hand out for the fly bar once more. One hand gripped it while the other hesitated. *How do you make the bar stop?*

The flying bar is tricky. There's a rope hooked up to each side. Stability isn't its thing. It's in flux, in flight. Swings.

I'll hold it for you. Spider's soothing songful accent. I re-chalk my hands.

Where are you from?

Brazil.

The instruction remembered – *lean hips forward.*

Spider yelled, *Hup*, the signal to leave the platform. Take off. Fly. The cue word 'hup' is used because 'go' can sound like 'no'. I hear myself say *NO*. Lean out. Hips forward. Jump.

There are twenty-one letters in the Italian alphabet. In Western society twenty-one symbolises adulthood. Twenty-one wins a blackjack hand but exceeding that number is a bust, an automatic loss. At twenty-one, my brother died from a 'gutshot', a horrible death. The stomach fills with hydrochloric acid as it intermixes with blood to produce fatal toxemia, leaving a person to bleed out in fifteen minutes. As I read about the slow and painful death from a bullet lodged into a belly, my gut told me that my brother's action was a cry for help. His favourite silk shirt had been deliberately draped over a chair and that gesture felt too sentimental and strangely composed. This person had hoped to be found, bandaged up and reunited with his shirt unstained, not turned scarlet. Even his suicide notes, with drawings, were detailed and instructional, and overstated his case. Dramatic depression. I can't erase the feeling that he sought rescue over death.

After my brother died, I concluded I wasn't likely to live to twenty-one. Before he was even buried, Dad contacted a life insurance company about his other children. He was briefed on the 'suicide clause' which required survival of two years to be eligible for payout. My height and weight were noted. *You're small for fifteen. Do you throw up after eating? Have you had your menses?* My blank face prompted the insurance agent to say *period.* Exhausted at the need to protect myself from my family, I shook my head no.

For years afterwards, I acted normal – *ssh-shush-shut up* – scared, sealed up, shamed and stigmatised by an imaginary questionnaire that sought to trace how abuse made me susceptible to suicidal thoughts.

Management has not sent out a building memo. Every day since the fall, new details jiggle, not babble, into elevator and mailroom conversations: the apartment owner's name, witnesses to the chilling event, who identified the Brazilian guest to the police, what time it occurred (9:45 a.m.), where the body landed (not near the pool), and a gruesome detail about the impact (███████████████). Part of me is happy to know that my views have not been disturbed since the apartment line of the fatal fall was on the opposite side of the building. That feels wrong, selfish.

'A guest, not an owner. Why didn't he take his business elsewhere?' The person I spoke to sounded Australian, though he was from London and his statement was not made out of anger, but more as a steely annoyance. It made me laugh because I'm certain he thought it was a valid point.

BLANK SPACES

Didn't I agree? What is said can't be unsaid. I flung out an offhanded quip over lunch, some gallows humour, but by dinner I was numb and silent. Survivors feel the stares and sense the dialogue that goes on behind closed doors as people play guessing games about the circumstances. Stage whispers are intended to be heard.

Tomorrow, on the lot adjacent to our building, an abandoned hospital is scheduled to be imploded at 9:45 a.m., a week on from the jumper. Preparations to secure the area have been detailed and residents advised to make changes to their departure times to avoid traffic delays. When the dust and debris settles and is removed, the plot of land that remains will become the location of Miami Beach's tallest building. Local activists like myself fought the developer, who found a way to make a mockery of zoned height restrictions. The skyscraper will have magnificent views of 'Cruise Ship Alley' where luxury liners pass, the Miami skyline, Biscayne Bay and the Art Deco glamour and glitz of South Beach with its impeccably beautiful beaches. According to the American Foundation for Suicide Prevention, it also risks becoming a suicide spot.

Ssh-shush-shut up – no building memo has gone out. When I asked if our staff who witnessed the incident were okay, I was told *yes.* Have they been offered counselling? *They're fine.* Scared, sealed up, shamed and stigmatised – suicide's standard silences. Tomorrow when the hospital is blown up, I will watch from my balcony and say a prayer for the fallen flock. Aloud.

WE AWFUL, AWFUL
Ian Boulton

Now I don't know but I was told that in your deepest distress your personal culture can turn on you and bite you on the bum. I asked a friend of mine – an experienced madman – about this and he went further.

It's much worse than that, he said. The bastard fires up the barbecue, sharpens a massive fuck-off blade and slices great chunky steaks off your arse to throw on the flames. Listen to this:

outofstateplatespoolofbloodallwhitejurytenfootcelltakeaman outfalselyforpaywentalongfortherideguesswhoArthur! Dexter!theregisterPattyGentlemanJiminflamedrunkards fromtheslums. Can you imagine having that ringing round your head twenty-odd hours a day, day after day, for weeks?

Horrible, I said.

Well, the first time I broke that's what happened to me, he said.

WE AWFUL, AWFUL

Did you ever find out what it was? I said.

O I knew what it was all right, he said. If I hadn't known it so well, if I hadn't absorbed it and made it part of my being, then it couldn't have shown up to torment me. It was a scrambled version of Dylan's 'Hurricane'. My too-literary mind had decided to mirror my own fragmented state by fracturing the narrative, turning something I loved against me. It thought it was being clever, I realise, but I had given it the ammunition it needed. The words were all in there, waiting to be turned into shrapnel. It happened again – Frightened Rabbit almost did for me a few years back – but eventually I learned my lesson.

Which is? I said.

Avoid the words, he said. And repetition. No Philip Glass. No Terry Riley. Earworms lie in wait under all harmony. Oddly, the more mad-sounding the music, the harder it is for it to attack you when you break. So embrace discord. Stockhausen. Soft Machine. There's nothing your head can do to make them sound worse. My tip to the future mad is this: don't give your bastard mind the base materials to work with and you'll be fine. Take control of the soundtrack and choose stuff that is already in tatters. If it ain't broke then don't go anywhere near it.

That's funny, I said.

Yes, that is funny, he said.

What about enjoyment, pleasure? I said.

That's funny, too, he said.

On the other hand I've heard it said that in times of darkness it is possible to turn to your store of art and that it will act as the source of nourishment it was meant to be. This view was put to me by another friend who senses her anxiety is rising up to strike her down when she finds that she is reluctant to enter a certain room in her own house. You'll think me quite mad if I tell you which one, she said. As soon as she feels this happening, she takes action.

I leave the house, she said, get on the tube to Charing Cross and walk up to the National Portrait Gallery. There is a photograph there taken by Camille Silvy in 1860 named *Two Unknown Women.* I feel that I resemble both of them. Looking at the picture has a soothing effect on me and my state of my mind. I don't quite know how to describe it.

Please try, I said.

It's a sort of calming sense of my own insignificance, she said. I feel like one of a vast crowd in which we are all fundamentally the same. Looking at the photo is my version of standing on top of a skyscraper and seeing the people on the pavement as tiny forms of insect life. Or gazing into the night sky when there are no clouds and having that realisation that we are little more than a speck in the galaxy.

And you find this calming, I said.

Immensely, she said. Why should an insignificant life form worry? What concerns can a speck have?

Why do you need to go to the gallery, I said. Couldn't you just take a photo of the photo on your phone and look at it at home whenever you felt anxious?

O no! she said. That wouldn't work at all. I need the cathedral experience, the vastness of God's creation, so that I know my place. In my own home, I am a giant. I am the God. Albeit one with crippling doubts about my own existence.

As for me, my own little quirks are not so debilitating. Obviously I cannot go to the cinema at night. I need to sit on the end of the fourth row on the left-hand side and that seat is not always available in the evenings. Also, entering a building in daylight and leaving to find it is dark disturbs me. I feel that too much time has passed and this sensation can stay with me for several days. The theatre, of course, is out of the question, even matinees where you can book online and choose your seat. Like many people, I'm sure, I find the notion of repeated performance deeply depressing. And that's about it. O and literary works that mention burned legs can set off something in me that I don't want to look at too closely. And that is definitely it.

I bumped into my friend who thinks she looks like two unknown women recently and she was on good form. She appeared little more than a mite, microscopically content.

And my friend who has a complicated relationship with music came to visit me at the seaside a few days back. I took him to a pub on the beach so we could catch up. The pub is named after a between-wars spy thriller that was partly written in the town. On the walls hang posters of the various film versions that used the book as a source.

The barman that evening was someone I knew to talk to though I never remembered his name. I did remember that he was the main writer and performer in a local punk rap band called The Ragged-Trousered Thoughtless Bastards. He came with heavy red beard and Buddhist tats. The rule in the pub was that the bar staff controlled the music so, cognizant of my friend's difficulties in this area, I asked him if he would be okay with that.

Will you be okay with that, I said.

No problem, he said. I have become adept at tuning out background noise.

I made sure that I was sitting facing the posters of the classic black-and-white version of the film. Behind me I knew there was an upsetting image produced in the mid-1970s but I put it out of my mind. I placed my pint glass on a beer mat to my right and my empty half pint glass on a beer mat to my left. As usual, I poured half of my beer into the smaller glass.

We filled each other in on recent cultural happenings that the other had been unable to consume. My friend told me of some movies for grown-ups he had sat through and I brought him up to date on current lesbian confessional break-up albums I had been able to listen to. A familiar song played over the pub's speakers and I found my left foot moving in time to its rhythms. I told this friend about my other friend and he seemed interested. It was pleasant. We moved on to other topics.

Are you able to work now, I said.

Yes I am able to work, he said.

Do you travel as much now, I said.

No not as much, he said.

Do you have any plans for the future, I said.

Yes I have plans, he said.

You must be feeling better, I said.

Yes I am feeling better, he said.

And better and better, I said.

Andbetterandbetterandbetterandbetterandbetter, he said.

AS DEEP AS THE ATLANTIC: ON GRIEF AND WRITING

Kirsty Logan and Paul McQuade

KL: I wrote my first novel, *The Gracekeepers*, in the strange stop-start of grief after my dad's sudden and unexpected death. I was twenty-seven; he was fifty-eight. I knew he was going to die, because everybody dies, but I had no warning and I wasn't ready. I guess we're never ready. I guess he wasn't ready either. I didn't know how to grieve, because I'd never had to before, not like that. There had been deaths: big ones, small ones, unexpected ones, drawn-out ones; my grandparents, several cats, a friend at school – in fact, two friends at school, one to suicide and one to drowning. But this was different. This grief was overwhelming, and it was drowning me, and I didn't know what to do. All I wanted to know was: how long will this last? What am I to expect from grief, and when? I was envious of religions and cultures with structures of mourning, as I'd been raised with neither. The only thing I did know was how to make up stories and write them down, so I tried to make that my way to grieve. One

158

day I was out on a sailboat off the south coast of England with my uncle, and I saw a buoy that looked like a huge birdcage. I often went sailing as a child with my dad, and being near water always makes me think of him – and so I thought of him then, though of course I was grieving for him so a part of me was always thinking of him. I wrote a world where death is marked by capturing a bird in a cage, and grief is timed by the lifespan of that unfed, untended bird. I knew that a starved bird wouldn't last long, and I didn't want my grief to last long either. But it did. Seven years on and I'm beginning to see how my grief has grown up with me. How I've grown with it. Been changed by it. How it nourishes me, opens my eyes, enlarges me. How we work together, me and it.

PM: Trauma is mischaracterised in our culture. We think of it in quantitative terms: such and such an experience, in the dimension of its displeasure, the magnitude of its horror, is traumatic. In this logic, all bad events are traumatic, and we would all be traumatised by the death of a loved one. But trauma is not dependent on a qualitative judgement or a physical cause. It was Freud who looked most in depth beyond the anatomic rationale of 'shell shock' to see the psychic mechanism of trauma. And what he found there, and what has been elaborated upon by later developments in the treatment and study of trauma, is that it is not the qualitative nor quantitative dimension that marks an event as traumatic, but an *unpreparedness* of the subject. A traumatic event overwhelms all the defences laid out in advance against the encroachment of negative experience.

This is why different people, undergoing similar events, are affected differently: some are traumatised, others not. What we find in the testimony of trauma, where such testimony is even possible, is that the mind is thrown back to the scene of a 'missed encounter'. Nightmares, hallucinations, and traumatic memories caused by the trigger all bring the subject back to a point in time in which something is missing. These symptoms play out bodily, in the form of anxiety, an upsurge in energy designed to defend the subject from the event's repetition, to make the subject ready for an overwhelming that has already happened. This is bound to a 'repetition compulsion' to return to the moment, to fix it, to survive it, intentionally. This is why trauma cannot be outrun but only worked through – *durcharbeiten* is the term Freud used. But the analytic clinic has been transformed since Freud's time, and 'working through' existed long before Freud. What was there before? What cultural practice helped? In all cultures we find sympathetic magic, or what we might extend into the work of metaphor. Burial is this kind of magic: I say goodbye to the body and I begin to say goodbye to the dead. I transfer my connections. I give votives, I suffer, I pray: I give up a piece of myself, a little bird left to die in the open sea.

KL: Partway through writing *The Gracekeepers*, I went on a month-long writing residency at an eighteenth-century castle. It was January. It snowed. It was so beautiful that the photos I took looked fake. I was there to write the scenes where one of the characters dies suddenly and unexpectedly, which leads to the meeting between the two protagonists.

AS DEEP AS THE ATLANTIC: ON GRIEF AND WRITING

Halfway through the month, I went home for the night to get my cat euthanised. He was eighteen years old and had been on the edge of death for many months. He could barely move his back legs and there was blood in his pee, and I spent a fortune on vet bills trying to fix him.

It will come as no surprise to learn that he was the family cat, and had lived with my dad before he died; I was determined to keep him alive in a way that I now see was not good for him (or for me, probably).

At the same time I broke up with my girlfriend of five years. It had been coming for a while, but I'd been pretending it wasn't; not that everything in my life can be traced back to my dad's death, but also it kind of can, because after losing him I was terrified of losing anyone else. My (ex-)girlfriend and I shared a flat; when I left the castle, I'd need to find a new place to live.

I did a lot of crying. I did a lot of crying while walking, which is soothing when the tears warm your cold cheeks but later terrible when your skin chaps and reddens in brackets around your nose and mouth. I did a lot of crying in the bath, which was huge and Victorian with taps that juddered and cried along with me. I cried and I wrote. I don't think I wrote myself out of anything, but maybe I wrote myself through. Or maybe things were just shit, but I wrote, because me writing or not writing wasn't going to affect the level of shit.

TRAUMA

PM: Catharsis, or in more psychoanalytic terms, cathexis, is an action in which psychic energy can be safely discharged from a subject: self-harm, for example, transforms emotional turmoil into form. A clean line, the first step in a written character. This is writing on the body: a message we want to send. A prayer for intervention. *Help me.* An extreme example. In another case, say that of depression, writing can bring some fire into the cold hearth of the heart. It makes me think of Plath's 'Munich Mannequins' when she talks about black phones glittering and digesting voicelessness. 'The snow has no voice,' she says. Though Plath's most famous image is the bell jar, I think of depression most often as being like snow: everything blank and unfeeling and mute and numb. But also strangely serene and untouched. Snowbanked, white, unwritten. It is hard to come back from that place. And then there is this: the little spark of the letter. Like flint and tinder I put words together, living off the heat, until at last there is enough. Enough to survive. And when we make it through, work through, *durcharbeit,* maybe things are better. Or maybe it's just that we are better, if never really cured.

KL: Apparently one novel with a heavy-handed grief metaphor wasn't enough for me. Next I wrote *The Gloaming*, which is set on a small (fictional) Scottish island where people gradually turn to stone. When they feel their time is coming, which can happen at any age and at any moment, they slowly make their way up to the cliff overlooking the sea, and there their bodies turn to stone. They become their own gravestones. Part of the narrative focuses on Peter, the father of the family, who is turning to stone throughout the novel; his daughter, Mara, is the main focus of the story, and she feels a churn of emotions as she observes both his change and his eventual stone form. He moves stiffly and can't grip things. He becomes forgetful and emotional. Finally his body, previously so fit and golden and unbreakable, becomes something outwith his control. Readers can choose to either attribute Peter's condition to the novel's conceit of stone people, or, less fantastically, to the *dementia pugilistica* he developed from hundreds of blows to the head during his career as a boxer. A few years before he died, my dad developed Parkinson's. He moved stiffly and couldn't grip things. He became forgetful and emotional. Finally his body, previously so fit and golden and unbreakable, became something outwith his control. Readers can also choose to attribute Peter's condition to this.

PM: It was Medusa's curse to turn living flesh to stone. There is something about immobility, stone, fossilisation, that is always tied, on its underside, to the idea of monstrous femininity. Both Freud and Marx used the word 'fetish' and brought it into European thought, though its origins lie in the writings of Charles de Brosses on the Yoruba in Nigeria. De Brosses argued that the fetish was a protean form of worship which deified the animal and the inanimate, and his work is drawn on by later commentators, such as August Comte, to place fetishist ritual – and with it African religions as much as Africans – into the mythic past of humanity. These commentators blatantly attempted to place the fetish outside of white European modernity. The fetish was, to them, a piece of magical savagery. It is Marx who points out the hypocrisy of this: here in industrial modernity is this strange metaphysical object circulating as the very lifeblood of capitalism, while those who worship it deny the very nature of the commodity itself, i.e. that it is a fetish at all. The fetish, like trauma, now lies in a very different usage in our everyday speech. We use it to mean fetishism, kink, etc. But the fetish has a religious, metaphysical force, and a peculiar relation to time: it suspends it. Nowhere is this more apparent than the man from whom we derive the term *masochism,* Leopold von Sacher-Masoch, particularly in the book *Venus in Furs.* The whole text revolves around contracts and women turned to stone. The unliving object which, in its very death, its petrification, is transformed into an icon, an idol, a golden calf. Desire is tricky. The object of desire oscillates, it repels us, repulses it. A person can draw us towards them all the while making us suffer. The fetish – this object outside time – solves this difficulty. What resistance is there in a foot? A shoe? Fetishism forms a religion in itself. Mourning does the same. Perhaps there is no greater act of adoration than to turn what one loves to stone. That way it remains untouched. It remains forever. In its very death, it is made immortal.

KL: I'm now writing my third novel, the last in a loose trilogy: *The Gracekeepers*, *The Gloaming*, and now this one with the working title of *The Gramarye*. The novels take place hundreds of years apart: *The Gracekeepers* in a post-apocalyptic future, *The Gloaming* in the present, and *The Gramarye* in the late medieval period. There are no characters in common and the narratives don't follow on from one another; each novel is completely standalone. Those are the differences. Here are the similarities. All three novels are coming-of-age stories about young women who leave their homes to go on a quest. All three novels are about women struggling in a world that feels simultaneously too big and too small; too looming and too confined; agoraphobic and claustrophobic. All three novels are set in liminal spaces where the sea meets the land. All three novels are about parents who are present, but lost – not dead, necessarily, but absent in some way. And all three novels are about grief. I didn't mean to write three novels about grief. I don't want to write about grief. I don't want to think about grief. I want to write about love and surprise and joy and betrayal and wonder and bravery and cruelty and hate. Not grief; please, anything but that. I've had quite enough. Yet here I am, three novels in, still creating characters only to kill them so I can make readers feel sad about it.

PM: Writing is its own form of magic, and metaphor, especially, is related to the plasticity of the brain – neuroplasticity. To the human animal there is no distinction in the body between metaphor and reality. Different ways of thinking literally rework the neural pathways of the brain. Writing leaves the mark of this working-through; the reader can follow, and in finding this ritual, like the codification of burial rites, finds a way to shed their own grief. We share our own coping strategies in writing. And yet, writing this way is always caught in the paradox of traumatic time, a paradox of time that is proper to human psychic life and which Freud called *Nachträglichkeit*, translated most often as 'belatedness', but literally meaning *carrying after it*, like the figure of the wake of a ship. In trauma, the subject is forced to return to a point in time always after the fact, harnessing the energies it knows it requires to be unaffected by that moment. And yet the moment has always already passed. It is too late to get ready and yet that is all we do, trapped in the compulsion to repeat. I don't *want* to write about grief, and yet I am here, again, trying to find my way through. We often say that writers are always writing the same book again and again, and maybe this is true. It's like the structure of trauma: we keep coming back to it, again and again, hoping, this time, we'll get it right.

KL: I haven't yet finished this last novel, but already I've noticed a difference: while the first two novels were love stories, this last one is not. I couldn't even retrofit it to be a love story; I've written literally no character that my protagonist could feasibly be with, and there's no way for the narrative to turn in that direction without breaking the whole thing. I always intended for her to end the story alone. In fact, the entire point of the story is that she finds out she always was alone, although she didn't know it. The whole time she's thought that someone was with her, helping her, guiding her, doing the things she didn't think she was capable of doing; she finds strength in that companionship, and it makes her do things she'd never do alone. But she finds out that all along it was her, always her, only her.

PM: When we dream we see ourselves with many faces. I dream of my father, say, but behind that father-mask is me; I dream of a baby, and that baby is me. The dream is a stage play in which the different parts of us act out, reveal themselves in the truth of their mask. Who is the audience of this? Who do we play for? In writing, much like the dream, every character is a piece of ourselves. Phantasmatic, of course: more moral, more just, smarter, more beautiful, more capable, while the other is despised, scorned, hateful, malicious. They are all a piece of us. All parts of us. We embrace them, in writing and in dreams, because we know that no story can exist without them: conflict is the animation of story, being more than one is the animation of ourselves. It's strange to say: *I am alone.* Who are we speaking to? Our words come from someone else and they go somewhere else. When we speak of doing things not with or for another, but alone, especially in a story like the one we find in a *Bildungsroman,* we are speaking about cohesion: of making sense of all the parts of us that remain inchoate. Where Jung's shadow says, in the dream you will find a mirror image of yourself, Freud says the dream shows pieces of ourselves refused entry into conscience, and granted entry to the dream-work only in distorted form. The dream remains a message nonetheless. Writing, even if it purports to be telegraphic or realistic, touches the same place as the dream. In this way, writing teaches us lessons in how to be what we might yet become.

KL: A lot has happened in my career since my first book came out five years ago. I won't list it all. I'm a writer and

I live a writer's life, just as I imagined I someday could, but more. In the dining room of my childhood home was a wall of floor-to-ceiling bookshelves, packed tight with my dad's books. Every mealtime I'd read the spines and try to imagine what stories lived inside; what worlds my dad went into when he sat silently reading. Recently I gave a copy of *The Gracekeepers* to someone as a thank-you; she emailed a few weeks later asking if it was suitable for an eight-year-old, as her daughter was obsessed with the cover image and title, and kept coming up with more and more elaborate ideas of what the story might be about. I said it was fine for her to read, but honestly, I wish I hadn't, so she could keep imagining. And through it all, a few times a week the thought floats through: I wish my dad could see this. When he died I'd had a few pieces in magazines and small anthologies, done a couple of readings, had a short story on the radio. But I hadn't published a book; hadn't won any prizes; hadn't performed at a festival; hadn't had my name spoken in a breath with other, proper writers. And I wish he could see me doing those things. I wish he could hear me read from *The Gracekeepers* and see that I had dedicated it to him. I wish he could see my book on other people's bookshelves; hear about a child staring at the spine and imagining the story inside. But I've caught myself in a paradox. Because the book is about him, for him; it's written because I didn't know how to grieve for him. If he was alive to read it, he couldn't read it, because I never would have written it. The very fact that he's not here to read my writing is why that writing exists.

PM: What is magical about writing is that it always goes astray. I send it to the dead and it comes back, thumb-printed, annotated, bearing itself away. It is free in a way that we are not. It means more than us. It becomes something more than us.

It is our privilege, as writers, that we get to make language our own. And in the nature of all great paradoxes: in making it our own, we share it. We open it. We invite the reader to follow. Down the rabbit hole, into the dark, where the truth and the shadows meet. We may never be able to be done with grieving, but in the attempt to face it, we break a path to make it easier for others to walk. When we use language to heal, when we light a fire or cling to it as a means of discharging the terrible excess of our lives, it always arrives too late. When we write a book to grieve it is always too late to pass it over, to the one we want to read it, to the only one to whom it is addressed. And yet there it is: waiting to be read by someone else, carrying with it a history and a grief as deep as the Atlantic.

'WHAT ARE WE LOOKING FOR HERE?'

Juliet Jacques

A simple line drawing shows an empty bowl at an otherwise empty table, in a space deserted apart from a chair left on its side, below a simple inscription: 'What are we looking for here?'

The graffiti is by street artist Hamlet Zinkovsky, left on a wall in Pripyat – a new city founded in 1970 for workers at the recently established Vladimir Ilyich Lenin nuclear power plant (known as Chernobyl, after the nearby town). Zinkovsky produces most of his work in Kharkiv, where he was born in 1986 – the year that reactor no. 4 exploded during a late-night safety test, and Pripyat was hurriedly abandoned.

Originally, the Soviets planned to put the plant 16 miles (25km) from Kyiv, but the Ukrainian Academy of Sciences, amongst others, warned against building so close to such a major city. Instead, they chose a sparsely populated site on the border of the Ukrainian and Belarussian Soviet Socialist Republics, 62 miles (100km) from the Ukrainian capital. This proved wise: it took just forty-eight hours to evacuate the 50,000 residents of Pripyat from the 10km 'exclusion zone' (literally 'zone of alienation'), in an operation that began at 2 p.m. on 27 April 1986 – the day after the catastrophe. Initially, they were told that they would return after three days; in the event, they were placed with host families in Kyiv and elsewhere, often separated from their spouses or siblings, and only allowed to return, briefly, two months later, to pick up essential belongings before leaving for good. In October 1988, they began to relocate to Pripyat's replacement town, Slavutych, built 50km from the nuclear site – which continued to function until the final reactor was closed in 2000. The logistics of doing similar with Kyiv's population, which currently stands at around 2.8 million, hardly bear thinking about.

Linked to the disaster by time and place, Zinkovsky still felt compelled to ask *why* people want to visit somewhere so melancholic and morbid. What are we hoping to see, feel or think? Even if Pripyat is safe enough for organised tours like the one I was on, what are the psychological effects of visiting? For me, Zinkovsky's question felt unanswerable, though it was in the air as soon as we boarded the bus in Kyiv. 'When else am I going to visit a nuclear exclusion zone?' I asked another British tourist, joking that Sellafield didn't quite cut it. I wasn't surprised that Angelina, our guide, shared this sense of humour – a deflective tactic against daily immersion in this horror – constantly joking about potential encounters with the zone's border guards, nuclear waste, radioactive wolves or the zombies from the 2012 horror film *Chernobyl Diaries*. (It was not the day's only US pop culture reference: by the river after which Pripyat was named, I had a laugh about the three-eyed fish spotted near Mr Burns' nuclear plant in *The Simpsons*.) We may even, she said, meet one of the few people who accepted the risks and returned to their lifelong homes in one of the abandoned villages within the 30km exclusion zone, although they have mostly died of old age – or slow, radiation-related illnesses – in the last twenty years.

Many aspects of the tragedy felt hard to comprehend. I don't have a head for science, so could not get my head around the plant's workings or the explosion's causes, let alone the emergency operations carried out to prevent a second explosion that would have rendered half of Europe uninhabitable, even when they are explained in the Discovery Channel documentary shown during our two-hour drive. I was more interested in the politics – both within the Soviet Union, where they continued with the 1986 May Day celebrations in Kyiv despite the risks, and evacuated Pripyat faster than necessary, without telling the wider public – and internationally, with the Soviet government being forced to confess after Swedish workers detected high radiation levels that could not have emanated from local plants. Refusal to admit the consequences cut across Cold War lines: the French were loath to concede any contamination, despite the radioactive cloud drifting over Corsica, whilst Soviet scientists played up the potential health damages to the international community. I was struck by the ghostly apparition of Mikhail Gorbachev, who said that the disaster's

18-billion-rouble cost tanked his *perestroika* programme and contributed significantly to the Soviet Union's collapse, but more so by Hans Blix, who was involved in the efforts to make the site safe. I was born in 1981, so was too young to remember Chernobyl, but Blix's doomed attempts to inspect Saddam Hussein's chemical weapons in 2002 are etched on my memory, leading as they did to one of the defining political catastrophes of my lifetime – one that killed hundreds of thousands more than the explosion of reactor no. 4.

As soon as we entered the deserted village of Zalissia, I realised that the emotional devastation would be in the details. It was in the doctor's surgery, with medical records scattered, its chairs strewn across the floor as in Zinkovsky's image. It was in the supermarket, with all its windows smashed: for the salvage teams who came first, and the looters who followed, it was quicker to throw things through the glass than carry them out through the door – the first step towards contaminated furniture ending up all over the Soviet Union during its last five years. It was in the 1986 calendar left in a broken window frame. It was in the stuffed toy on a table in someone's home – Cheburashka, the most popular Soviet children's character – although this was soon topped by the smashed-up doll on a rusty bedframe in the kindergarten in the next town, Kopachi, just inside the 10km exclusion zone.

For me, above all, it was in the concrete sign that said 'Pripyat, 1970', and the town behind it. Too much had passed in the Soviet Union for me to feel the same kind of nostalgia that I hold for the art and architecture of the USSR's first decade, crushed by the dead hand of Stalinist cultural policy after the 1920s. Mainly I felt the intense sadness of each person who died, and everyone who was rushed onto a bus with just their papers and whatever food they could carry, and then driven out of their home. I felt it in every derelict building in the post-war brutalist style I like so much, all of which are now so structurally unsound that visitors are barred from entering; in every panel that has fallen off each mosaic; every textbook on the floor of the partially collapsed school. I had never visited a ghost town before – doubtless it's upsetting anywhere, but to see such a model city in ruins, grass growing through some of its flagship buildings, was unbearable to me. I imagined someone more right-wing being as triumphalist as I was distraught, and that made me feel even sadder.

Metal signs still hung over the aisles of the supermarket, above upturned cabinets and shopping trolleys. Propaganda posters, including Lenin's imperative to 'learn, learn, learn!', remained in the Palace of Culture, having never been displayed. The derelict main stand at the Avanhard Stadium, home of FC Stroitel (Builder) Pripyat faced an area overgrown with trees and weeds, unrecognisable as a pitch. The funfair, due to open for the May Day celebrations, sits on the edge of the city. Security recently had to be increased after several 'stalkers' (named after the Tarkovsky film, which predates the Chornobyl disaster by seven years but describes a similar scenario) broke in and somehow got the Ferris wheel moving for a quick 'ride'.

These were quite melancholic, while other places were deeply harrowing. The doctor's surgery in Zalissia was one thing; the hospital in Pripyat quite another. The only Soviet facility able to treat radiation poisoning was in Moscow, one thousand kilometres away; the one here was intensely busy for a few days in April 1986, providing first aid to burns victims, and then abandoned, and is now in the same desperate state as everything else. The last building I saw here was the fire station, whose workers – like the hospital's – did all they could in a situation that was almost beyond human comprehension, let alone control, and yet they helped to avert a catastrophe from which Europe might never have recovered.

That night, I returned to my filmmaking residency at Izolyatsia – the cultural platform set up in an old Soviet shipyard in an industrial region of Kyiv after the Russian invasion of Donbas forced them to evacuate their original home in Donetsk in 2014. I put the image I'd seen on Facebook: one friend at Izolyatsia pointed out that it was Zinkovsky's work; another translated the caption. Another simply replied: *'This is going to haunt me.'* Why single out Zinkovsky's drawing when I had uploaded an album full of smashed-up houses and collapsing buildings, overgrown plazas and radioactive forests? It's not just because one doesn't expect to find any surviving art here, let alone not something so starkly contemporary in a zone that functions as a time capsule. Nor is it especially surprising that someone should use graffiti here as a way of striking any tourists who have not considered their motives out of their complacency – although it definitely managed that. At first glance, Zinkovsky's drawing struck me as a replication of the destruction I'd seen in the exclusion zone's villages, its stark simplicity designed to raise my awareness of how each house had been left as it was to maximise its impact on visitors. Learning what his caption meant heightened the emotional impact of seeing this destitution, which only belatedly hit me: thinking primarily about what an 'interesting' experience it would be, I had neglected to even consider it.

Since my visit, tourism to the zone has spiked, partly because of the recent HBO series about it, and partly because, as part of a less spectacular environmental disaster, Kyiv has become another city in Europe easily accessible by cheap flights. This industry functions on stark visual contrasts: between the post-Cold War present and the crumbling Soviet infrastructure; the uncanniness of the abandoned environment and the school-trip feel of the coach journey, tour and canteen lunch; the (potential and actual) severity of the disaster and the tacky tat on sale to tourists, such as the Chernobyl ice cream and 'Radioactive Wolf' T-shirts. Zinkovsky's image provided the only contrast that I hadn't anticipated in advance – none of the many journalists who were writing about Chernobyl tourism had picked up on it – which made it feel more personal to me: it was as if Zinkovsky had taken me aside and told me that *you, in particular, should not be holidaying in other people's misery, nor helping others to profit from it.*

I spent two months in Ukraine, making a documentary about the country's contemporary art scene, and especially its queer and feminist strands, but the two hours I spent in Pripyat stayed with me the longest. Talking about it to friends, I was told that some people become obsessed with the zone, continually returning to it, and I wondered if those people would be any more able to answer Zinkovsky's question than I was. If I had been nostalgically looking for a Soviet city, I had already visited several others that hadn't changed much since 1991, and still had statues and symbols everywhere, so it wasn't (just) that. I wasn't looking for the same thing that I might find in Auschwitz or Hiroshima – sobering evidence of man's inhumanity to man. No, the yawning realisation prompted by Zinkovsky was that really, I was seeking out trauma in and of itself, to immerse myself in it, to appropriate it for myself, and the haunted sense of despair I felt for weeks, months afterwards was exactly what I deserved.

ON CREATIVITY AND MEDITATION
David Lynch

'Know that all of nature is but a magic theatre.'
The Upanishads

Cinema is a language. It can say things, big abstract things, and I love that about it. Some people are poets and have a beautiful way of saying things with words, but cinema is its own language and so you can express a feeling and a thought that can't be conveyed in any other way. It's a magical medium.

For me it's so beautiful to think about these pictures and sounds flowing together in time and in sequence, making something that can be done only through cinema. It's so magical, I don't know why, to go into a theatre and have the lights go down. It's very quiet and then the curtains start to open and you go into another world.

ON CREATIVITY AND MEDITATION

Although the frames of a film are always the same – the same number, in the same sequence, and with the same sounds – every screening is different. There's a circle that goes from the audience to the film and back. Each person is looking and thinking and feeling and coming up with their own sense of things. I like a story that holds abstractions and that's what cinema can do.

I was a painter. I painted and I went to art school. I had no interest in film. One day I was sitting in a big studio room and I had a painting on the go which was of a garden at night. It had a lot of black with green plants emerging out of the darkness. All of a sudden these plants started to move and I heard a wind. I thought, 'Oh how fantastic this is!' And I began to wonder if film could be a way to make paintings move.

An idea is a thought. It's a thought that holds more than you think it does when you receive it, but in that first moment there's a spark. Desire for an idea is like bait. You bait your hook and then you wait. The desire is the bait that pulls those fish in, those ideas. Little fish swim on the surface but the big ones swim down below. If you can expand the container you're fishing in – your consciousness – you can catch bigger fish.

I started Transcendental Meditation in 1973 and I have not missed a single meditation ever since. Twice a day, every day. It has given me effortless access to unlimited reserves of energy, creativity and happiness deep within.

TRAUMA

When I started practising meditation, I was filled with anxieties and fears. I felt a sense of depression and anger. Anger and depression and sorrow are beautiful things in a story, but they are like poison to the filmmaker or artist. You must have clarity to create; you have to be able to catch ideas.

Life is filled with abstractions and the only way we make heads or tails of it is through intuition. Intuition is seeing the solution, it's emotion and intellect coming together. Personally, I think intuition can be sharpened and expanded through Transcendental Meditation. By diving into the self: there's an ocean of consciousness inside each of us and it's an ocean of solutions. When you dive into that ocean, that consciousness, you enliven it. It grows, and the final outcome of this growth of consciousness is called enlightenment, which is the full potential for us all.

There are many, many dark things flowing around in this world now and most films reflect the world in which we live. In stories, in the worlds that we go into, there's suffering, confusion, darkness, tension, and anger, but the filmmaker doesn't have to be suffering to show suffering. Negativity is like darkness: you turn on the light and darkness goes. We're like light bulbs. If bliss starts growing inside you it's like a light. You enjoy that light inside and if you ramp it up brighter and brighter you enjoy more and more of it, and that light will extend out farther and farther.

Maybe enlightenment is far away but it is said that when you walk towards the light, with every step, things get brighter.

Every day for me gets better and better and I believe that enlivening unity in the world will bring peace on earth. So I say 'peace to all of you'.

www.davidlynchfoundation.org.uk

'Time to dive within and let go of that castle.'

HALLELUJAH

Emma Jane Unsworth

'Give me three words to describe childbirth,' the antenatal course leader says brightly.

'Life-affirming,' someone shouts. She writes it on the board.

'Emotional!' shouts someone else. She writes this, too. 'Terrifying, traumatic and agonising!' I shout – you know, just to balance things out.

Is she living in cloud cuckoo land or what? I've seen *One Born Every Minute*. (I watched it obsessively throughout my pregnancy, all the previous series. I don't watch it once after I've given birth.)

A major tumbleweed moment. She stares at me. Buzz-kill in row three! 'Let's not write those down just yet,' she says, 'let's keep them as "maybes".'

Huh. This was just a few weeks after I made a cocaine joke at pregnancy yoga (THAT went down like a lead balloon, let me tell you). I won't even tell you about going on a weaning course when I was hungover. All I will say is: puree and poo are not what you want to ponder at those times. Just call me the queen of baby-group faux pas.

But there was a bigger issue. Bigger than my public embarrassment, even. I was irked by the baby-brainwashing. The PR sheen-y bullshit that painted, from the start, a perfect depiction of motherhood and niceyniceness that – well, made me personally feel utterly unprepared for childbirth and the aftermath. I'm all for positive thinking. But, you know, laced with a good dose of reality. It's not gloomy to recognise that a huge thing can comprise bad as well as good, is it? But where babies are involved it's like we've got to slap on a rictus grin and chant, 'Everything's lovely!' Which is dangerous on so many levels. I've recently read a number of excellent books and articles (Lucy Jones, Maggie Nelson, Polly Clark, to name a few) that have done great things in terms of broadening the childbirth chat. They acknowledge the joy and the wonder of such a significant experience – but also the terror and trauma, too. Because I think women are often being sold something else, something untenable (and don't even get me started on breastfeeding. Oh mama).

Anyway – let's rewind to last November, the 8th to be precise, a day of very good and very bad things. Donald Trump took the White House, Leonard Cohen had just died, and my son Leonard Fox was born (we were hoping he'd be the reincarnation, but then I read LC had vowed to come back as his sister's dog). I was in a crazy daze, waiting to be stitched up. Because despite all my best efforts (more on these later), I had torn, quite badly. Here are some words you don't want to hear when someone is between your legs, holding a needle, aimed at your vagina: 'Should I put a stitch there or there do you think?' Woah! Shouldn't you be practising on, I dunno, a chicken breast or something? But this was how I found myself, an hour after the birth. High on gas and air, trying to patch my psyche together in order to mentally grapple with the fact that the midwife attending to me had called in someone more experienced to 'guide her through it'. In one way, it was good she was asking the question, and I know everyone has to learn, but there seemed to be no acknowledgment of the fact that this might have been absolutely fucking terrifying for me. And it was, absolutely fucking terrifying. I lay there mute, in stirrups, feeling very much like I was in the film *Saw*, where you have to do some hideous mutilating challenge to get out of the room.

I'm not writing this as a horror story. I have no desire to frighten anyone. But according to a study in the *British Journal of Gynaecology*, 85 per cent of women suffer some form of tear during their first vaginal birth. That's a lot of women getting injured! Not only that, but the number of women suffering severe third and fourth degree tears (from vagina to anus) tripled from 2 per cent to 6 per cent between 2000 and 2012. The rise has been put down to tears being better diagnosed, but also to women having babies later in life, and bigger babies at that. I wasn't prepared for this. In fact, I felt weirdly pressured to not tear, to not have stitches, because that was so doable, right? I even bought a stupid blue balloon machine to stretch my perineum every day:

TRAUMA

The 'Epino'! As in: Say NO to that episiotomy! (For those blissfully ignorant, an episiotomy is when they cut you open widthways at your vagina so that you don't split along your entire perineum.) Such contraptions don't come cheap. My partner found me trawling eBay looking for a bargain. 'Are you nuts?' he said. 'That's like buying a second-hand dildo.'

'But there's one here that has been "fully sterilised" and it's only £30 instead of £120!' I cried. In the end, I bought a new one. But just as I was deluded about the hygiene of genital equipment, I was deluded about the potential elasticity of my vajayjay. I felt as though it was a real likelihood that I wouldn't tear. When in fact, it was the most likely thing to happen. And it did.

Before I go on, I want to say that the midwives in general were brilliant (especially once we got home, and we got a visit every day for a week). I love the NHS. I'm furious at the Tories for dismantling it (and they are, as we speak). But I wanted to tear and share (sorry), because in terms of that initial time period, those injuries were as affecting as meeting my baby. And, once I started talking to people about it, the stories flooded in (birth stories in general seem to do this – women hold back, but the stories are there, waiting, like dammed water).

One friend had her labia accidentally stitched together and had to go back, be cut apart and re-stitched correctly. Another friend had a large knot at the end of her stitches that had to be snipped off before she could sit down in comfort. Things go wrong in medicine because it's human beings practising the medicine, I understand that. But it strikes me that the injuries and repairs women receive during and after childbirth are talked about even less than childbirth itself. So much so that I didn't even think about them when I was writing my birth plan. All I could think of was my friend's mum who, after giving birth in the 1970s, was brought a cig and an ashtray and a box of matches on a wheelie trolley. I wanted that kind of afterbirth. Hell, I was so out of it that I forgot to ask to see the placenta (something I HAD been looking forward to). My partner didn't even take a photo! He was so engrossed in the baby. I'm still pretty pissed off about that. But back to the main event.

My baby blazed out of me in three hours. This was not a desirably fast birth. This was chaos. The doctors and midwives were overwhelmed. I was stratospheric with pain. It didn't feel like a birth as much as an evacuation. My body wanted the baby out. My contractions were coming so fast that I didn't have time to eat a chocolate brazil in between (this was how I measured them – I kept getting halfway and spitting the half-chewed nut out, scared of choking; even more scared of not sucking on the delicious gas and air in time). I dilated five centimetres in half an hour. It was a far cry from the chilled candlelit pool birth I'd envisaged – I'd even made a Spotify playlist, hilariously entitled 'Labour Party'. None of this was to be. As soon as the pool was a no-go, I asked for all the drugs. I was in agony! But the epidural failed. I was like a marauding ox, stampeding around, hooked up to god knows how many machines, unable to squat and push. I pulled out cannulas, sprayed blood everywhere. I bellowed so insistently that a registrar came running in off the corridor to ask, 'Why she was making that noise?' ('She' was making that noise because the baby's head was crowning and her gas and air tank had just run out.) Little wonder, then, that afterwards I had a deep tear on the posterior wall of my vagina and a badly 'grazed labia' (new band name, anyone?).

Pregnancy was a time when I shared my body with someone else, but I still felt like a sealed unit. In fact, it blew my mind that my body was growing another body (inside! Like a meaty Russian doll!). During the birth, I felt like a tin can hacked apart by a knife. I'd never even been in hospital before (except for a fractured wrist when I was twelve). For weeks after the birth I was convinced I had a womb infection, that something had *got in*, such was my feeling of wide-open vulnerability. Early in pregnancy, a friend gave me a book called *The Orgasmic Birth*. Optimistic? Ludicrous! Also: no pressure! I appreciated her intention, though – to remind me that my vagina was more than an escape chute for a tiny human. And I think this is what concerned me most about the stitching. This afterthought, this add-on, this potential botch-job, would determine part of my identity – my sex life – for the rest of my life. If men birthed babies, there would be some kind of Nobel Prize for Penis Repair. But women? Nah. Look at the baby, they say – look at the baby! In a sort of 'watch-the-birdy' kind of way. Doesn't it all just melt into insignificance when you see your beautiful baby? The subtext being that it *should*, if you are not a selfish creature; if you are *worthy* of motherhood. Well, I love my baby, but I also love my vagina, and myself. If that makes me a bad mother, so be it. And when I got home and the drugs wore off and I settled into that wildest mix of bliss and dread that would colour the next few months, I found I was angry. Like, livid. Roiling with rage. That there was no trust established. Not enough anaesthetic. That even though I pride myself on being assertive, in those stirrups, I hadn't spoken up. So I thought I'd write this, because I think we all need to talk more about all of this stuff.

TESLA, MURDERED BY SOCIETY

Seraphina Madsen

*'No one has ever written, painted, sculpted, modelled, built,
or invented except literally to get out of hell.'*
– Antonin Artaud, *Van Gogh, the Man Suicided by Society*

They won't give me pens or pencils. I'm forced to write with crayons, which, in this heat, are soft and melting and already making it a challenge to write these words down. I don't have the patience to convince someone to let me put them in the refrigerator for a bit. I will instead let my hand fly wild and free. My blood is boiling.

There are some who say all writing is pig shit, that words are no more than tacky drapery attempting to give form to the obscure phantoms of the mind. Phantoms which, with their rich and varied interior lives, propagate in our heads. In my head. Nikola Tesla is one of them. Along with Van Gogh, but Tesla is haunting me now.

TESLA, MURDERED BY SOCIETY

They say that anyone who writes is the worst kind of maggot. But I am compelled to write the story of this inventor, suicided by society, just as Van Gogh was. Tesla, a person of superior lucidity, which enabled him, in any circumstances, to see further, infinitely and dangerously further than the immediate and apparent reality of 'facts' that seethe and multiply all around us. That hum and sting. In all honesty, I would go so far as to say that words, far from being pig shit, when used in certain ways, have occult properties capable of creating reality. But that is another matter. I will, nevertheless, attempt to bring something of this man, this inventor, ultimately murdered by society, by xenophobic American Industrialists, onto the page and alive in your imagination.

Because he is also one of us and we can find parts of ourselves within him. And because he brought wireless technology, the radio, neon lights, and so much else to the world, for which all of us are no doubt grateful...

The austere cottage where the infant Tesla was born stood in wooded, hilly countryside next to a neat, modest, whitewashed Serbian Orthodox church. This church was presided over by his father, the Reverend Milutin Tesla, who secretly wrote articles under the pseudonym 'Man of Justice' and poetry he would never publish. One hot summer night in 1856, during a lightning storm, the child was born. The midwife declared, 'He will be a child of the storm,' to which his mother countered prophetically, 'No, of the light.'

The family was part of an ethnic and religious minority in the province, then under the rule of the Hapsburg Empire. For generations, men in both his father's and mother's families were sent to serve in the Army or the Church. The women were packed off to become wives of officers or ministers. Little Tesla and his elder brother were destined to follow their father into the ministry. They watched their father, erect at the pulpit, orating Bible verses with his voice raised like a heavy, jewelled sword, fierce and shining in the face of battle, cleaving the air and all that comes into contact with it, including, more importantly, people's hearts, and souls.

Both boys inherited their mother's extraordinary memory. Washing the kitchen floor, darning socks, milking the cow, she recited whole volumes of native and European poetry to her children, whose eager ears and keen minds absorbed the words that conveyed phantasmagorical images lit up with emotion and ideas, stirring them in her clear, soft voice, 'I am the daughter of Earth and Water/And the nursling of the Sky; I pass through the pores of the ocean and shores; I change, but I cannot die...'.* She sang the verses to the cow, pumping its silky teats, the warm milk spurting through her hands, the pealing rhythm sounding into the metal pail.

When the child was out from under his mother's skirts, he was sent to feed the hens and collect their eggs. At five he was old enough to follow his brother. Young Tesla was in thrall, spellbound by his elder brother. He circled him like a moon. They walked the grounds, hauled grain and water, mucked out the stalls, kept the tack and saddle oiled,

* From 'The Cloud', by Percy Bysshe Shelley

fed and watered the animals, turned the cow and the fine Arabian stallion out to pasture.

The stallion was the most magnificent creature either boy had ever seen. Dappled silver, it had been a gift from one of their father's closest friends. The beauty and power, lustre and terror the animal exuded held them, bewitched. In its immense eyes pooled a sensitivity, a liquid chiming, that communicated directly to their souls. While his elder brother brushed the stallion's coat to a high shine young Tesla learned to be gentle enough to approach the animal and feed it apples, stroking its downy, fluid nose. The little boy thought he loved the horse nearly as much as he loved his brother.

Each morning the two brothers stood in the field at daybreak to watch the geese rise into the clouds, everything gold and crimson in the mist, the birds' wing spans beating the air, toying with their ears, slipping over on the currents, feathers hissing, honking from on high, returning at sundown in perfect phalanxes above the hills, landing one by one across the field. Days were marked by the spectacle of the geese.

In the surrounding forest the brothers spent their free time building forts and swimming in the river, diving into the cool, emerald water, where they found another world, one that enwrapped them, sometimes so tightly they nearly drowned on more than one occasion. The forest was a ferocious place. They'd been chased by packs of mad dogs, and wild, solitary hogs with formidable tusks. And then there were the crows.

TRAUMA

The elder brother, with seven years on young Nikola, was an expert crow catcher. They hid in the bushes, mimicking their calls to draw them in. When one of the dark feathered creatures alighted, the elder boy threw a piece of cardboard to distract it, and grabbed the bird with his bare hands, quickly shoving it into a burlap sack where it beat its wings and wailed and wailed for help. Normally, one of two would come to its aid and the elder Tesla would have no problem catching it in the same manner and throwing it into the bag. However, on one occasion, hundreds and hundreds of them appeared, a mass of bloodthirsty crows, hovering, descending, blackening the sky. The two boys were knocked to the ground by the screeching, cackling horde, their beaks like arrows, piercing their flesh, ripping the hessian open, freeing their brethren who darted out into the safety of the air. The great murder, in a mass of wing and wind and dust, disappeared into the sky, leaving the two boys behind in the quiet beams of sunlight, bruised, pecked and scratched with bloody gouges and lacerations torn into their exposed flesh that would stay with them until their death.

The younger child watched as his elder brother shot up, growing as quickly as the corn stalks, standing like an angel before him, glowing in the dawn, with the softness and the fizzing of the goose flock's wings skimming the air overhead, until the last dissolved into the clouds, clouds which his brother's head seemed to touch. The little boy couldn't imagine a world in which he would ever be taller than his brother, or as strong and shining and brave. The elder boy was his father's, and everyone's, favourite. Their eyes sparkled when they looked at him.

As the young Tesla grew, there were still tasks too dangerous for him, such as cutting trees in the forest. On these days all he had were the simple chores on the farm, which left time for his own devices. He did what all the other boys did: he made fishhooks out of wire, tying them to a string to catch frogs in the pond. Here, he made a massacre with his superior hooks and technique, sharing his secrets with the other boys all but annihilating the frog population. Young Tesla continued in this way, observing nature, killing it with a tool or his bare hands. More and more, what he found he wanted was to harness the energy of the natural world and build machines that would give endless power to humanity. Observing the world around him, he saw it was teeming with energy.

One such energy came in the form of May bugs, descending upon the farm in clouds from across the hills. They covered the trees, the branches heaving with their weight. Young Tesla stood in the middle of this spectacle, the insect white noise filling his head, vibrating the downy hairs on his neck. The air crackled with electricity. He would harness the power of the beetles to run a simple machine.

Taking a glass jar from the kitchen, he plucked the most robust specimens out of the humming, crawling, probing masses. Attaching a cross-piece to a thin, rotating spindle at the centre of a disc, he then glued the thoraxes of as many as four of the beetles at a time to the contraption. Once started, the beasts were tireless. For hours on end Tesla watched them whirl round and round, faster and faster, even as the day grew hotter. His 'apparatus', as he called it, was a success. It generated power. The creation and application of this device thrilled him.

This, the young Tesla's first experiment, came to an abrupt halt when one of his father's flock, the child of a soldier, wandered into his room one Sunday, saw the jar of beetles on the table, unscrewed the lid, reached in and popped one of the insects into his mouth, crunching it in his teeth, and swallowing. After this, the young Tesla never wanted to see a beetle again. He turned to dismantling his grandfather's clocks.

The success rate for putting these clocks back together again was negligible. All clocks in the house were taken down and locked away. Tesla then took to making pop guns, which went well until he shot a hole through a window. Next, he carved swords from his parents' furniture to wield in battle against the corn stalks, his enemy. Shouting verses from the Serbian national poetry his mother had recited to him from infancy, (verses with motifs of 'national sacrifice' and five 'tragic centuries' marked by suffering and destruction, the systematic Ottoman oppression, massacres and forced conversions) he cut down the crops, for which he received a beating, something which was by then a regular occurrence.

One fateful morning, the Reverend Milutin Tesla left at dawn on the magnificent Arabian to visit one of his flock on the other side of the hills. The boys watched their father ride away, the geese honking overhead, then went to milk the cow. In the late morning the horse returned riderless, tearing out of the forest, whinnying and snorting, circling the area between the house, the church and the barn. The two boys were the first to hear it, and felt the ground vibrating beneath them. Racing out of the barn like two shots, they stood on the peripheries, the elder brother pushing the younger away as he approached the animal to take its reins. Visibly distraught, eyes rolling in its skull, the Arabian whinnied, reared and kicked his elder brother in the head. He fell to the ground, trampled, his limp body flailing like a doll between the stallion's legs, in a fit of hysteria. The young Tesla did not look away, but remained fixed to the spot until his mother grabbed him and carried him into the house.

The family buried their eldest boy in the church graveyard, then piled their belongings into a cart and left for the nearby city of Gospic. The first-born son, the golden child, was gone. Young Tesla was now the eldest. He was the one who would carry his father's name into the next generation. He had been his brother's shadow, following him in and out of their world of farm and wood. Now he was alone, cramped between labyrinthine city walls. He could no longer be the shadow. Or the moon. All he wanted to do was hide. The world became a torment to him.

Afflicted by unwanted scenes and images, accompanied by blinding flashes of light, young Tesla now stood on the knife's edge of anxiety and suffering. He was losing his grasp. His own mind was beyond his control. These manifestations always took him back in time, to events which had already happened, never imagined. As well as the visions, another curiosity manifested. When someone said a word, 'apple' or 'spoon' for example, the object would materialise before him, so lifelike he wanted to reach out and touch it, hovering there in the air. Tesla lay in bed each night, going over strategies to gain supremacy over his mind and the visions that plagued him. Eventually, he struck on the idea of focusing his will to change the structure of the hallucination, in order to banish it.

In the city, young Tesla was sent to school. He excelled in his lessons, completing the four-year gymnasium at the top of his class, where he also distinguished himself as champion crow catcher of the Empire. At this school, his attention was captured by water turbines, inspired by the mechanical models on display there. He took great pleasure in constructing his own turbines, fascinated by the Niagara Falls, the tallest waterfall in the world, and dreamt of one day installing a turbine there to create power for the area (something he was to do thirty years later).

Tesla became obsessed with crafting the perfect arrow in the school's archery club, surpassing everyone, his arrows capable of penetrating a plank of pine one inch thick at close range. Later he would write a series of articles called *My Inventions and Other Writings* for an American scientific magazine and recall, 'Thru the continuous tightening of the bows I developed skin on my stomach very much like that of a crocodile and I am often wondering whether it is due to this exercise that I am able even now to digest cobble stones!'

I am no longer using crayons, I've managed to get my hands on a pencil, one that I had forgotten about, in one of my hides around this institution when they move us from place to place, doctor to doctor, in groups, and can't keep their eyes on me constantly. But I have run out of paper and they aren't going to give me more because they're always complaining about the number of sheets I use. So, I'm now writing on the wall behind my bed, in awe of how Tesla shone, despite the grief and the mental fits that plagued him, the visions and excruciating bolts of lightning that shot through his head.

Eventually, Tesla landed on a technique that tricked the visions, dissolving them. What he also discovered was that, in controlling the manifestations, he could conjure whatever he wanted with his mind, watch it hover and spin in four dimensions before his eyes. Like this, he didn't need to make models of his inventions in wood and metal. Whatever he imagined would materialise out of thin air. His three-dimensional prototypes hovered and spun around him, controlled by the sheer force of his mind, where they were later stored for future reference.

During his spell in Gospic, Tesla's sense of hearing also proved to be extraordinary. Several times, he saved neighbours from fire, hearing faint crackling noises coming from their buildings, which they themselves had ignored in their sleep, and called the fire brigade. (Later, much later, when he was a man and living in Colorado with a sizable laboratory, he found could hear thunderclaps at a distance of five hundred miles, whereas his assistants could hear no more than one hundred and fifty miles away. He was to notice that while under nervous strain, his hearing became even more acute.)

TRAUMA

At the age of ten, Tesla was sent to a secondary gymnasium in Carlstadt, Croatia where he lived with his aunt, a distinguished lady married to a retired colonel. They led a regimented life. The family ate the finest food in the smallest of portions. Tesla was always hungry. At this school the department of physics had various models of classical scientific apparatus, electrical and mechanical, which ignited his obsession with the ideal of continual motion through steady air pressure. He wanted, more than anything, to create a flying machine.

Not long after arriving, he contracted malaria. Much of the three years he studied in Carlstadt was spent at home, in his bed, in convalescence, yet he was again at the top of his class. Obsessed with the flying machine, he created many models, all in vain. When he thought that, at long last, he had produced something viable, he was shocked and deflated to discover its success was due to a leak, and only gave the illusion of working.

His parents had not wavered in their desire for their son to enter the clergy. This fact was very clear. The thought of entering the Church made young Tesla break into a sweat and his heart race with terror and panic. He had become fixated on the mysteries of electricity and was dead set on spending the rest of his life investigating this force of nature. He thought he might spontaneously combust if he wasn't allowed to become a physicist. At thirteen, a particularly serious bout of malaria took hold of Tesla and nearly killed him. From what everyone had assumed was his deathbed, the teenager asked if he could study engineering. His father consented, vowing to send him to the best technical institution in the world.

Against expectations, after a long convalescence, Tesla regained his health. His father sent him to one of the oldest and most esteemed institutions, the polytechnic school in Gratz, Styria, where he reeled with ecstasy in anticipation of the knowledge that would be made available to him. He was not disappointed. His professors were of the highest calibre. They immediately saw his excellence and potential and took him under their wing. Here, Tesla became obsessed with magnetics and incorporating a rotating magnetic field into his next invention.

Struck by another affliction, with a wildly varying pulse, he was set upon by tremors; the sun's rays were blows to his brain, leaving him stunned. When passing under a bridge, he would suffer a crushing pressure to the skull. In the dark he found he had the echolocation of a bat and could sense an object at a distance of twelve feet by a particular, creepy sensation on the forehead. The sight of pearls, the touch of skin or hair from another human being, made him physically ill. Before he ate, he had to calculate the food's exact cubic volume. Everything had to be done in threes, divisible by three. He was prescribed Bromide of Potassium in one large daily dose. When he became too weak to leave his bed, the doctor declared Tesla incurable. It was the second time he had been told he was at death's door.

One of his friends wouldn't give up on him. He visited Tesla every day, brought him herbs and healthy food to eat, nursing him back to health. They took walks in the park to help him regain his strength, and it was on one of these walks at dusk, reciting from Goethe's *Faust*, that out of the blue Tesla was struck with the solution to a problem he had been unable to resolve. He picked up a stick, drew his machine in the sand, and took his friend through its motions. It was the first drawing of the same machine that would become the basis for modern electricity. Tesla was thrilled. It was his first great invention.

Recovered and invigorated, his degree from the polytechnic school in hand, Tesla took a position in a telegraph office in Budapest, then later in Paris, quickly moving up in the company and being given a position as an engineer. When he felt the United States of America calling, he bought a ticket and sailed to New York City with a few cents in his pocket and a letter of introduction to Thomas Edison.

'I wish that I could put to words, my first impressions of this country. In the *Arabian Tales* I read how genii transported people into a land of dreams to live through delightful adventures. My case was just the reverse,' Tesla wrote of his American experience. Thomas Edison played Tesla for a fool, being himself, in the end, the real fool. 'When you become a full-fledged American, you will appreciate an American joke,' Edison told him, refusing to pay Tesla the grand sum he'd promised for a job he'd imagined was too difficult for the young man. In a fury, Tesla left Edison and took a job digging ditches. Day in, day out he kept to himself, digging, thinking of alternating current and how it was far superior to Edison's method, which was ridiculous and childish, like the man himself (not to mention pig-headed and a scoundrel).

However, word had already spread of Tesla's genius. He was contacted by the industrial giant George Westinghouse, who wanted to use Tesla's AC powered machines to compete with Thomas Edison's company. The two went into business together. Tesla cut a tall, elegant form, feted as a genius inventor in New York City's elite circles, invited to all the parties. Women adored him. They admired his graceful figure, chiselled face, the spark in his eye. He could not get to close to them, however; he couldn't bear the touch of human skin or hair. The sight of pearls made him want to be sick.

Surrounded by industrial giants and their adoring daughters, Tesla demonstrated his astounding achievements in his Manhattan laboratory. The most magnificent machine, the one they had all come to see, was the monstrous, humming, crackling orb that spat twenty-foot ribbons of blue-white lightning like discharges of ectoplasm. Police came to his door regularly with noise complaints from the furthest corners of the neighbourhood, at all hours of the night. The bolts of lightning coming into existence from out of the orb shook the ground.

During this time Tesla also gave lectures, pursued wireless lighting and world-wide electric power distribution. He opened another laboratory in Colorado Springs. Edison watched from the sidelines and seethed. Edison, like Tesla, was a showman. He did not like having the spotlight taken away, and even less, his business. Tesla's inventions for harnessing AC current, his motor, coil, and generator, produced far more energy at a lesser expense than Edison's DC system. And now Edison was vying for a contract with the Chicago Columbian Exhibition of 1893–94 against Tesla and Westinghouse's joint company. Thus began the 'War of the Currents'.

It was rumoured Edison had a friend who worked in a correctional facility about to execute a man. He asked the officer to use a Tesla AC motor to do it. Whether the prison officer used the motor of his own accord or was pushed by Edison, the result was that Tesla's motor first became known to the public as an instrument of death. Not long after this, Edison took a contract to kill an elephant and used Tesla's AC system, causing a sensation in the papers. Edison then publicly executed dogs and a horse with AC electricity to further frighten the general public away from Tesla and his inventions.

Meanwhile, Tesla invented a coil more powerful than any that had come before it, capable of generating high voltages and frequencies which led to new forms of light, such as neon and fluorescent, as well as X-rays. The coils made it possible to send and receive radio signals. He quickly filed for American patents in 1897, beating the Italian Marconi to the chase, who was nevertheless awarded the Nobel Prize for the invention of the wireless radio. Tesla muttered to people he knew that Marconi had used seventeen of his patents to make his radio, and eventually took Marconi to court. Litigation favoured the Italian. However, in 1943, after

Tesla's death, the US Supreme Court ultimately decided in Tesla's favour.

By 1915, Westinghouse asked Tesla to return his stocks and bonds in the company, or the enterprise would go under. He handed over what would have eventually yielded a fortune, hundreds of millions of dollars. This left him with his only investment, the famous Wardenclyffe tower plant. The plant kept him going fifteen years, until he had to sell it to pay a $20,000 debt to the Waldorf-Astoria Hotel.

During this time, Tesla became an American citizen. His fervour for bringing light, information and energy to the world for the benefit of humankind was as alive as ever, but he was alone. Abandoned and cheated out of his just rewards by Westinghouse, his name dragged through the mud by Edison, Tesla had had a few successes but ultimately failed in finding collaborators to achieve what he believed was possible.

The powerful men in that country, the industrial giants he'd had so much hope for, along with fellow inventor Edison, were truly like the evil genii, out for his pound of flesh. Each had turned a foe. They murdered his trust and his hope and made him an exile. The afflictions continued to plague him, the bolts of light, hallucinations, anxiety, the aversion to pearls and human hair. He consulted students of psychology and physiology and found no relief. After a lifetime of fighting, it is the general consensus that he descended into madness.

In Tesla's final days, love-starved and alone, getting by on the joys of a hallucinated love affair with a pigeon he rescued in a nearby park, he slipped away in his sleep: gaunt, angular, his grey, cavernous face frozen by death. He was found by a maid in his hotel room, alone in his bed. Just before he died at the Governor Clinton Hotel in Manhattan, he had offered the management his 'Death Beam', capable of blasting ten thousand enemy planes out of the sky, in lieu of his $10,000 debt. The machine had been reported on in the *New York Times* as an invention he was working on in his efforts to secure world peace. No one knows why, but the hotel management accepted the 'Death Beam' as payment. Later, it was discovered the box he gave them contained a standard piece of electrical equipment.

So you see, he was murdered. Murdered by society. Murdered because he wasn't murderous himself. And this is the shard in my heart I cannot pull out, which will not push its way out of me. Again and again, *he* gave *his heart*, the Tesla coil, wireless electricity technology – all the prototypes spinning in his mind he gave to the world. Meant for the betterment of humankind. Over three hundred patents at the time of his death. They knew what they were doing.

IN ORDER TO LIVE
Anna Vaught

'Do not read, as children do, for the sake of entertainment, or, like the ambitious, for the purpose of instruction. No, read in order to live.'
Flaubert

And read, read, read in order to build and rebuild. Listen, too, to stories, to new words and worlds. This is how it was for me, reading to set the darkness echoing and to know that I was not alone. You may think (as Flaubert did) that young children do not feel this way about books, but even as a young child, I read both for entertainment and safety, because I could find spaces with characters, or just linger with the feelings that words gave me when I ate them or jumbled them about in my mouth. I would talk to the characters in books and ask their advice; tell them how I felt. Or read passages again and again for security; they were a private talisman to me. I think, looking back, that I savoured scansion or the weight of a line for its mnemonic qualities and the comfort that afforded.

In bed, as a kid, I would hear shouting or groaning, diffuse sounds. Arguments. Later, my father whimpering and screaming, because he went mad before he died, though no one spoke about it. I would hear stertorous breathing and feel frightened, but there was no one to tell. And I think that the sounds outside my room got mixed up with the sounds in my head. When I was very young, I also began a series of rebarbative and ruminating thoughts, the roots of obsessive compulsive patterns, I suppose, in which I imagined that if I thought something bad, then it would happen to someone. That if I thought something unkind, or even allowed the words access into my mind, then those words would billow out and do things. This was, I knew even then, because my mother had instilled in me an idea that I was the bringer of bad things. Looking back, I don't know why she did this; I don't know why she wasn't prevented. Even now, if I am not careful, I slip into this mindset if someone is particularly caustic to me. I may struggle to believe, despite the pressing of my rational mind, that it could be them, and not me. I turn to reading. Every time.

When my youngest child, now eight, was six months old, I had a nervous breakdown. As I recovered, I wanted to assemble my thoughts and turn them, if I could, into something more productive. *My* story. I also wanted my three boys, when they were older, to understand who or what their mother was a little bit better. They are aware that their mum struggles with mental health conditions and I wanted the boys to see something of how this happened to me, but also – and this was really important – to understand that, in our darkest times, our creativity and imagination are resources. I put it all into an autobiographical novel and that became my first book, *Killing Hapless Ally*.

I found, recalling, that there were turning points for me and here was an early one: memories of the intense morbidity, the dripping taps, and the strange muffled noises in my paternal grandfather's house. And yet, and yet. *They were storytellers*, my lot. My God. Both sides of my family were. The stories were often ghastly, and I am staggered, looking back, that anyone thought they were acceptable for a young child to listen to. My maternal grandmother's tales of poltergeists summoned up by the beatings within the house; my great-grandmother's visions of the Virgin Mary; the little white woman in the corner of the room who was smiling and beckoning: it was, she told me, the most beautiful thing she had ever seen. My family keened of loss and disappointment, of deaths of baby at breast and a lost lover round the point at sea. I was drenched in melancholy and let me tell you that there is a strange anomaly here: no one else can remember these stories. Of club-footed boatmen in love with wall-eyed women; of wraiths, and screaming, invisible cats; of a moss at foot that tried to draw you into the Pembrokeshire mud and people, of generations gone, taken to the asylum and left there by misunderstanding, or the unwatchful doctor who'd missed a goitre. *Why? Why can't they remember?* Or did they not listen? The stories were macabre, often raggedly inappropriate but nonetheless, within these times, there was nourishment, because my imagination was incandescent from an early age; storied. And not scared of death, because we had rehearsed it often enough.

Looking back, I feel that I was ready to become a writer years ago, but what burned in me, in terms of linguistic excitement, trope and landscape, was also part of a wider life of brutality and being crushed, so I thought that writing was what clever and decent people did; what the other did, not an eldritch child, eldritch woman, like me. I battled years of mental health problems, it's just that, gradually, I was able to process it all and begin to turn it into a manageable, readable product. Or to put it another way, my poison is part of my cure; or, as William Empson had it in *Villanelle*, 'My stare drank deep beauty that still allures./My heart pumps yet the poison draught of you.' Oh, it does. And anyway, love is complicated sometimes.

Although he was not entirely literate, my paternal grandfather could turn a story and recite many lines of poetry. So, as I wrote in *Killing Hapless Ally* (in which I unpicked the origins of my mental health problems and got rid of a troubling alter ego): '…here, all the skewering and squishing death-stories were told as gentle reminiscence, horrible endings so comforting over an otherwise silent dinner on the huge table by the old range with the clothes on the Sheila Maid hanging overhead. Frequently, in this exposed position on The Hill, the wind would whip up, Grandpa's chickens screamed like banshees, timbers creaked and doors quivered and smashed shut: perhaps the unquiet souls of the dead, disliking the cheery retellings of their worldly extinction.'

It was horror, but poetically so.

My paternal grandpa would recite poems by Tennyson and Arnold and the whole of Browning's *The Pied Piper of Hamelin*. To me, *those were the spellbound, golden moments*. And it was hard to imagine Arnold's *Sohrab and Rustum* told with anything other than a broad North Somerset accent, a bit of a dribble and a touch of snuff on the lip and septum. That is how I received the magic, which he delivered with his eyes closed, in the unquiet house. Because, here is the thing: words can heal. They can make you soar, whether read or heard. And you cannot take them away once brought into the world. Sometimes they are good even if a bad person said them; because the words can exist independently of the mouth that uttered them or the horrid geography that spawned them. It is magic. Yes. It is *magic*. Even, I am convinced, when you hear or read those words in extremis or in a risibly dysfunctional home; or even if those words are a conduit to the words you need.

I can feel my grandfather's words now; I am bathed in them. It was, and is, magic. To stay well, I take medicine every day. My medicine is – antidepressants and mood stabilisers have been duds for me, and you probably know it is hard to access appropriate mental health care on the NHS – *I read*, but I also read aloud. My older boys laugh at the fact that I can recite reams of poetry; my husband is aware that, watching *King Lear* or *The Winter's Tale* with me, I am mouthing the words. I can do that with a good part of the first folio. Not because I've rehearsed at the RSC, but because words were what kept me safe and gave me happiness. I also know textual variants between quarto and folio texts because I was interested in the gaps, the changes between lines; grace notes, elisions, ellipses. Does that make any sense to you?

There was a good deal of insanity in my paternal family. Of people who went to bed because of 'overwork'; of relatives suddenly dead of illness, with no apparent lead time. Two suicides were ascribed to brain tumours. Why did someone think that was a better way to describe it all, to a young child? Looking back, I lived a weird old life, even when people were being nice to me. That was why reading was so important as a child.

An episode in my autobiographical novel recalled a Sunday over Christmas. I was visiting my paternal grandparents, *sans* my mother because my grandmother was a downy-knuckled terror of a woman who hated outsiders; I was allowed into her world for a short while but only because I was a kid; when I got older, I was expelled. She died first; then Grandpa and, after that, I lost a whole side of my family because, as my father's siblings (the ones who weren't on closed psychiatric wards) sensitively announced at my mother's funeral, I wouldn't be seeing them again. No: do not cry for me. There are plenty of people in the world; your family is huge, if you look for it: love it like everyone's life depended on it and perhaps what you read in a book can be your blueprint for that.

But back to Christmas. A curious thing about the child-battery in one house and the darkness and acute psychiatric conditions that lived, often unspoken yet palpable, in both, was that it was all survived. When I had, for the first time, some effective psychological support, I remember the team being impressed that I had stayed off the ward and remained, in most ways, fully functional. It had not occurred to me that this might be a surprise. If it is, then the books in which I could find refuge were integral to its genesis. There was a Christmas which, when my senses are provoked by the smell of cinnamon or the alabaster texture of a sugared almond, could have been yesterday. I remember that I had overheard mutterings in the kitchen, with scary-sounding phrases and words like *personality disorder, manic depressive* and *psychosis*. I heard the voice of Uncle John, saying of his keening wife, to my terrifying grandmother, '... And Mother, I did think when I married her she might have been a sociopath, but she was cheerful enough then and anyway folks don't mind that in these parts.' I knew a lot of words, but not that. It sounded cheerful anyway. Kind of chatty. Then I looked it up.

I recall that, after a curious but normal Christmas break, I went back to school with the customary sense of being just a bit separate. To get away from mad aunt-women (who lived in depressing slapdash-mortared bungalows, which after all weren't interesting in a pointy, Gothic sort of way and where there was no hint of left-behind Caribbean heat on the top floor), and death-warbling grandparents, I furiously and hungrily read and re-read that bit in *The Wind in the Willows* (it's at the end of *Dulce Domum* if you care to look) where Rat manages to make a cheering little feast for Mole and the field mice who have come to sing carols at Mole End. I would race in after school to read, fast as I could, like gulping air. For added reassurance, I read *The*

Wild Wood – with particular emphasis on the moment when Badger opens his front door and the two animals tumble in out of the snow. There are hams hanging from the ceiling, a big fire, the plates wink in a kindly, anthropomorphic way, and when the famished animals are fed and ready for bed, their sheets are coarse but clean and smell of lavender. I felt that a hybrid of the two chapters connoted Christmas; the word *cosy*; into life came a wafting amorphous thing which some might have called happiness.

What was happiness? It was a place where no ringing curses from my mother were invited. Because, in *The Wind in the Willows*, the creatures veritably fall upon one another in a riot of being pleased to see you, which felt like an unfamiliar construct beyond the books. No. That is not entirely true: there was one person who ran to twirl me in the air and that was Helen, my father's sister. She was the first person in the family to go to university (I was the second) and she was radically clever. She married an arctic man when she, full of life, was dying; she showed me more tenderness than my own mother and there's not a day when I don't think of her.

Over a four-year period, I lost all my grandparents, the person I loved most in the world (Helen), two cousins and both my parents, followed by my much older brother breaking contact without explanation. I'm not sure I'd have survived it, already mired in OCD and dissociative episodes as a teenager and young woman, without the books, the reading that opened doors, the possibility of rebuilding and, if not a solution, then at least a hiatus from whirling griefs and trauma. I had to grieve for my mother – who was sainted in our community because of her teaching, her campaigning and the way she coped with chronic physical illness; her name was Mary and that's why she's Santa Maria in the book – and not divulge a word of what she had done to me.

Eventually, I began to write about it, as well as to find relief through reading. For instance, a childhood holiday that kept cropping up in nightmares, spent in the caravan, the memory of which makes me shudder to this day. Here are some fragments of memory. My mother was thumping me on the back.

'Mummy, should I cook the bacon? Mummy, isn't this violence?'

'No this is not violence!' With the un-pounding hand, Santa Maria fried bacon in the warped and blackened pan. More fat. Dad disinfected the cramped little toilet. Thus, the afternoon segued, incongruously, into tea, bacon sandwiches and a box of Mr Kipling's while my parents listened to Alastair Cook's *Letter from America* on Radio 4. It was, as I reflected in later years, a childhood replete with incongruity; compounded of beauty and horror. While my back throbbed, I ate a second cake. Outside, the stream thundered on to the kind and distant sea. Wales. Because, thank God, and *Diolch i Dduw*, always there was Wales. And in Wales there were more stories than you could ever imagine and so much to say aloud, so that it rang with a sonorous music which gave breath and life.

I took up words like mnemonics and talismans and on I went. I would say to myself, 'Oh, I want to dip my hand in that icy sea like boy-Dylan Thomas. I want to be in the sea town away from monsters and throw stones at cats and meet Mrs Prothero as she beats the dinner gong. Her daughter, Miss Prothero, would look at me kindly and ask if I'd like something from her bookshelf to read because Miss Prothero always knew what to say and I would say back to her, *Oh yes, I would and I would and can I come up to your bedroom and we can talk about all the books you have and I can borrow and come back? Can I maybe stay forever? You could read the Mabinogion to me! Oh, I would, and I would!*' And from such things was my better world constructed when, at night, my parents impressed on me that maybe I could wake up as a different person. A better person. A not-me person is what I heard.

On another 'holiday', parked up by the Seine and sitting under the willows for days, I began a roaring and extraordinary affair with Camus. It was a reading summer, between the two sixth form years. All around was the sense that people were dropping like flies and the deaths of Dad and Mum must surely be imminent. But the reading: for days on end by the river: Sartre's *Nausea*, Genet's *The Thief*, and, best of all, Camus's *The Plague*, *The Fall*, *The Outsider* and *Selected Essays and Notebooks*. Also, at speed on the journey home, Simone de Beauvoir's *The Force of Circumstance* and, cheerily, *A Very Easy Death*. When I got home, I devoured Gide's *Straight is the Gate* and *Fruits of the Earth*: *Nathaniel – I will teach you fervour! Fervour.* Holy fuck – what was *fervour*? What was *lust for life*? Were those things somewhere in the unknowable distance, just visible beyond the bacon grease of The Fucking Caravan? I was intoxicated: dislocated entirely from my surroundings and, thus, safe. The dislocation did not provide a new or unfamiliar sensation, but this kind of dislocation was one in which I was on fire and in splendid company. If you feel very alone and are told you cannot speak, perhaps it is not so odd that you borrow people and populate your mind with books, those in them and those who wrote them.

I possessed a lot of influential imaginary friends.

I had two nervous breakdowns when my first and third children were babies. You know, that time when it's supposed to be dreamy eyes and chequered Moses basket and all that? When the first happened, something snapped inside. It was like a pop and then a torrent. At the time I was in the car, driving past Westbury White Horse in Wiltshire with my three-month-old baby beside me. And when the snap came, my mind was deluged with images and sounds; it was like a synesthetic flood, tasting fear and seeing words with colours, and damn me it was being expressed with literary figures and images from my family life. I could hear my mother screeching and mocking; my sweet father saying I was not loved, but tolerated, and he was about to hit me. Cold grey eyes, globed shoulders like Atlas: powerful man. I was recalling things I was taken to and things I was banned from because I was *horrid child*. Changeling, or eldritch. Try and follow this. I wrote down what was in my head. John Skelton is a medieval poet, known for his rhythmic play dubbed *Skeltonics*; in Michael Ondaatje's book *The English Patient*, Kirpal Singh, the Sikh sapper, is walking on the headland about Westbury White Horse; both appeared in a moment of terrifying and colourful derangement, thus:

'So, on it went: "Helter skelter. Ha ha Hapless Ally. Helter Skelter–John Skelton–Skeletonics–Helter Skelter John–helter skelter at the fair. I was banned from the fair and the helter skelter at the fair with Santa Maria and she is still here as Dead Santa Maria. Slap. And she said then and she says now, *You are a little bitch and so you will never go to a fair again and you will never have a goldfish, little bitch! But Mummy what about the other children and the grinning red-haired boy with a fish in a bag? Was he really really bad, too?* Slap. *I was right all along! You should have been left in a bucket and also your babies will come to hate you!* Helter Skelter John–skeltonics–John Skelton at the funeral of Edward IV: *Where is now my conquest and victory?/Where is my riches and my royal array?* And again he comes, worrying: *Humbly beseeching thee, God, of thy grace!/O ye courteous commons, your hearts unbrace.* And again, *Et ecce, nunc in pulvere dormio!* Slap.

"Why do I remember all these bloody quotations and I have no one to tell? And Kirpal Singh is standing in the chalk-white, where the saddle of the horse would have been – and I am so alone and I am so, so wrong. The ways, the roads, the littoral and the mountain and on the chalky downs are so deep and the weather is so harsh and the concrete white horse does not rear and run and now Kirpal Singh is striding down across the huge animal that looks like a child's paper cut-out and he will fall and he will be hurt – and now I am falling on the helter skelter and I cannot control this speed – And the old white horse wants to gallop away into a sweet meadow but he cannot: he is mired in shiny white concrete...'

I recollect that the baby woke up and the surprise and sudden shock of it made the word association stop. I took him from the back seat and cradled him in my arms, fed him and settled him and began driving home: a terrible, important moment. Rounding a corner nearer to their house, the sulphurous-yellow light of the Co-op supermarket hurt my eyes after the darkness – mental health problems are truly an assault on your senses. It was just one of a series of yellow lights punched into the black, with a pattern continuing until they met the lane to the house. Home, I held my baby tightly; he was asleep again, and I know, because I can sense the physical sensation I write this, that I sat down heavily in an armchair, exhausted by the helter skelter moments and the depressing, jarring movements from dark to ugly yellow light on the journey, and rang my husband. I said, 'Come for me. I am losing my mind – or it is already gone.'

I am sorry if that was a hard read, or hard to read because so very stream of consciousness, but this is how the experience was. And the medieval poet and the novel sprang up to me: it was very frightening – they were here, this time, not as comfort, but to help me corral my thoughts. Like a transliteration, almost: or an iteration. This is also what my reading has brought me to.

I still read. About three books a week usually and often, in a busy life, at furious pace. I also return to the dog-eared corners and marked passages in emergencies. I have been delighted, over the four and a half years that I have been writing books, to discover a whole new diverse and enlightening world in the texts of our indie presses. Yes, I still suck words in my mouth like sweeties and I think I always will. I love a new word, too – and to observe language change, idiolect, slang, rhyme. Love it all. There is one more thing. I hope, as a writer, teacher and one to one tutor, that I have helped some to read and that, in joy, or crisis, it was where they went. I hope that I brought alive the delicacy, the beauty, as well as the urgency.

Back to that Flaubert quotation at the beginning.

'Do not read, as children do, for the sake of entertainment, or, like the ambitious, for the purpose of instruction. No, read in order to live.'

I read for *all* those things. But most of all, I read in order to live.

And, without reading, I know that I would not be alive.

MADNESS AS SUCH
Neil Griffiths

(These fragments were written over the summer and autumn of 2019, during one of the most severe and extended episodes of depression I have experienced in forty years.)

—

No more life

Out there, along the river
The body might make a swerve, leaving the body
To go about its business,
To be in life.

But the mind stays deep in the body –,
The body that swerves
Into nothingness.

—

Write in numbered propositions like Wittgenstein, aphoristically like Nietzsche. Ha!

Like, like … not the same as … not as well … meaning as good … You can write 'as well' if you mean to say that they wrote and you are writing.

It is the case that I am writing. It is the case that I am writing. It is the case.

—

If we're not depressed, we're suffering from … what? I mean none of us is *well* well. None of us can be *well* well. None of us wants to be *well* well.

(The boy must be returned to the well.)

—

Overwhelm. I'm suffering 'overwhelm'. (There is no more space left in this emptiness.)

If the art of living is in being, then being would live artfully. Fuck your wellbeing. Fuck your rights to it.

Be unwell.

No more life.

—

Bring back madness. I mean, that's what it is, right? … what this is, in my head. *Madness*. In both senses: 'this is madness – I can't believe it's happening' and the other one … the one represented on this page. There is a third, of course: 'He/she is mad', meaning, sometimes at least, full of life.

—

I am not in the world. (that first off, that first is the case)

If I am depressed and you are not, we are not alike. (that is also the case)

(Say it, say it) If you have never been depressed, we are not alike. (can never be alike, that is key)

(Make it plain) We are ontologically different. The question of the meaning of being is different.

That is the case. (what befalls us is the case, can't argue with that)

(Depression is knowledge)

Not being in the world is different from being in a dissociative state. (been in that, have you)

(Sorry) Psychic pain is not observable phenomena. (no inflammation or lesion is present, sir)

Deep in the body.

—

Freud was a hard determinist. He believed wholly in impersonal causes. Which means no one is to blame.

—

We are object-seeking. Not pleasure-seeking.

Or: Object-seeking is pleasure-seeking.

(We live in hope.)

Object here means a *person*.

(Surely the proof of this is Transference.)

Enticing object/rejecting object – our relations to a ...

... Love-object. I like the hyphen in love-object. We turn it into an arrow, to show the direction of our yearning. Seeking. Love→object.

(Except that love can miss its mark. Or not. Let's not forget (admit) we can be mistaken as to the nature of our love and the damage it will do.)

Desire starts from inside, a residuum of the primal agony in the gut. The impossibility of the fulfilment of desire is also felt in the gut.

It's not that we can't escape our desire, it's that our desire can't escape us.

It is in the body. Deep in the body. Boundless Limit.

—

Forgive me, but I want to be precise. Let's say there is a cline of lived experience, and at one pole we have joy in all its forms and at the other we have despair in its simplest form. I contend that the depression I am describing cannot be found here, it cannot be plotted. Which is to say ... depression is beyond despair. (There is a psychiatric model for this, at least for mood, where Euphoria and Tension are represented algebraically $y = 1/x$, suggesting depression is categorically different. After all, depression is not the highest expression of Tension. Depression is not a state of feeling.)

Boundless limit.
Deep in the body.

It's the discontinuity that is important. The cline breaking off, falling away. And us with it. Me in this instance, and I mean now, where I am now, in this moment, writing this ...

MADNESS AS SUCH

(It is the case that I am writing now, here.)

Joy and despair are for others. In this moment at least. For others who live in the world and each day ask for more life. The mad ones.

Chaos theory: sensitive dependence on initial condition.

Saying 'Yes, yes!' to Nietzsche's notion of 'the eternal recurrence of the same' is to live in good faith. To live in good faith is to accept your life as your own (to be owned by you) and as such if you are offered the chance to live your life over again (the same life, eternally recurring) you will choose to do so as it was, is and will be, with no alteration, variation or change, and you will do this because you understand that your life and you are indissoluble (intrinsically not dispositionally), and to want your life to be different (to regret) in whatever small way is to want *not to be you* ...
No more life.

—

The pain feels unbearable, which is to say, you can imagine it as life-ending. A notch more and ...

You curl up in bed, knees up, arms around your head, gripping your head, pulling your head tight in. (The body is a gesture.) Where is the pain, inside or out?

It is in the head and in the gut. It is in the darkness that is the world leaking into the mind and the gut, taking up the new space, the enlarging space (the nothingness into which the universe is expanding) that is within you ...

The darkness of the nothingness within you, the enlarging darkness within you, its impossibility as a *feeling*, as a fact, as truth ... it is that which causes the pain.

—

I am not in the world but it cannot be said that I am in another place because 'in' suggests a structure within which one might exist and no such a structure exists.

'What is There?' – Quine.

Over there, outside the body. Along the river. The world that we're in. *There.*

'Every structure is habitable.' – Roland Barthes, *A Lover's Discourse*. He was wrong.

Structure in this instance being meaning. Meaning meaning. What it means for the world to have meaning.

To be in the world is to inhabit structures of meaning and habits of meaning structure the world. To have both is what being in the world is.

(What is it builders say? We need to do this and that and then 'make good'. Build and make good. Make habitable first. Then make meaningful.)

Yes, yes.

Let me make this plain: the there where I am ... all meaning has gone.

MADNESS AS SUCH

No more life.
Boundless limit.

—

It's interesting as much as anything is interesting that in this madness I am numb and yet the pain

is in the body. Deep in the body.

—

There is no skyhook to keep me up. To keep me there, to carry me through, to march me on.

—

Here's a thought experiment. Pick a thing, a notion, a concept, and imagine its opposite. I suspect your first inclination is some phenomenal version of $y = 1/x$, where zero and infinity are never observed. Or put more simply, the opposite of thin is fat, short is tall, stupid is clever. But that is wrong. Of course it is. The opposite of all things is *nothing* ... it is *nothingness*.

Not being in the world is to encounter nothingness.
Nothingness is an encounter with a new truth, a new *half to the truth*. (Truth reduced, then added to, doubled. Truth redux.)

'And the earth was without form, and void; and darkness was upon the face of the deep.'

This is where I find myself. Faced with. Facing.

In truth all truth. Waxing crescent, waning crescent.

Dostoyevsky: 'If someone proved to me that Christ is outside the truth and that in reality the truth were outside of Christ, then I should prefer to remain with Christ rather than with the truth.' And now we know why. (Although in fairness, he mainly remained with the truth, poor soul.)

—

The lived experience of madness is to be in a logically impossible place and yet to look down and (not be dead) see one's body in the world going about its business.

The body is done, the heart is in the stomach, the heart is broken.

Depression is knowledge.

—

Something must end. Something must end. Something must end. Something must end. Something. Shush. It must end. It must end. It must end. I'm telling you. I'm telling you. Something. Something must ... end. Right? What are you looking at? I'm telling you. Something must end or it must end. See? Easy. Shush. That makes it clear. That makes it clear. (I could walk forever. Forever. Never go home. Never go home.) Do you get it? Do you? I bet you do. I bet you do. Except, you really don't. You can't. How about this? How about this? If I were to turn here. Here. If I were to swerve. Here. Just a little bit. Here. Now. See. Just like this. (Arms out as if I were an aeroplane.) If I were to angle myself and swerve. Away. Turn a little and swerve. (Make a swerve.) Off the path here. Just here. Just this spot. Here. And leave the path. Here. Do you see? Do you see? I mean I know you can't, but can you see that I can see? That I can see it here. The opportunity. That I can see the opportunity. To swerve away. Off this path. Here. Here in the park. Just here. And if I were to. If I were to. I mean … make that decision. To finally swerve away

Deep in the body. No more life. Boundless limit.

———

The world cannot be otherwise.
Nothing is otherwise.
Depression is to know that it is possible to live otherwise.
The un-fact in the world.
The choice unmade.
The world as otherwise.

I am not in the world.

———

Please, picture this. Picture the years you have ahead of you and picture each year as a flat thing, a rectangle, a rectangular-shaped piece of … metal (silver, tin, it doesn't matter), and that each rectangle is hinged to the next, creating a chain of say (at least in my case) around twenty-five pieces, so twenty-five years hinged together and laid out before you like a path (if you will), and then picture yourself thinking of a thing to do, something, anything, in the future, moment's time, or in an hour, or a week, but something that implicitly acknowledges futurity … that in all likelihood you will be around, in time, moving forward into, over, through (it doesn't matter), but able to do this thing, but now rather than picture all those years laid out and linked together like chain or path, time to do the thing you've thought of to do, picture the chain or path rising up before you, rising and curling up (like a scorpion's tail) or rearing up and bearing down (like Wordsworth's mountain), and that somehow suddenly all the time you thought you had before you is now right in front of you, rearing up and bearing down, and now picture (imagine) this happening every time you think of a thing to do, every time you acknowledge the future by thinking of a thing to do, the *whole of* the rest of your life becomes *in an instant* a reared up, huge, ugly, stubborn, impenetrable wall bearing down on you, collapsing down on you, and revealing behind it (because it doesn't end with collapse) nothing but timelessness, space without time, which is no space at all ... so nothingness in all its dark and dimensionless purity ...all this is what you face when you picture what you might do ... its impossibility, its straightforward impossibility because you have run out of time to do it in, there is no time left, there is nothing laid out, only nothing. No life left.

Please, picture this.

(Imagine.)

—

It is banal to talk about blankness, but this is what one is faced with, and into which all things fall. Of course, the world persists, visible on the periphery, a grey corona around a dark centre. But the world is a noisy, cold place, worse than the blank.

The blank is a new thing, there because nothingness has been encountered, after which the world cannot be faced. You cannot be in possession of the whole truth and face the world.

(Only one half of the truth contains the whole truth; the other half is too full of sunlight.)

(Plato's Sunlight.)

The pain this causes is a kind of negative surprise at coming face to face with the whole truth as a blank in the centre of the world into which all things fall and still find yourself to be alive and going about your business with this knowledge.

The impossibility of being present when pressed over against nothingness. (The side of face pressed to a window at night, pressed hard, forced against the black pane. The blank pane.)

Do I repeat myself?
Very well then I repeat myself.
(I am nothing, I contain nothing.)

Whitman is a poet of enthusiasm, an optimist. In that sense he is no poet at all.

—

Boundless Limit. Deep in the body. No more life.

—

'What do you *feel*? How does it make you *feel*?'
I have no feelings. I do not exist.

That I am writing is the case. That I am writing this. In the world.

—

TRAUMA

Your existence isn't real to me. Your subjectivity. Your agency. Your body. You. You in the light. You in the glare. The 3-D you. The live-action you. In the world.

—

(Before the universe. Before time. Before God.)
How is it that we know nothingness? What is it a percept of?
'And the earth was without form, and void; and darkness was upon the face of the deep.'
Ontogeny recapitulates cosmogeny
Deep in the body.

—

Freud believed the objective of the death drive is to return us to nothing, that as an organism we possess a trace memory of non-existence, of a time before the genesis of life, and that that has a kind of hold over us ... it beckons us back.

—

I am the universe
Deep in the body
Boundless limit
Deep in the body
I am not in the world
Deep in the body
Depression is knowledge

No more life.

WE STILL WENT TO THE MOVIES

Momina Masood

We found a way to our bodies and to each other in darkened cinema halls. You remember when the city had been shut down by religious extremists two years ago, and the very next day you went to the movies. There hidden in a corner you watched two men make out and held your breath. The film played on, a biopic of some musician, and as the two men moved in their seats dancing to the music, you danced quietly in the back as well. Look at us, you thought, in the dark. We're here.

'You buy a ticket to watch a film, but what you are really buying is time.'*

Time. X drags you to the newest John Wick playing in CineStar because they need something to take their mind off of things. It's a smaller cinema, more intimate, a strange

---

* Hira Nabi, *Transient Spaces and Places: Inside an 80s Cinema Hall in Lahore*. BioScope.

place to be watching a film like that, but nothing about this city ever made sense to begin with. There X rolls their pants up as they pull their feet up to the seat crossing their legs underneath them and gripping your hand. It doesn't matter here, our bodies, the bits we usually hide, the hands we aren't brave enough to hold outside. Nothing matters here in the dark. X lets out a breath as the screen lights up, and lets their dupatta fall. You grip their hand tighter.

'Instead of time, perhaps you were buying space?'*

***

When cinemas closed down under General Zia-ul-Haq's military dictatorship in the 1970s, going to the movies became something more than seeking entertainment. Under Zia's Islamisation project, going to the movies was deemed an 'un-Islamic' activity and cinemas were often vulnerable to police raids. The films that were made during this period were mostly low-budget exploitation-style films and are remembered for being quite transgressive. As cinemas were often raided, and many were burnt and destroyed, the few remaining had to navigate a time of extreme censorship and surveillance quite strategically. The marquee would advertise a tame, innocent title from the last few decades to ward off potential raids, meanwhile inside something far less innocent would be playing. Some cinema operators were cleverer – they would play the film advertised and insert clips from a recently released low-budget horror or softcore porn at various intervals. These were called cut-pieces. Sometimes a

* Ibid.

whole separate film would be shown this way, in the form of cut-pieces spliced onto and inserted in another wholesome state-approved social drama. Never had cinemagoing been this dangerous, this thrilling, this *queer*.

We still went to the movies. When the cinemas were burning, we went to the movies anyway. It made much more sense then to go. Something important was happening, we didn't know what exactly, and even if it wasn't, we wanted to pretend anyway. To pretend this mattered, that we could get away with a little bit at least. I remember during Ramadan once, it was sehri and we couldn't find your uncle anywhere. Your Nano literally walked all the way to the cinema near the train station and found him sitting there all alone in one of the halls. It wasn't weird at all. The people of Jammu, after migrating to Pakistan during Partition, didn't know weird. They were used to slipping away when things got difficult.

Part of my work has been collecting stories from those who lived through the coup, All stories eventually lead us back to *Maula Jatt,** a low-budget Punjabi film which riled up enough people for Zia to eventually ban it. Working-class men who frequented cinema halls found in Maula an anarchist who helped them process the times that had suddenly come upon them. When Maula spoke up against oppression, when he hoodwinked the police and killed in the name of justice, audiences felt strangely represented. The masses are being radicalised and encouraged towards violence against the state, they said, but several Lakshmi chowk cinemas kept

---

* A Pakistani Punjabi-language film, released in 1979. A cult classic and one of the most seminal films in the history of Pakistani cinema.

playing the film, maybe for that very reason. The Red Light District in Lahore spanning Lakshmi chowk and Royal Park, known for their cinemas and brothels, was a strange place during Zia. I wonder why this is where we decided to hide. When your uncle was dragged back to the house, no one asked him what he had gone to see. As long as he was found and came back home. Many didn't. It was easier this way though. Pretending the thousands who disappeared were just hiding and scattered across the city watching a pirated monster movie in a nameless cinema.

***

Cut to the early 1990s and you are a young girl from a lower middle-class background in a small town in Pakistan, and you didn't go to the movies. Nobody did. On your way to more posh bits of the city, you'd ogle the huge billboards and fight your brother to get the better seat on the tonga trying to get a view of half-naked women, their cleavage painted over black by the local religious group, wielding guns, staring back at you grinning. Those who were respectable had stopped going to the cinemas since Zia had deemed them un-Islamic, and you were respectable. You took out the Quran from your room whenever you jerked off to the fantasy of having a different body. You were respectable like that.

'Zia had banned all types of collectivization. Cinema was the only space where you could be a part of a public, without it being a *jalsa* (protest rally) or a *janaza* (funeral).'*

---

* Hira Nabi, *Transient Spaces and Places: Inside an 80s Cinema Hall in Lahore*. BioScope.

WE STILL WENT TO THE MOVIES

One of the Lakshmi chowk cinemas is playing the original cut of *Maula Jatt* celebrating its anniversary and you quietly slip inside the Odeon, taking a seat at the back. The girl beside you holds on to her niqab a little tighter this time but eventually lets it fall as the screen lights up. You think of the trans women who hung Sultan Rahi* posters in their quarters and wonder who else snuck inside the cinemas to hide when the country was burning. Your mother tells you stories of rebellions and cinemagoing and *Haseena Atom Bomb*[†] and you wonder when the fear finally stuck. Now no longer a child on a tonga, you infiltrate spaces too and have your little rebellions, find your own darkened rooms to let your dupatta fall where it may. When *Maula Jatt* plays, you know all the lines. Everyone does. Something lifts and lightens.

***

We found our way to our bodies through cinema. We hid in dark rooms to hold hands and let our bodies breathe, retracing steps of those before us and the paths of rebellion they left scattered across the city. The country never fully healed from Zia, they'll tell you. I'm not sure if you and I have either, from the fear passed down to us from our mothers. Something woman in us broke a long time ago and everything since then has been a violent act of imagining our bodies and desires anew in languages half-learnt, half-forgotten. We rebuild. In the light of the cinema hall, hiding

---

* A well-known Pakistani actor who starred in several Punjabi-language films in the 1970s, including *Maula Jatt*.

† A Pakistani Pashto-language film, released in 1990. It was a massive hit, and was even dubbed in Urdu for a wider re-release.

in the back, we rebuild and find each other. X still asks me out to the newer cinemas that keep opening across the city to watch foreign films that mostly play out to half empty halls, just to hold hands. We heal, we find kinder ways back to our bodies, to our mothers, to our collective and historical pasts. Like our dead uncles who once wandered the city before us, we too somehow keep finding our way back home.

QUITE COLLECTED...
MEANWHILE...

Rowena Macdonald

'Quite collected at cocktail parties,
meanwhile in my head
I'm undergoing open-heart surgery.'
Anne Sexton, 'Red Riding Hood'

startle awake heart pounding butterflies butterflies butterflies in chest bitter tension in pit of stomach butterflies is it starting again? butterflies is it? is it? butterflies butterflies oh god please let it not why am i feeling this? is it the novel re-write? i don't need to think about the novel re-write now, butterflies i can do it i

5 a.m.: She wakes up in bed next to her boyfriend. Her daughter sleeps in a bunk bed in the same room. The room is well-proportioned, high ceilinged and airy with red velvet curtains and vintage furniture. The flat overlooks a large beautiful park in a fashionable part of east London. Beyond the curtains is a calming

can't do it i can do it, it will be fine it won't be fine it'll be fine it won't be i won't be able to do it butterflies butterflies should i try and get back to sleep or just get up? get up? stay? up? not up? i might be able to catch another couple of hours lie with eyes closed butterflies butterflies butterflies until...

L wakes and comes into our bed no point in lying here any more

lie on sofa while L watches cbeebies heart pounds cheerful brightness parades past hold on is that lorraine kelly narrating raa raa the noisy lion? lovely calm lorraine kelly lorraine would never feel like this tough impenetrable cheerful successful type not stymied by doubts oh to be lorraine kelly

wrangle L into clothes and through weetabix-eating hair-brushing teeth-cleaning and face-washing butterflies butterflies no appetite mouth

view of the lake and a café where you can eat plant-based breakfasts, heavy on avocado. The sun is rising. The three figures inside the room lie in apparent peace

6 a.m.: The little girl wakes up and climbs into her parents' bed.

6 – 7 a.m.: Her mother takes her downstairs and switches on the TV. Sunlight floods through the muslin curtains. The mother lies on the sofa while her daughter snuggles against her and watches CBeebies; they are a picture of warmth and togetherness.

7 – 8.40 a.m.: With brisk efficiency the woman propels her daughter through the usual morning routine while simultaneously getting

dry force down bowl of muesli immediately feel sick

wrangle L to school other mothers exchange pleasantries all small talk gone sure i seem weird unfriendly stand-offish must escape

should i go to work? am i up to it? will normality make me feel normal? am i going to freak out at work? am i going to have a panic attack? burst into tears? seem like a nutter? end up shunned by colleagues?

on tube wish someone would give me a seat knees weak need to sit down exhausted not enough sleep 12pm to 5am onetwothreefourfive only five hours eightminusfiveequalsthree three hours fewer than the optimum am i going to be able to get through the day? everyone else is calm and together some have their eyes peacefully closed others

herself ready, unloading and reloading the dishwasher and making the beds.

8.40 – 9 a.m.: At her daughter's school she does not look out of place among the other middle-class mothers in mutedly tasteful workwear, who have had their children late.

9 – 9.15 a.m.: On the road to the Tube, she does not look out of place among the other locals walking at a purposeful pace, with recyclable cups of coffee and phones in hand.

9.15 – 9.45 a.m.: On the Tube, she does not look out of place among the other commuters, with their unreadable, expressionless faces and eyes and bodies held carefully against accidental contact.

are playing games on their
phone or reading absorbed
concentrating   sweating
sweating mouth feels dry
butterflies am i going to be
able to work? am i going
to freak out? is it starting
again? should i go to the
doctor's? increase my pills?
should have increased them
last week before this started
happening again why didn't
i increase them then? why?
butterflies enter office
thankfully don't bump into
anyone no need for small talk
colleagues ask how weekend
was pretend it was okay ask
how their weekends were
can't concentrate on their
answers start computer
heart pounds deep breaths
in through nose out through
mouth in through nose out
through mouth shoulders
are up round ears make
conscious effort to slacken
them in out in out heart
quells butterflies subside
computer uploads log into
outlook sixty-five unread

10 a.m. – 12.30 p.m.: She
enters an office building
in central London. Her
workplace is high profile; the
kind that prompts people to
say, 'that must be interesting,
working there'. Her
colleagues are intelligent,
pleasant people. They greet
their teammates as they
arrive, bring in homemade
cakes and ask about their
weekends and if anyone else
wants a coffee as they go
downstairs to the canteen.
Again, she does not look out
of place among them as she
sits at her desk, switches on

emails click through them problems demands queries deadlines heart pounds can't remember how to do job get up go to toilet sit on toilet wonder if i should go home now what should i say to boss? wash hands, eyes look huge and scared face tense smile unconvincing

make phone calls send emails voice sounds querulous palms sweaty colleagues lounge with headphones on enviably relaxed overhear small talk with each other join in but intonation sounds odd and forced

walk around the lake in park try to notice nature try to ignore tightness in chest and head bursting with fear of future try to be pleased by sight of pelican take photo of pelican sit on bench and eat sandwich bought from canteen tastes of sawdust mouth dry glug bottle of water weight loss is the only silver lining

her computer and appears to work steadily throughout the morning.

12.30 – 1 p.m.: She walks around the famous park, sits on a bench and eats a sandwich. The sun is shining, flowers are blooming, birds are building nests on the lake. Runners in bright Lycra dodge tourists posing for photos. Ice creams are being licked. Picnickers sprawl on the grass.

open gmail write to mum: *I'm not feeling very well* mum writes back worried email tears spring to eyes heart pounds with renewed vigour scroll through work emails vision blurs blink tears away turn in chair to boss who sits behind me i'm going to tell him how i'm feeling i'm going to come out with it he looks up i take a deep breath swallow and say

1 p.m.: She returns to her office, taps the keyboard to wake her computer and opens Gmail. Sometime later, she turns to her boss. Her eyes are wide with anxiety and glittering with unshed tears. When her boss looks up she takes a deep breath, swallows and says,

'Can I have a word? In private.'

We go into the meeting space with the sofas, known as the soft play area. My boss regards me with quizzical concern. 'Is everything okay?' he asks.

My face crumples and I say, 'I'm not feeling too good.'

SLEEP NO MORE
Rhiannon L. Cosslett

'I've dreamt in my life dreams that have stayed with me ever after, and changed my ideas: they've gone through and through me, like wine through water, and altered the colour of my mind.'
– Chapter IX, *Wuthering Heights*

I am walking to work one sunny morning when the man comes up behind me and holds the pistol to my head. I can feel the coldness of the barrel against my warm skin and he whispers in my ear not to move, his breath tickling the insides of my ears. All is still and silent as we stand there. Time takes on a viscous quality. We are alone in this concrete landscape that I have come to know so well.

I look down towards the railway bridge, knowing that these moments will be my last ones on this planet. How sad I am that my life will end this way; alongside the terror there is also a profound sense of regret. I do not want to die, I think, closing my eyes. My limbs are frozen. Still he does not shoot the gun. Instead, I stand waiting for it, knowing that it is coming. I do not know how long the waiting and the knowing lasts in real time, before he puts the bullet in my brain and I wake up gasping, but it feels like hours and hours.

***

Henry James said, 'tell a dream, lose a reader'. I disagree, though I may be at odds with those readers who have been defeated by *Finnegans Wake*. It has become common orthodoxy that it's tedious to talk about your dreams, and yet I am always fascinated by them when they are offered to me. Even more so when it comes to literature: my favourite plays and novels are littered with dreams. 'Last night I dreamed I went to Manderley again...' is an opening line that almost dares the reader to lose interest. Put the book down then and there if you must be so unimaginative. Your loss.

Rebecca of course harks back to *Jane Eyre*, whose heroine has an active and persistent dream life, perhaps a hint at what is referred to as her 'spiritual eye'. She dreams of children, a 'sure sign of trouble', and dreams the destruction of Thornfield before it occurs. She is dreaming when she wakes up to find Bertha tearing up her wedding dress. Her dreams have a premonitory quality, but at a time which followed an era when dreams were interpreted as otherworldly visitations by demonic, gargoyle-like creatures (see Henry Fuseli's much-reproduced *The Nightmare*), Brontë shows a more intuitive understanding of why we dream: Jane is, I believe, traumatised. She dreams of the red room in which the child Jane was locked by her awful guardians:

'I lifted up my head to look: the roof resolved to clouds, high and dim; the gleam was such as the moon imparts to vapours she is about to sever. I watched her come – watched with the strangest anticipation; as though some word of doom were to be written on her disk. She broke forth as never moon yet burst from cloud: a hand first penetrated the sable folds and waved them away; then, not a moon, but a white human form shone in the azure, inclining a glorious brow earthward.'

Is Jane's dream boring? I do not think it is. The interior dream-lives of female characters who were robbed by the patriarchy from leading fulfilling exterior lives take on untold significance for me both as a reader and as a woman. It is no wonder that they feature so frequently in Gothic novels, those haunted dreamscapes of repressed femininity.

But even more relevant to my interest is my own diagnosis; dreams, or more accurately nightmares, are a central component of post-traumatic stress disorder. We read novels partly as a means of understanding the human psyche, and we all dream. To omit the dream, particularly when it is a factor in that most atavistic of human responses, the trauma response, is to construct a house with a wall missing.

***

I dreamt the gun-to-my-head dream when I was at my worst, during the second flare up of post-traumatic stress disorder. The initial trauma was an attack in the street involving strangulation. This was treated and, while not cured, my day-to-day life was made manageable once more. The second flare-up was trigged by my unlucky proximity to the Paris attacks of November 2015. This is the point at which guns started appearing in my nightmares.

PTSD can develop when a person has been in a situation where they have felt threat to their life (though not everyone who has been in a life-threatening situation will necessarily develop it). It often involves the intrusive reliving of the trauma, sometimes in the form of nightmares, but I rarely dreamed of my attacker or the feel of his hands around my neck. My dreams would certainly be defined as nightmares – long, frightening dreams involving threats to survival or security, from which I would awaken – but I was not reliving my trauma, at least not in the strictest sense.

Long before I was ever traumatised by the attack, I was a sensitive and vivid dreamer. Nightmares about the deaths of family members, most often my younger brother, who is severely disabled (a different sort of trauma, it could be argued) would see me wake sobbing, and, overtaken by feelings of profound sadness, I would be unable to achieve much the following day. I would also have the occasional bad dream – an important distinction from the nightmare. Trauma nightmares were something else. They were lengthy and relentless, and felt entirely real. Often I was being chased, often by a gunman, and trying to run would feel like moving through toffee, my muscles refusing to cooperate. The images in the nightmares – of torture, shootings, rape, dead bodies – were worse than any horror film. Hangings featured particularly strongly, which makes sense considering the nature of the original trauma. The Holocaust was also often present, despite my not having ever had a personal connection with it, other than it having haunted me as a child. Clearly certain images, stumbled upon far too young, had found fertile ground in which to flourish.

***

I am being taken to a camp, and I am being forced to walk down a long, muddy track at the sides of which are poles, and from each pole a human body is hanging by its neck. I know that when we reach the end of this road I too am to be hanged by the neck from one of these poles, but when I try to run it is as though I have forgotten how to move my limbs, have become somehow paralysed. This feeling of immobile terror continues for many hours, until I wake sobbing and unable to breathe.

***

Humans make art for a number of reasons, and one of those is to make sense of trauma. The Surrealist artist Rene Magritte was, like his contemporaries, influenced by the psychoanalytic preoccupation with the unconscious and dreams (incidentally, anyone in search of a visual echo of Jane Eyre's 'roof resolved to clouds' need only look at one of his paintings). His most famous dream-work is perhaps the suitably titled *Key to Dreams* (1930), consisting of several objects – an egg, a shoe, a bowler hat, a candle, a glass, and a hammer– framed by a grid-like structure. Underneath are what look like captions, but the words bear no ostensible relevance to the objects themselves. For example, the shoe is designated *La Lune*.

The painting has become well known perhaps thanks to its placement on the cover of John Berger's *Ways of Seeing*, and its use at the start of the book to explain how 'the relation between what we see and what we know is never settled'. In dreams, that which we know but never see can become manifest, and there is much that we see but do not understand. Freud, whose theories inspired the Surrealist movement, initially believed all dreams were a form of wish fulfillment whose symbols and images could be interpreted by the patient with their analyst through free association. It was only after the First World War, when the repetitive nightmares of shell-shocked soldiers were brought to his attention, that he made an exception, writing that: 'it is impossible to classify as wish fulfillments the dreams we have been discussing which occur in traumatic neurosis, or the dreams during psychoanalysis which bring to memory the psychical traumas of childhood.'

Magritte himself was probably traumatised. His mother drowned herself when he was fourteen and he watched as her body was dragged from the River Sambre, her nightgown rucked up over her face like a shroud. The swaddled heads that appear in several of his paintings have been posited as a nightmarish echo of this, but less has been said of the naked, fragmented female forms in several of his works, which to me seem to be in the process of decomposition, like a corpse rotting away.

***

In Deborah Levy's *Swimming Home*, a group's villa holiday in the South of France is disrupted by the discovery of what appears to be a woman's naked body floating in the pool. Kitty Finch, it turns out, is very much alive, and her arrival is the catalyst that sets the others on a course that will end in tragedy.

Finch is fragile (or 'mental' as another character describes her) and has not long returned from being sectioned and treated with ECT (electroconvulsive therapy). After being invited to stay at the villa, she experiences dreams (nightmares), or hallucinations:

'When Kitty Finch woke up, she felt someone breathing on her face. At first she thought the window had blown open during the night, but then she saw him and had to shove her hair into her mouth to stop herself screaming out loud. A black-haired boy was standing by her bed and he was waving to her.'

I suspect Henry James would not approve, but Kitty Finch's 'nightmare' is interesting. The boy, who we come to understand is a younger Joe Jacobs – the poet who has let the house and with whom Kitty is obsessed – disappears through walls. He is not a ghost, but Jacobs, Finch concludes, who has 'trance-journeyed into her mind' Jacobs is haunted by his own trauma, the trauma of being left in the Polish forest by his family in the hope that he will escape the Nazis. This overlapping of two traumatised minds, and how they become dangerously drawn to one another, is at the heart of the novel.

In *Swimming Home*, the character of Mitchell also has a nightmare, about hacking at a centipede which multiplies until 'he was up to his ears in centipedes. They were crawling into his nostrils and trying to get into his mouth.' Mitchell is, as far as we know, not traumatised, though his attempts to have a normal holiday are increasingly thwarted and it emerges that he and his wife are significantly in debt. Mitchell's nightmare, like him, is more typical than Kitty Finch's, and yet it serves to show us that even he, this unpleasant character with simple desires, has an active dream life that tells us something about his unconscious motivations. As Kitty Finch has told him:

'It's rude to be so normal, Mitchell. Even you must have been a child once. Even you might have thought there were monsters lurking under your bed. Now that you are such an impeccably normal adult you probably take a discreet look under your bed and tell yourself, well, maybe the monster is invisible!'

***

I am falling down the hole in the middle of a very high staircase. The staircase exists in a vacuum, no surrounding walls or windows or ceilings are visible, only the velvet blackness of space. Nor is there sound. Occasionally, as I fall, I glimpse another item that is floating in space (how these float and I do not is not a question that occurs to me): a kitchen chair, a rolling pin, a teddy bear. It is as though a house has been exploded like Cornelia Parker's shed, and I am falling through the universe, the flotsam and jetsam of domesticity around me, the staircase curling around like a spine. But I am falling and I am afraid because I know that when I hit the ground, I will die. This feeling seems to last all night, until I do.

***

Deborah Eisenberg's adult narrator in *All Around Atlantis* recalls, 'Yes, I had nightmares – children do. After all, it takes some time to get used to being alive. And how else, except in the clarity of dreams, are you supposed to see the world all around you that's hidden by the light of day?'

***

Deborah Levy, when asked by a reader on Radio 4 about her dream-writing: 'I don't want characters in my novels telling each other their dreams, but I am interested in dream and I think I believe Freud when he told us that a dream is an illustration of an anxiety or a wish. Also dreams tell us things that we don't want to know.

'This is a book not really about depression but about repression, pushing away really difficult things that are hard to bear.'

Just before the publication of my first novel, *The Tyranny of Lost Things*, I went to see Levy speak at a psychoanalytic conference. I had poured everything I knew about trauma into this novel, and in so doing it had been necessary to include dreams and nightmares. It went against all the writing advice, but as a trauma victim I knew that not to include them would result in portrayal of trauma that was too flat. My character, Harmony, has repressed her trauma. Unlike my own reality, which had been plagued with flashbacks which made the reasons behind my anxiety very plain, her dream-world is telling her the things that, as Levy describes it, she doesn't want to know. She finds this frightening; as Freud notes, the element of the *unheimlich*, or the uncanny, which scares us, is 'something that has been repressed that now returns'.

Despite being comfortable with the psychological and psychoanalytic rationale behind my dream-writing, I had yet again come across the 'no dreams in fiction' rule and will admit that, as an inexperienced novelist just embarking on her career, I was worried by it. What, I asked, did Levy think of this rule?

She told me that she kept the dreams in her novels to no longer than a paragraph, and that it was important to distinguish a dream retold at a cocktail party from a dream in a work of fiction. Good dream writing, she said, adds a dimension. It tells us something about a character.

I came away from this interaction feeling less worried and, if anything, slightly vindicated, not only about my own writing, but also about the literary propensity to pronounce rules. The problem with rules is that they can operate perfectly well for as long as you are able to follow them, and even if the rules frighten or annoy you, you can make a conscious, considered departure from them provided you have a rationale for doing this (and adhere to certain other rules). But when you are severely mentally ill, the rules don't just cease to apply, but following them becomes impossible. How to convey the ruleless state of a psyche in distress in a literary form? The answer that I came to was that you look elsewhere for guidance: to other writers, more specifically, to women writers.

***

Perhaps, in order to inscribe the feminine as Helene Cixous asks of us in *The Laugh of the Medusa*, to lay bare those 'unheard-of songs', to convey the history of 'life somewhere else', we also need to inscribe our dreams. It is thought that everybody dreams. Women, however, are more likely than men to remember their dreams, and are probably more likely to admit to having them. They certainly have more nightmares than men, starting in adolescence. The most common scenario – across cultures – is that the dreamer is being pursued or attacked.

Jung's theory of dreams as part of the collective unconscious, the inherited experiential record of the human species in the form of archetypes – those symbols that also appear throughout religion and myth – has been scientifically disproven. We do not inherit symbols in the way we inherit eye colour. And yet I am drawn to the notion of a collective unconscious, at least one formed through living in the world – socialisation. That collective unconscious is not static; it shifts as the world changes. The patients' dreams with which early psychoanalysts were confronted would not be the same now. Then they dreamed of ghosts. According to a 2009 *New Yorker* piece on the treatment of nightmares, Voldemort now crops up. Interesting, modern dreams are becoming more fragmented, as though responding to the development of technology.

While researching this essay, I stumbled across a notebook I had kept from when I was living in Paris in 2005. Alongside some poetry that I reminded myself needed to be burnt, I found a record of a nightmare that I had experienced, in which I am stabbed by a man in a dark tunnel (I am then at a registry office with my then-boyfriend, but I am wearing a funeral hat instead of a veil, a symbol which speaks for itself). Were I to have this dream now, I would tell myself that it were a result of post-traumatic stress. But what this note told me was that I felt the trauma of being a woman in a world in which some men wanted to hurt me more acutely than was clear to me in my waking life at the time.

'We meet our unconscious in our own destinies,' a psychologist once told me. He said it was a quote from Jung but I have never found it anywhere. At the time it felt like he was blaming me for what had happened to me.

***

What are dreams for? It's an argument that is still raging. The Freudian 'wish fulfilment' hypothesis and the Jungian notion that dreams have a 'compensatory' function, reflecting aspects of the unconscious that are not adequately developed when awake, are no longer fashionable as scientists find continuity between dreams and people's waking lives.

And because dreams do not provide us with solutions to our problems, they are not thought to have an adaptive function. Even Freud excluded the nightmares of traumatised, shell-shocked soldiers from his wish fulfilment hypothesis, saying that they had more to do with the mind compulsively repeating events in an attempt to create stability. Indeed, it has been posited that the repetitive nightmares of PTSD sufferers should occupy a different category entirely. Dream researcher Dr Ernest Hartmann has suggested the term 'memory intrusions'. Such trauma nightmares have been compared to broken records, 'stuck in a groove and unable to play on...'

And yet, my trauma nightmares (and I would argue those of Jane Eyre) are not simply repetitions of events that have occurred. Jane is not dreaming of the exact scenario she experienced, when she was locked in the red room as a child, and I was not dreaming about the man who placed his hands around my neck on the pavement that night in North London, though I did experience similar emotions in those dreams. Even my most repetitive nightmares still changed settings and locations: new material was being added.

***

A 2018 study into the nightmares of Holocaust survivors, conducted by Wojciech Owczarski at the University of Gdansk, affirmed Hartmann's theory that even terrifying nightmares, such as those suffered by survivors of Auschwitz, could have healing or adaptive potential. Instead of displaying the trauma exactly as it occurred, these dreams weave in new experiences. This has a quasi-therapeutic function, allowing the trauma to be less overwhelming the more it mixes with more recent experiences and emotions.

This is especially the case, Owczarski argues, when it comes to those nightmares categorised as 'comeback dreams', dreams in which survivors are sent to Auschwitz, or told that they will be sent to Auschwitz a second, third, or sixth time. These sound like horrific nightmares, but they are actually far more cheerful in character than the other nightmares of survivors – the dreamer knows he is there for a limited time and will one day go home, or no longer feels fear, or knows that he and his wife will survive. It's still a nightmare, but the reality of the camp has changed.

***

Dr Barry Krakow, a US-based sleep doctor, believed that the repetitive nightmares of trauma survivors have little use to sufferers, and wondered if patients could be trained to rewrite them in a technique that came to be called imagery-rehearsal therapy. Patients undertake a similar process to that which a writer might – writing out their nightmare scenario as a narrative. Then, like a novelist being told by their agent that their book will not sell without a happy ending, they are asked to amend the nightmare, editing it to give a more prosaic or pleasant outcome. And so blades turn to leaves, planes that are nosediving right themselves, one woman's nightmare concentration camp becomes a summer camp, and the gun pointed at my head would become a fluorescent water pistol.

As part of this treatment, the new revised dream scenario is then conjured on a daily basis. And it appears to work: the patients' nightmares are transformed, neutralised. They become manageable.

***

I am standing in a hospital waiting room, having just had a routine blood test. The doctor comes over to me with a grave face. I suspect that she is about to tell me and my husband that I am pregnant, but instead I am ushered into a small anteroom and informed that I have advanced cancer of the uterus and have mere weeks to live. I collapse, crying, on the floor, knowing that I will never be able to do any of the things that I have wanted to do in my life, that I will never write another novel, or have a baby, or grow old alongside the people I love.

There is always so much death in my dreams, usually, but not always my own. And this nightmare is going the same way. I am prone, hysterical, on the hospital floor. And then I think: no.

Somewhere in the back room of my unconscious, I have retained the article about imagery-rehearsal therapy. No, I say to myself, this doesn't have to be this way. I do not have to die. This is only a dream, and I can snip and paste and make a different ending.

And so I do: the blood test results are a false positive. The hospital made a mistake, and we go home holding hands.

***

Walking through a recent exhibition of the work of Edvard Munch, an artist who was plagued with nightmares and visions of death – and whose self-portrait *The Night Wanderer* captures the gaunt desolation of sleep deprivation – I wondered what art we would have been left with had he been cured. Mary Shelley famously dreamed Frankenstein's creation. Perhaps one day we will succeed in eradicating all nightmares, and be able to improve the lives of the people who suffer them. But what else will be lost?

By the time I learned to lucid dream, the treatment I had been having for PTSD was over. I sometimes wonder how I would have responded to reading about imagery-rehearsal therapy when I was mired in the whirlwind of severe mental illness, agoraphobic and terrified, insomniac for fear of sleep. Perhaps it would have made no difference.

Or perhaps it would have cured me, and those nightmares, which, to quote Catherine Earnshaw in *Wuthering Heights*, 'altered the colour of my mind' and changed my ideas, and which I have remembered for ever after, even inspiring a novel about trauma, would, like the novel I would write, never have existed.

A RECIPE FOR MADNESS
Naomi Frisby

1. Woman meets man, whisk rapidly

J stands by the hob, nurturing a mushroom risotto. Risotto's the most tedious of dishes; hours spent ladling small amounts of stock into the pan, waiting for it to be absorbed before adding another tiny spoonful. If I was making it, I'd pour all the liquid in at once, take my chances. J isn't me; he's got some patience. I don't know what I've done to deserve this man who's taken a train from another city to come and cook dinner. I'm not even paying him any attention; I'm marking exam papers.

He'd messaged me a few weeks earlier, told me I sounded like someone he wanted to get to know. J's profile said he liked walks in the rain, fry-ups for breakfast, staring at the sea, going to gigs. It was so similar to my own, I wondered whether I'd written it, if I'd imagined him into existence.

Friends at work convinced me to try online dating. I resisted, my excuses well-practised: I was fine on my own. I had a career. I earned good money. I took myself to gigs. I sat and read in the pub. My complaints about being single told a different story, they said.

I wasn't going to admit that I was lonely. That I didn't know how to share a life, a home, my heart. Since the end of my previous relationship, I'd built a wall around myself. I was too scared of having my heart broken again. When I signed up to the dating site, I told my colleagues it was to stop them from nagging. I told myself I'd get some good anecdotes from it, that the stories would be worth a few terrible dates. I wasn't expecting anything else. Ten days later I met J; my defences weren't as secure as I'd thought.

Cooking is J's thing and I love that about him. I can make a handful of reasonable dishes, all of them vegetarian: lasagne, spaghetti bolognaise, macaroni cheese, stir-fry with a packet sauce, curry from a jar. Feminism's my excuse for not learning to cook; I've been too busy having a career to care about being in the kitchen.

The risotto's delicious. We talk while we eat. What we were like as kids, who we wanted to be, where we've travelled, how we've lived. We talk a lot in the early days, revealing ourselves layer by layer.

That evening, it's my boss's fortieth birthday party. J tells me he's shy around people he doesn't know very well but he chats and dances with my colleagues. They like him. They're thrilled I've met someone. It feels strange being seen as part of a couple. I'm strong, independent. I can take care of myself.

My attitude doesn't bother J. He's always there, holding my hand, telling me I'm fantastic. When we're apart, texts and emails arrive throughout the day. He's attentive and available. Other men I'd dated could be standoffish at first, probably mirroring my own approach. J makes it clear he wants me, but his directness makes me uncomfortable. Over time I grow used to it and I like it. I know I can fall and he'll catch me. It feels good to trust someone again.

The morning after the party, J and I lie in bed talking about our fears. Mine is being financially dependent on someone who's abusive. Trapped with no way to leave.

I tell him about my dad. How I'd woken up one morning to find him still at home. He worked in the local foundry. To me, his days seemed regimented: he left for work at seven a.m., holding his plastic lunchbox, and returned around six. I can't remember what he said to me, but I could see he'd been crying. My mum sobbed as she brushed my hair for school, told me it was grown-up stuff. I was ten.

The arguments that followed were ferocious. At night, I lay in bed terrified, not understanding why this was happening. One day Mum packed a suitcase. She told me Dad was having an affair with someone at work and she was leaving. I cried. Begged her to stay. She put the case in her wardrobe but she never really seemed happy after that. Years later, I asked my mum why she'd stayed. 'I couldn't afford to go,' she said. I swore I'd never allow myself to end up in that position.

J listens. When I've finished, he tells me his biggest fear is being cheated on. His last partner was unfaithful and it devastated him. 'I'd never put anyone through that,' he says. To show how serious he is, he offers me all of his online passwords. I don't want them; I trust him.

We fall fast. While we still live apart, we imagine a future together, a life shared. A house filled with books and CDs and love. Evenings spent listening to music; Sunday afternoons watching old films. I've never dated anyone with so many shared interests, the same hopes and dreams.

For Christmas that year, he buys me a knife. 'If I'm going to cook at your place,' he says, 'I want decent equipment to prep with.' On New Year's Eve, he arrives with quiche he's made and carried across two cities. I tell my oldest friend I've met the love of my life.

2. Add a pinch of fear, stirring continuously

I move to J's city. We're desperate to live together and it makes sense that I'm the one to relocate: my landlord's selling the place I live in and it doesn't take me long to get a new job. We find a house, fill it with books and CDs and love. As we slip into a routine, the passion and intensity of those early weeks fades, but we're making it work. At least I think we are.

We've been living together for a year. It's a bank holiday and we're lying in bed. I reach out, touch J's skin. I want him. He covers himself with his hands, curls up like an animal under attack. I move away, stunned. While J has a shower, I sit in the kitchen, coffee going cold in front of me. He walks into the room. 'I don't love you anymore,' he says.

I don't understand what I've done to make him fall out of love. I beg him to tell me what the problem is; we can fix it. I can fix it. We've built a home and a life together. I'm not going to let us fail.

We go for a walk and talk more than we have in months. J says I'm too wrapped up in my work. I've stopped paying him attention. It all makes sense. My previous relationship ended for similar reasons. This is my fault.

I promise I'll be kinder, more thoughtful. When J agrees to try again, I'm thrilled. At the beginning of the relationship, when we'd exchanged parts of ourselves, I thought I'd learned how to share my heart. What I hadn't learned is that you can't just cross those things off your to-do list. Finally, I understand. Love is a work in progress.

The following day, to show I'm sincere, I decide to cook. Roasted vegetables with Quorn sausages. Simple but tasty. J returns from work, an atmosphere hanging over him. I'm in the living room; he sits in the kitchen. Dinner's in the oven, but I'm too scared to check it. I don't want to hear him say the words I know are coming. The house is choking. The oven timer goes off. I'm shaking. I silence the timer without looking at him. 'There's someone else,' he says.

For ten days, I take Valium and sleeping pills. I drink until I can't stand up. I walk and walk and walk. A never-ending stream of texts and phone calls come from family and friends checking how I'm feeling – *awful, I'm trembling and I can't stop* – whether I'm eating – *not really* – if I want somewhere else to go – *but this is my home.*

My reaction surprises me. I'm the woman who would walk away – no exceptions. But I can't go. J is my rock. It isn't just love, it's fear. I'm afraid of being without him.

On day ten, J sends me a text: *Have I made a mistake?*

While I wait for him to get back to the house I veer between excitement – he's realised that we're great together and this is meant to be – and nerves – what really led to his decision?

When I ask why he had an affair, J says I look miserable all the time, I don't smile at him, I wear my pyjamas until teatime on Sunday, I don't seem bothered about sex anymore. His words are sharp, each one stabbing deeper. I'm selfish. I'm withdrawn. I've stopped making an effort. But all those things can be resolved. I can show J how much I care about him and he'll love me again. I just need another chance.

I suggest we should have counselling. J says he doesn't need counselling, implying that I do. I make an appointment just for me the following day. If I can mend myself, everything will be fine. We will be fine.

After my counselling sessions, J asks what we talk about. I tell him we talk about me. How sad I am. How I'm scared of losing him. How coming home makes me anxious. How I have to force myself to walk up the street while my body resists. How I'm certain he'll have gone. How I shake as I put my key in the lock. I don't tell him that the counsellor asked whether we'd cried together and that I said yes when the answer was no. I know what she's suggesting but, even though her question worries me, I'm not prepared to believe it. We love each other. We have a solid foundation. I just need to be more considerate.

I start to do things to win him back. I leave love notes around the house for him to find. I smile and hug and kiss him when he comes home from work. I get dressed on Sundays. I buy tickets for gigs and plays I know he'll like. I make sure I don't go for longer than a week without instigating sex. And then I decide to cook him an elaborate meal.

We talked about Valentine's Day when we first met. J said he didn't do it, that it was a commercial construct. Better to show someone you love them every day. I went along with it, said I felt the same. But it isn't true. I like the cards and the flowers. I like going out on a date. I like the focus on love, the visibility of it. *Look, world! Somebody loves me!* I took my previous partner to Venice for Valentine's weekend. I keep that from J. I don't want him to think that I'm a fool who's been taken in by advertising. But if I do something special to show how much I love him, maybe I'll be forgiven.

When I tell him I've planned a three-course meal, J looks surprised. Not only because I'm cooking, but because of the day on which I'm doing it. I preempt his response, pretending I don't know it's Valentine's. 'I want to do something nice for you,' I say.

I'm nervous. Cooking makes me stressed and angry because it requires patience. Cooking for J is the biggest gesture I can think of: I love you. I relinquish control. I'm spending my time doing something I hate to make you happy.

The menu is ambitious: roasted asparagus with poached eggs and orange hollandaise followed by feta, chilli and mint-filled aubergine escalopes, and panna cotta with poached nectarines to finish.

I create the meal backwards. Starting early afternoon, I poach nectarines in a rosé wine sauce, make panna cotta and sieve it into ramekins I've bought especially.

At 4 p.m., I prep the aubergines with salt and place them in the oven. While they're roasting, I crumble, chop and juice the ingredients for the filling. I line up three bowls and place flour in the first, beaten egg in the second, breadcrumbs in the third, dipping the escalopes into each bowl in turn. It takes two hours. Dinner will be late and I'm panicking.

The starter is where it falls apart completely. I've chosen it unaware that hollandaise is the most difficult sauce to make.

The egg yolks and vinegar are supposed to triple in volume and turn pale. I'm not sure how you judge the increase, so I remove them from the heat when they look lighter. I add butter and carry on whisking, waiting for the sauce to thicken. Nothing happens. I keep whisking. It's still runny so I whisk some more. The sauce drips from the wire loops. It's a mess. I can't do this on my own.

If I'd done one course it would be manageable. Instead, by making a grand gesture, I've set myself up to fail. This wasn't about J. Like everything that's wrong with our relationship, this is about me.

I concede defeat and ask J for help. He tries the electric whisk, but the sauce still won't thicken. Too late to start again, I know my only option is to abandon it. We have the roasted asparagus – ten minutes in the oven – and poached eggs – which are perfect, the whites are firm and the yolks are runny. The starter's fresh and tasty, but it's a failure as far as I'm concerned.

When we've finished eating, I ask J what he thought of the meal. He says it was nice, gives me a perfunctory kiss on the lips and goes to play games on his computer. I do the washing up and go to bed alone.

3. Place in a warm room, leave to rise

Six months later and I'm in bed on a Friday evening, fully clothed, a migraine starting to form. I've had a disastrous day at work and don't know how I'm going to get past it. J sits beside me, holding my hand. 'I love you,' he says. 'You can't go on like this.'

I love being a teacher. It isn't just a job, it's a vocation. It gives me status. I'm brilliant at it. My results – grades for lesson observations, pupil progress, exam results – are outstanding. I'm the first person in my family to go to university. I'm the first person in my family to have a profession. I think I've made it. The price I've paid – relationships, friendships, migraines, chronic insomnia, anxiety – is worth it. I've escaped, risen far above my roots.

My classroom is my safe space. It's the one place I allow myself to experiment, to be vulnerable, to be wrong. I can't anticipate all the ways in which my classes will react to creative, challenging tasks, but I'm secure in my ability to engage with their ideas. We work as a team and learn from each other.

Now, my classroom is no longer my sanctuary. I've been told my lesson observation is inadequate. The head suggests I might require some coaching from one of the consultants. It's a step away from competency proceedings. I cry. Teaching is my identity. I don't know who I'll be without it.

When I tell J, he offers me a solution. 'We need to get you out of there,' he says. He knows my dream is to be a writer. He's read some of my fiction and says I should apply for a creative writing course. I can get an admin job, work part-time. He's been promoted recently and can cover the rent and bills if I can pay the course fees.

We've talked about buying a house one day. J says he can still afford to save some of his salary for a deposit. I can contribute when I've finished the course.

I don't want to be reliant on someone else. I earn my own money, pay my own way. But I'm miserable. The school's in special measures, the pressure is crippling. I've been crying in the car on the way to work for weeks. My confidence is so low, I can't face applying for another teaching job. No one will employ someone who's gone from outstanding to inadequate in a matter of months.

As I lie in bed, J next to me, I make the decision to resign. Our relationship's good and the change will stop me from becoming self-absorbed again. I don't need a classroom anymore, I have a new safe space now.

4. Sprinkle with lies

I stand at the threshold to the bedroom, frozen, fear coursing through me, head to toe.

What if I go down to the kitchen?

A RECIPE FOR MADNESS

What if pick up the knife he gave me?

I can see myself in the bedroom.

I can see myself standing over him.

I can see blood everywhere.

It feels like there's a stranger inside my head.

I push my back against the wall and force myself to take deep breaths. The house is still and quiet. Minutes pass. When I've calmed down, I walk into the room, lie next to J. In the six months since I started my writing course, I've become unrecognisable and so has my life.

Four weeks earlier, a letter arrived. Standard A4 white envelope with window, return address on the back. Letters tend to hang around in our house. They live on the windowsill until someone can be bothered to sort them out. But this letter disappears. It's fear that makes me search for it. Since J's returned from a work trip the previous week, I know something's changed. My body trembles with anxiety when he's at home.

Before the letter arrives, J becomes withdrawn. He goes for walks on his own, works late, comes to bed after he thinks I'm asleep. When I ask about his day the replies are one word, nothing more. When I ask if there's anything I can do for him, the answer is always no. I stop trying to talk to him. I think if I give him space, he might recover himself. I'm also scared. Scared that if I push him he'll say that I'm the problem, that my writing course and lack of contributions to our finances are the issue. If our situations were reversed, I'd be jealous of him having time to do something he loves and not worry about paying the rent. I wonder if he's jealous of me.

My search uncovers three things: the envelope, empty, in the bin; a spent match under the bowl in the sink; a scattering of ashes next to one of the hobs, small charred pieces that crumble when I attempt to pick them up. I google the address on the back of the envelope. It's the mortgage department of a bank.

The conclusion I draw – that J's trying to buy a house behind my back – seems far-fetched, although I'm absolutely certain it's the truth. He told me he was saving for a deposit and then announced at dinner with friends that he wasn't; it was the first – and last – I heard of it.

The position I've put us in means I can't confront J about the letter. If I'm wrong about it, I don't know what I'm going to unleash. Instead, I send him an email, tell him I'm worried. That I think he's unhappy and I don't know what to do about it. Perhaps he might think about talking to someone, someone who isn't me. He doesn't reply.

A week later, he ends our relationship.

He says he's been for a counselling session and hasn't discovered anything he didn't already know. Our relationship is over. He wants to come home to someone he feels passionate about.

I'm devastated. I love him. Why doesn't he love me? I don't know what I'm going to do without his support, how I will survive.

Knowing this is my last chance, I ask the questions I've been holding back.

I ask whether they talked about his affair in counselling, if he's worked out why he did it. 'It just happened,' he says. I tell him these things don't just happen, he's in denial about his own behaviour, can't face himself. I think he can't look at me anymore because I remind him of what he's done.

I keep going. I ask about the envelope. He denies its existence. I ask him why he burnt it on the hob. He denies lighting it. I ask him why there was a match in the sink. He says he heated some food when he got in from work. A lie. He ate the goat's cheese tart I'd left in the fridge, cold. He changes his story and says he used the hob the previous day to warm some baked beans. Another lie. But his responses are impossible to disprove, the evidence already destroyed.

J asks me if I want to stay in the house, although he knows I can't pay the rent. I tell him it might take me a while to find somewhere else. I don't know what I can afford, whether I'll need a guarantor. I don't tell him that I don't want to move, that I don't know where to go, what I'll do. We agree to a civil coexistence in the meantime.

A week after our relationship ends, J tells me he's had an offer accepted on a house. 'So you did have an agreement in principle,' I say. J denies it, tells me you do it all online now. You don't need any paperwork. More lies. Google reveals the truth.

That night, I tell J he needs to sleep downstairs. He refuses. 'There isn't enough room,' he says. I won't move out of stubbornness. I lie by his side, although now the space feels anything but safe. I'm furious, indignant and frightened.

I start going to bed earlier so I can doze for a bit before J comes up. Once he's next to me, I'm too afraid to sleep. What else is he capable of? How many more lies are there to be exposed? Who is this person I've been sharing my life with?

The day after I stand in the dark and imagine stabbing him to death in his sleep, I borrow enough from my parents to cover a deposit and six months' rent and move out. I leave the knife he'd given me.

5. Separate into pieces

Moving into the flat alone is tough. J is in my head and my broken heart; I think about him incessantly. I need to do something to get him out of my mind so I return to teaching and am surprised to learn a few things about myself: I haven't lost my skills in the classroom; not only can I cook but I really enjoy it; and that I'm in love with a narcissist.

A RECIPE FOR MADNESS

Once I realise that my relationship with J is emotionally abusive, I read everything I can find. There are three stages to a relationship with a narcissist: idolisation, devaluation, discard. A poisonous recipe.

From the day we met, J and I emailed constantly, from the moment one of us woke up until the moment we fell asleep. He cooked for me and told me he loved me in the first week. It's a technique called lovebombing where a narcissist bombards their target with adoration to keep their attention and create a dependency.

J's declarations were too fast for me. I was afraid of losing my independence, but I was scared that if I said I wanted to go slower, the relationship would fall apart. I was probably right. But there wasn't time to think about the consequences. He didn't allow me any. I moved in with him after a few months.

In the devaluation stage, a narcissist emotionally withdraws from the lover they've made codependent. We went through it twice: before J's affair and before he bought the house. The first time, J's criticisms were confusing; I was miserable partly because he was making me miserable. The circular nature of his comments meant I couldn't argue against them. He told me he loved me, he just wanted me to be happy, and I believed him. The second time, having lost friends and colleagues, I was isolated. It was part of his plan. I felt lonelier than I had before I met him. I was trapped, emotionally and financially dependent. It was then I understood my mum had been telling a half-truth; it wasn't purely because she couldn't afford it, she didn't leave because she couldn't imagine life without my dad.

When J initially tried to discard me, it didn't work. I wasn't humiliated by his affair, I believed it was my fault. I was so in love with him and so desperate for the relationship to be a success I couldn't see that I was being manipulated.

It isn't until I realise the relationship is abusive that I feel humiliated. I feel ashamed I fell for his scheme, that I opened my heart to someone who was planning to shatter it for his own validation. The more I read, the more I come to realise the version of J I fell in love with didn't exist. It was a facade designed to lure me in. He mirrored my hobbies, exploited my vulnerabilities, pretended to share my hopes and dreams. But J had never loved me. Narcissists aren't capable of it.

I feel another wave of shame when I think about my feminism. It was so binary, so divorced from any context. Having read white middle-class feminists discussing how women are suppressed by domesticity, I simply decided anything to do with the home was restrictive and I wasn't going to allow it to hold me back. This approach enabled me to believe J, with his cooking and apparent support of my goals, was good and my mum's reaction to my dad's affair was bad. I prided myself on being independent, educated, strong, but my response to J pushing me away was to cling harder, to give more and more of myself to him. By doing everything I could think of to try and stop J abandoning me, I abandoned myself.

Finding myself again takes time. I have to learn who I've become and why. Teaching shows me that the way I approach learning with my pupils can apply in other areas of my life. In my classroom we take risks, we explore. We don't fear failure; we know we can learn from our mistakes. Expanding my reading to incorporate feminists from a range of backgrounds forces me to consider what liberation might really look like – for others as well as myself. It's Audre Lorde's much-quoted statement – 'Caring for myself is not self-indulgence. It is self-preservation, and that is an act of political warfare' – that helps me to decide to make better use of my kitchen. Cooking teaches me patience and perseverance. I stop valuing myself by my achievements and start allowing myself space to relax, to feel, to grow.

6. Cook until golden

A year on, I stand in the kitchen of my rented flat, feeding dough through a pasta machine. I watch it become thinner and thinner until it's just right for ravioli.

I cut circles from the dough, spoon goat's cheese filling into the middle and seal them together. It's fiddly and I worry they'll split when I cook them. I persevere, boiling a pan of water, sliding the pasta in. The edges, uneven, fragile, hold fine.

Sitting at the table with the dish I've made from scratch, I feel proud of how far I've come. I've learned that you can balance career and home. All or nothing isn't healthy.

The ravioli doesn't look as neat or glossy as the picture in the book. It won't win any competitions, but I'm not looking for external rewards anymore. I take a bite and savour the taste. Maybe one day I'll make these for someone else, share my life, my home, my heart. But, for now, finally, I'm learning to take care of myself.

'It's not a Members' Club. As it's our third date, I booked a couples' therapy session, to see if we're trauma-compatible.'

THE FISH BOWL
OR, SOME NOTES ON
EVERYDAY SEXUAL TRAUMA
Monique Roffey

I was thirteen. It happened in a large swimming pool in
Trinidad, in an erstwhile bastion of the colonial era, the
Country Club. Their huge Olympic-sized pool was famous
in Port of Spain. At the snack bar, flying fish and chips was
my favourite meal, ever. With ketchup. A small group of us
girls, four of us, black, brown and white, had gathered to
spend the day together, liming and swimming and generally
hanging out. We were skinny, nubile, nervy and fizzing with
a nascent sexuality we knew not what to do with. Two
of the girls were a lot more confident; they were already
'hot'. Another girl was Canadian, a friend of mine; she was
very blond and already glamorous. I was the gawky, ugly
duckling: mono-brow, lazy eye, overbite and breasts still
two jutting, pink nubs.

It was a Saturday. We'd been allowed, for some reason, to
go to the pool unaccompanied by adults. It was agreed that

we could spend the day together at the pool. However, none of us had told our parents that we'd invited a group of boys to join us.

Before I go any further, let me deconstruct what I have just written.

I have used the word 'girls' to describe us, a group of thirteen-year-olds.

Thirteen: can you call a thirteen-year-old a girl, still? At twelve, you are a girl, at least in the West. At thirteen, is that still true? We'd arranged for the boys to be there. We'd asked the cocks to the hen party. What had we been planning, really? To be admired, to have fun, to tease and rehearse for adulthood? Who was the alpha amongst us, which one would secure the attentions of the alpha boy? I am fifty-five now and never had children. But I remember that younger me, like Bambi, all legs and innocence. I remember that day. And, while I wanted 'the boys' to look at me, all I wanted then was for them to look. And yes, it's my opinion that we were all still girls. Pre-sexual, not able to vote. Not legally allowed to have sex. The law protects girls till they are sixteen. We were girls who were in the process of forming; we were in-progress, apolitical, we weren't feminists. We weren't anything, not remotely conscious of the wider world. We were girls; we were 'coming to come' still, but – and – all of us had bodies which were already childbearing and even womanly. However, in parts of the developed world and almost all the developing and/or subaltern world, it's all a mother can hope for, that her daughter won't have a baby before she's sixteen.

Even so, I was a girl then. I didn't know what I wanted from those boys, then. That took decades to work out.

I have used the words 'nubile' and 'glamorous' and 'ugly'. Yes. I have used these words of objectification often ascribed to women and girls by men. These words sexualise us, rank us and rate us. I was the 'ugly' one. This one was 'hot'. That one was 'blond'. It starts to happen from the get-go, this 'who is who' in the sexuality stakes of womanhood. Who is going to do well, attract a mate, and so on. It's Darwinian, I guess. Women self-relegate according to internalised patriarchal conditioning. Women do not set our own rules and standards. If we could, I doubt I could have even thought them up, aged thirteen. This ranking and rating talk happens from the get-go, so much so, that girls and women talk like men talk about us.

So: catch yourself, Roffey. Rewind. Write again. And it is hard to rewrite patriarchy, even though the feminists have been doing it for a hundred years or so, in the West and elsewhere too: Dworkin, Chakravorty Spivak, bell hooks, de Beauvoir, Steinham et al. Let me say it all differently. Start again.

We were girls. We were all still fairly innocent. Virginal. We had made a covert plan to liaise with boys. We hadn't much more planned than that.

THE FISH BOWL

***

I'd separated from the pack and was swimming alone in the middle of the pool. I didn't see the boys coming till they came, all splashing and loud and boisterous and full of testosterone.

The 'ugly' one, I was suddenly the centre of attention and for these first few moments, I think I was very surprised, maybe even happy. Three boys had arrived from nowhere (actually, they'd been draped around the other girls), and they'd come to shower me with attention?

I began to swim away from them, hoping what? That they'd follow my skinny-arsed mermaid self and pay court like knights or princes?

The boys had a ringleader. He was a white boy with a freckly face and he was about fifteen, a man-boy. The other two boys were brothers; brown and pencil thin with straight brown-black hair, maybe Indian or a Creole mix. All were local Trini boys from a neighbouring school. I knew the white boy. I knew him from riding horses at a stud farm in Arima. I still remember his name. I've never seen him since, but if I ever see him again, I will surely tackle him.

I know your name, dick head, and I remember your face like it was yesterday.

The white man-boy was confident and mimicking the everyday adult, male Trini machismo; he was also in the process of forming and learning his own way of being in the world, no doubt from the men around him. I'll call him DJ. He was the harder one, the alpha boy, the cool one, leading the others on.

It was DJ who put his hands in my bikini pants.

It was DJ who shoved his index and second finger up and hard into my virginal vagina. It all happened in a flash. A sudden sharp stabbing, up... and up... and in. Two quick bayonet stabs.

The other two boys knew what he'd been planning; they all started shouting the word 'Penguin!' at me. To this day, I've no idea what they were implying. That I was frigid? The others two boys jumped on me too and then all three of them pulled me under. For a few moments I was being drowned by the small gang. First violated, then humiliated verbally, then penetrated. Then half-drowned.

Underwater, I freaked. I fought and lashed out and struggled and made myself a thrashing tiger shark they couldn't hold on to.

When we all broke for the surface again there were more 'Penguin' taunts. But by then I was leaden and lethal. I would kill them. A strong swimmer, I tore away from them and got out of the pool, smouldering with rage.

Day over. For me.

THE FISH BOWL

Why me?

Mortified, I never told the other girls about what happened.

Decades later, I wrote about this event in my memoir, *With the Kisses of His Mouth*. It was the opening event of my sexual career. My mother read it and never even asked about that day. She was much more concerned with the shame I had brought on myself for writing about sex generally. What would people think? Later, much later, I found out that the three boys, led by DJ, had also jumped on and violated my 'blond' friend that day. I've no idea if they did the same with the other girls there; maybe.

I was outnumbered. It was non-consenting. It was a pre-mediated attack.

Was it rape?

Answers on a postcard, please.

It was also *no big thing*.

These things happen. Every. Day.

Don't leave your daughters unattended till you teach them karate? Maybe.

I never had a daughter. But if I had, I would have definitely taken her to karate lessons. And I would have bought her pepper spray.

My first sexual experience was this attack. And this kind of thing is commonplace. Sexual trauma is everywhere and every day. We just don't know about how common it is because of the shame. We keep quiet about it because of the shame. These are the stories we never tell, and they are mainstream. And, as a result, mainstream culture is as holey as Swiss cheese. This is why I'm passionate about teaching memoir these days. To fill in the holes. Get people writing about difficult things. Telling their stories. Then society will look different. What is normal? Every day sexual trauma like this is normal; it is everyday. But I grew up reading magazines like *Cosmopolitan* and *Marie Claire*, and in these magazines, aimed at the mainstream girl-to-woman, everyone is fine. Everything is marvellous. We all learn how to have a good time, mimic the lives of the rich and famous. Tips on 'giving your fella a terrific blowjob' are strap lines on the cover. There's a big gap in society, with regards to sexuality, between what we are told is everyday, and what really is.

But we all get to figure this out, in time. Most abuse (and the stats are high for women, and for men, in the UK alone) falls into the gap. We, in the developed West, are only just getting to grips with it now; abuse in institutions that we used to trust, the Catholic Church, the BBC, care homes, social services. Only now, early twenty-first Century, a digital, confessional, globalised age, are we losing our innocence. Sexual abuse and sexual trauma doesn't happen now and then; it isn't rare; isn't something that happens to bad and/or unlucky people, or poor people, and/or 'slags', loose women. Almost every woman I know, personally, has been molested.

Every woman I know has had rough and barely consented-to sex. Several women I know have been raped; one good friend has been raped twice; another friend got it worse than me and was raped, aged sixteen, after a party, again by boys, a small gang, and for her it was her first sexual experience, too. Not only was there the swimming pool incident, I've been kerb-crawled, verbally harassed, jeered at, also had rough sex I couldn't say 'no' to, and have been sexually objectified, generally, from the age of about fifteen.

It's everywhere. And everyday. #Metoo? Sure, it bust things open in Hollywood. But what is the scale of this everydayness of sexual abuse? We're only just coming to it. It's so common we don't see it, it's too big. Hiding in plain sight. It's in every other family; it's in one in four of your friends' childhood, or one in five; it's that common. So common, that my swimming pool attack wasn't even commented on by my own mother. She's internalised her own objectification and relegation; she hadn't even noticed that her teenage daughter had once been attacked. To a large degree I have internalised patriarchal norms too. We all have. We must forgive ourselves for this, and each other.

***

Decades later, I'm in group therapy.

I'm listening to a man, my age, late forties, sobbing about the abuse he suffered as a child, at the hands of his mother. In the group, almost everyone has been abused, some severely and systematically, and it has caused lasting psychological damage. Listening to these people, over the course of a year, my swimming pool attack seems impossible to count as serious. I have come to understand there is a 'spectrum of abuse', and my teenage event registers as mild or weak on this spectrum. Something to get over. It was only fingers. They didn't gang rape me with their teenage cocks. Then, I'd have something to write about.

In those workshops and therapy groups, I came across dire pain, historic pain, pain of the individual that carries over decades, and, sometimes, from another generation. One woman in our group barely spoke, her depression was so bad. Her trauma had been inherited from her European Jewish parents, or so she concluded, after years of therapy and lithium. I held a woman, once, who sobbed and sobbed because, after twenty years of faithful marriage, her cervix had been battered to pulp by her husband's large cock. I've held men who've wept in my arms and disclosed all manner of abuse, from men and from women. I have wept too.

So, so much pain we cause each other. We, sapiens, are aggressive, so much so, we even hurt our own children. It's common. It always had been common.

From my early forties, I began a process which really is a privilege. I began to 'work on myself'. Psychoanalysis, group therapy and many, many edge land workshops and trainings around sexuality and intimacy. But in one of these workshops something very rare happened, from which, to this day, I have drawn insight. It was something called 'the fish bowl' and it was very, very simple.

THE FISH BOWL

First, we women, about fifteen of us, sat on the floor. The men in the group sat around us. We women began to talk about ourselves, very much relating to men and to sex. But what we began to talk about wasn't sexy at all. It wasn't fun or titillating. One after the other, almost every woman relaxed and opened up and began to say the truth about their life as a woman and their everyday sexual lives, and sexual trauma, ranging from rape to painful sex. We talked for a long time. The men listened. They had no idea. No idea that PIV (penis in vagina) sex often hurts, that penetration doesn't make most women orgasm, that many of us don't even like it, that many of us have been molested, hurt. They didn't know how common it was. And how women stay silent. No woman wants to be seen as frigid. We want to like sex and be seen as sexy, enjoying it. If we don't then best shut up. Not one woman was pointing a finger at anyone in particular.

Why the fish bowl worked was because there was no blame; it was women's talk. For the first time in my entire life, men were allowed to eavesdrop on the secret and sacred world of women. Our yonis, our cunts, the – oh so irresistible – slash between our legs, the wound from which the whole world is born. We talked about how our vaginas had torn giving birth, and how it was hard not to pee ourselves when we cough, and how our breasts had sagged after childbirth and how we had grown older and wider and how men no longer looked at us anymore when to start with all they could do was gawp. Those dear fifteen men heard it all. We talked for hours. Red tent talk. And it was good to talk and have the men listen in. They wept. And so did we. So much pain we do to each other.

Then, after the lunch break, it was the women who surrounded the men. The men sat in the middle of the fish bowl. It was their turn.

Never before, or since, have I been privy to hearing about men's pain. The men spoke slowly, and very, very shyly, at first, about their own version of relegation, of always being measured against alpha males, of not being able to reach out to other men, of having few male friends, of lonely marriages and of erectile dysfunction, and of wives and partners who didn't know what they wanted in bed and didn't seem to want sex from them, how their wives had gone off sex, had gone through menopause, how they slept in separate rooms, separate beds. Most of these men said they had wanted sexual intimacy long after their partners had stopped wanting it. They spoke of being castrated, henpecked, rejected for being fat, old and stupid; their rage was palpable. They talked about always having to measure up, 'man up', never show their feelings, of being trapped again and again whichever way they turned. Too manly and that's not okay. Not manly enough wasn't okay either. How could they manage to please women, ever? They had lost their way. Many had also been beaten as children, hurt, abused. One man had only one eye; the other had been ripped out by his daughter, a fight when he'd been drinking. His own father had been violent and had taken a knife to his mother and siblings. We women listened in silence and held their pain like they had held ours.

I don't like the world 'healing'; it feels too New Age and generic. But this fish bowl thing was exactly that; it had a healing effect on this small group of men and women. We were so much more loving and careful with each other after the fish bowl.

***

We need a major rethink, don't we? Humanity, world over, has been recycling pain, violence and sexual trauma for millennia. The Buddha had a word for the suffering of humankind, this constant pain and craving: 'dukkha'. Round and round we go, on 'the wheel of life'. We don't get off the wheel until we have developed more consciousness and even then, it's still not easy to get off. The Buddha and almost every leader of every major world religion teaches compassion. And yet it still remains a kind of ideal, a state of consciousness which we cannot often reach. We have to practise compassion, because it doesn't come naturally or easily. We are all too busy trying to survive. Life is painful and the devil take the hindmost. It has ever been this way. In my life, I've had to be shown how to live compassionately, given ideas, a path to follow. Compassion for others wasn't really a thing, a practice, or a concept I found at home or at school. By the time I was in my early forties, I was well on my way to a toxic compassion-free existence.

Compassion and loving kindness were felt that day in the fish bowl when we men and women listened to each other and held space and time for each other's pain. I've been hurt by men, again and again: by my own father, by DJ and the boys in the swimming pool, boyfriends too. I've been hurt, sexually, and emotionally, let down and badly betrayed, and yet since that day of the fish bowl, I cannot find it in myself to hate men and rage against them, because *all of us* are in so much pain. DJ, if I ever meet him again, I won't attack. I'll ask and listen, I hope. Rage just begets more rage and hatred isn't any way to counter hatred. I only found this out the hard way and late in life. We can only hope to stop the cycle of abuse we do to each other one way: with love. And this means to love a lot and every day in order to combat our oh-so-common everyday pain.

LANDING IN POLAND
Tom Tomaszewski

My father and I had a curious relationship. Until yesterday, and I am fifty-two, I had thought it contained no love at all. When I was very young I was aware there had been something *like* love, but as I grew older it evaporated: a steam of sentimentality boiled off as the lie of *he* and *me*, *father-and-son*, cleared to reveal a couple of inconveniently related men most happy when they were apart.

He had a fondness for puppets, robots and that kind of thing. Soulless mechanical toys that paced through life as relentlessly as he did; there was a horrible, unfathomable energy to them, as if each had a strange heart to it. I found him and them unstoppable. Nothing would get in the way of him saying whatever he wanted to say. Not me, for sure, nor a searching for the right words. He spoke poor English, regularly lapsing into Polish or sometimes just awful, animalistic sounds as he shouted at me.

He was a frightening, noise-producing thing: a beehive or an alarm clanging on the wall, or a siren screaming. There

295

didn't seem to be any *background* to him beyond the kind of background you'd give a hive (bees) or an alarm (in those days, *Made in Hong Kong*). I couldn't find a clue to what he was thinking and why.

It felt as if he wasn't born anywhere, more as if he had been made, *made in Poland*, and what on earth was that? His father, some kind of wealthy Polish newspaper baron born in the 1850s, looked like an even more irascible and bloody-minded version of him. All I knew of his mother I drew from a photograph of my father kissing her – kissing her desperately, when he was a middle-aged man and she was very old, and kissing her unlike she was his mother.

Ideas?

I looked for thoughts, beliefs, the qualities I had found in writing, in characters and in scenes in books, that might show I was in the presence of a living, proper man rather than a frightening machine. But he behaved as automatically as his toys.

Where was the thought? Emotions seemed to come to him as they would to an animal and he'd usually have lashed out or moved on, literally or in the way his mind closed down to one thing and transferred to another as if someone had changed TV channels, before I knew what had happened.

There was nothing and nobody I could appeal to who I could imagine getting through to him. No, not my mother. I loved my mother but all she told me was that he loved me. I didn't discover he'd been to prison until I was almost an adult, but if I'd known that I'd have realised even Her Majesty hadn't found a way through. In my dreams even God couldn't sway him. I had one in which my father was Belshazzar seeing the writing on the wall. He didn't panic and call for his wise men, though, or for a Daniel. He swore and gnawed on a chicken wing.

I had no way of understanding my father and for a very long time I felt as if there was nothing intelligible to understand. There were reasons I came to know of at a steady rate, as I grew older, that might have explained how he was, but these only suggested to me that nothing would change. He was a madman and people who tried to stay close to him, to work him out, like my mother, seemed to be driven mad as well. Get drawn into thinking you understand someone like my father, that you feel safe around him, and you leave your sanity behind.

As I mentioned I am now fifty-two, a person successfully practising psychotherapy with people unlike my father (maybe one of the reasons I have been able to become successful is that he gave me a very good rule of thumb; an interesting form of counter-transference. If someone's at all like Dad, probably don't go there), and for the first time I am visiting Krakow, the city where my father grew up. He left in 1939, aged twenty, eventually reaching England as a member of the Polish armoured division following the evacuation at Dunkirk.

He never went back. I knew there were differences with his family, a horrible chaos of betrayal and abuse I have tried to understand but have never been able to absorb. It's as if I have been able to see inside a room but from far away, through a narrow window. I'm too far away to hear what is being said, only to see brief scenes that would break anybody's heart or leave them furious, or disgusted, or terrified as I was as a child.

My father left as the Germans and the Soviets invaded. There was a story, a scene I caught hold of, about his mother suddenly packing him a lunch of herring sandwiches and telling him to go, to get out of the way, which had stupid echoes of how I felt my own mother had behaved to me in relation to my father, the œdipal invader. Get away, find your own life. This will end terribly.

After my father escaped Poland his family fragmented. Some married Germans and some remained patriots like my grandfather had been. My grandfather had published a newspaper at the end of the nineteenth century when Poland was not, in its own right, a country and he was regularly issued with court orders instructing him to shut up, to close down, to stop.

In 1943 my father's sister was arrested in Krakow as part of a group of Catholic women who worked against the Germans and was sent to Auschwitz, where she died. I was told, and I can't even remember by whom, that she had been arrested because of something her younger sister had said.

That younger aunt of mine, denounced as a collaborator, escaped to live in New York at the end of the war. By then my father had settled in Scotland. She asked him if he could look after her teenage daughter.

He agreed.

What happened to her, his niece, was similar but far worse to what happened to me. On that occasion my father was sent to prison for nearly ten years for his violence towards her, and her sexual assault.

He always maintained that this was a miscarriage of justice. What happened to others in his family may have been, but even though the High Court eventually, in 2000, ruled in his favour, I noticed that the judges allowed his sentencing for assault to stand. His trial judge had made a mistake in the way the case was run, but the evidence wasn't called into question.

None of these scenes ever added up to a story. Every time I tried to create one it evaporated like the sense of father-and-son I mentioned at the start. There was no feeling of a single mind capable of holding onto everything without it potentially being driven crazy. Maybe someone like one of the filmmakers I came to adore, people like Jacques Rivette, David Lean, Agnès Varda, David Lynch, Claire Denis or Tsai Ming Liang, could have done something with it (the artists I come across, sometimes introduced to me by someone I love, often feel like the parents I never properly had), but it's the kind of story people shouldn't have to live with. It's why people dispose of the truth.

The truth is unbearable.

Anyway, yesterday as my plane landed in Krakow I started to cry. I had wondered what finally going to Poland would do to me, but this display of emotion was as unexpected as any of my father's mood changes.

I thought: *I've come back.*

My mind seemed to freeze a moment before delivering another thought, as if it had become stuck on something but had somehow recovered.

But it was Dad that left, and I've come back.

I felt something start to happen, a kind of rearrangement, like clouds forming a pattern after a storm, and holding it, holding it – holding it. Sometimes I've seen clouds holding shapes for so long after storms in which they've swirled and rolled from one moment to the next have ended.

The airport was busy, but leaving the main terminal, as I got closer to the train that would take me to the centre of town, the crowds thinned out. I went into a washroom and found that the doors opened in a different direction from what I was used to. You had to pull from the outside, not push, and as I did so the brightness of the empty room inside flooded me: a gallery, an operating theatre, a space in *Twin Peaks*. There was a hum of air or electricity. I couldn't work out which.

I stood in front of a sink and looked into a mirror, and there I was, after all that time, a man in his fifties, a white wall behind him, bald, lined, foreign and with an uncanny sense of not knowing *how* he was foreign. I don't look much like my father, but I could see my father in me.

I thought about him, about how he could be the best or the worst thing that ever happened to you. Even when he was happening to you, it sometimes depended on where you stood, and on how you took that in. I am the eldest of five, with four older half-siblings. My younger siblings still generally treat my father like a hero; the elder ones, they are usually hard pressed to think of anything good – and the bad things they, like me, remember are absolutely awful. I've noticed too how the people in my family who acknowledge the worst of my father and also, it seems, have some compassion, are the ones whose thoughts, whose memories are most reliable. The ones who seem to have also suffered but still cleave to his extraordinary specialness are the ones whose memories seem to me often like what you get when you start rotating a kaleidoscope: patterns and then different patterns from the same ingredients, all captivating, without there ever being one you could settle on as 'real'. I've heard them tell me stories about when we were children that I know are almost complete fantasies – if only because sometimes each of them tells me something different about the same thing.

I thought of how it was for my father after the war and what had happened to his Polish family, his country, his home, his new family in Scotland, his freedom and his future. I could see at once, looking into the mirror, why my father didn't think; why he liked to live his life automatically. I could see why he didn't seem to have any background. I could see why he hadn't wanted to come back to the city where his sister died like that and his family had behaved like that, and given him something to do that had almost been the end of him.

For me, growing up with him in London, there had been facts, like he was born in Krakow, and signs, like the way he took us all to church (as if we were being taken abroad but not on holiday) or how he'd decorate the house at Christmas (with tinsel, candles, lights and fake snow but not as I or any of my friends knew it). But it wasn't just him who had been unable to hold a story of his life together. There hadn't been anybody doing that. There had been nobody in a position to tell me why life was like it was and how different so much of my experience was from a boy whose father had been born in England.

All of these years, I realised, I had felt in some way foreign.

Landing in Krakow, there I was, invited into my father's world for what seemed like the first time. I may have felt foreign because of the un-Englishness that inflected everything my father did in England but, as I was coming to understand, there was more to it than that. We had thought in different languages. Most of the things that had come to him in English (what people had said to him and what he had done in England or Scotland) I wouldn't have wanted to come to me. The things that had come to him in Polish, in Poland, as a child and a young man before the war, these were different.

Being Polish meant that there was something else to him from before the war, prison and everything else, and it was something that the English world hadn't been able to take from him. It seems that it had been hidden away, maybe on purpose but more likely cut off without my father even realising it; unthought about in the way that almost every aspect of his life came to be. He grew into a kind of machine that cut off: a bench-saw to the present moment, slicing through connections before they spurred him into reflection. He kept his connection to something of the past through all those nods to his childhood I had been caught up in.

Today, as I move through Krakow, things keep coming to me. People start to speak to me, unprompted, in ways I am not used to. They talk in Polish, thinking I am one of them in ways, as far as I remember, that few English people ever have.

I'm told I look foreign. Here, in Krakow, whatever that means doesn't seem to apply. I feel as if I belong here, even though I know hardly any Polish.

But even this changes.

On the tram I listen to some children counting and realise I know how to count in Polish. I remember a Polish woman staying with us when I was a child and teaching me some of the words, and then my father carrying on, teaching me in the car as we drove to his warehouse at London Bridge.

TRAUMA

As the tram rattles across Krakow I find myself staring. *That tree must have been a hundred years old: Dad would have seen it. Those buildings, they're really old. He must have walked past them. That park. He must have walked there. That crack in the wall. The face on that statue. The curve of that street. That door. The rise of that hill.*

As a teenager I had given up trying to work out whatever was on my father's mind, but here I am with his thoughts, without even trying. Here I am in Poland with my father, the two of us holding things together somehow, and I find that extraordinary.

THANKS, I'LL
TAKE THE CHAIR

Jude Cook

For a brief period of time, the walk to my therapist's house was the only simple pleasure left in life. I was thirty, newly divorced, skint, and living (like the student I'd never been) in a Crouch End flatshare with two classical musicians and a very witty man who worked for Penguin Books. Without these staunch allies – met the day I crashed out of the marital home – I might have gone under. Because since separating from my wife – and the demise of the band I'd spent my twenties trying to make a success – life's mailman had delivered nothing but blues. Everything was broken. I was deeply depressed, occasionally suicidal, and worried enough to ask my GP for help.

She referred me at once to a local therapist. I hadn't asked for a strict Freudian, but that's what I got – a shock for someone who'd never so much as read a self-help book, and had always medicated their moods with drugs or alcohol. Art was also something I'd found healing in the past, but somehow art had begun to fail me recently. I needed something more urgent, more direct. I needed The Talking Cure. I ended up talking for nearly two years, and the ten-minute evening stroll to my therapist's place, along a reliably empty North London residential street, always did me good. It cleared my mind for the eviscerating hour ahead in the blank amber of the consultation room.

During the autumn months, the long curve of that street afforded a scintillating view of London, across a stretch of parkland which was, in fact, a reservoir. Being a Crouch End reservoir, it was discreetly covered in well-cut grass, and appeared to the casual observer to be a private games field or pricey sports annexe. From the elevation of the road, the blinking pyramidal tip of Canary Wharf Tower was always visible: a comforting sight – a beacon of hope, of human activity in the dead night of the soul I inhabited back then. Strange to get abstract emotions from an Aviation Warning Light, but I felt it every time. A piercing flash every six seconds, followed by a strange sensation of gratitude. A measure of how ill I was, perhaps.

Once at my therapist's, the 'work', as she called it, would begin. Even though the consultation room was on the ground floor of a solid family house, there was something of the courtesan's chamber about it. A small room at the back, with a bright downstairs loo adjacent; a gentleman's umbrella rack outside the door. This, coupled with handing over banknotes at the end of the session, sealed the impression of a furtive, sexual transaction. Of course, most of my therapist's wealthy clients didn't open their wallets and deal in cash – they paid by direct debit or transfer. I was a referral, and thus paying a drastically reduced rate. And anyway, my bank had closed my account the previous month.

At the first session, I had been given the option of reclining on the chaise longue – like all the clichéd representations of therapy in films – or sitting in the armchair.

'Thanks,' I said uncertainly. 'I'll take the chair...'

I didn't want to feel vulnerable, lying flat, unable to meet the eyes of my interlocutor.

But, as I would come to understand, this was the Freudian method. You weren't supposed to see your therapist and there was no real interlocution. You talked; you were regressed to childhood; you were made to feel your pain all over again.

I settled into the comfy upholstery, wearing my uniform of black leather jacket and black jeans, only to feel immediate social diminishment. It was a middle-class parlour, really, with soft lamps bearing saffron shades. Outside, a well-kept corner of garden could be seen: decking, urns, wisteria, crimson carnations. Inside, the only furniture aside from the chaise longue and the two chairs was a large mahogany bookshelf holding many heavy academic tomes and papers. It was like the set of *One Foot in the Grave*. How could my therapist ever have any understanding of the journey that had led me to her on a rainy Tuesday night?

On commencing, there was an unsettling five minutes' silence while I steadied myself and looked at the carpet. Finally, she said,

'So... How can I be of help?'

Where, oh where, to begin?

At the beginning, of course. Though she never said, 'Tell me about your childhood,' it was implicit from the start.

Over the coming weeks, I told her everything, and she listened inscrutably, saying a maximum of six or seven sentences per session. Highly unnerving, and a reaction I never really got used to. They were costly sentences – for the spirit, and for the wallet. I told her my twin brother and I were from a working-class/lower-middle-class background, and had grown up in a faceless Hertfordshire commuter town. My mother, the child of Irish immigrants, had been raised in Barnsley in impoverished conditions. She'd trained to be a midwife, and later became an NHS nurse, a job she did for over forty years. My father, by contrast, had grown up in leafy Pinner; a grammar-school boy who managed to get into Oxford on a scholarship. But his mother had been a dinner lady, and his father a pen-pushing civil servant, and he'd never felt at home in the ocean of privilege that was (and is) an Oxbridge college.

Our parents split up when we were six, and my mother's new partner (eventually our stepfather) entered our lives. A trainee nurse, he was an imposing, aggressive and paradoxically camp Yorkshireman. Over the fourteen years he was with us, he was consistently physically and emotionally abusive (and, on the one occasion I can remember, sexually abusive) towards me and my brother. He would nearly always mete out the violence behind our mother's back. Once, he kicked us both up the stairs to bed after a wedding in Yorkshire. You could always be sure of the back of his hand if you 'lipped' him. He was often absent from the house – where he went, we never knew. By the time we were eleven and starting the first year at the local single-sex state comp, we were used to his threatening presence – it was just the sea we swam in. The fact that most of our friends had parents who stayed together, and treated them with kindness and respect, should have made our situation seem stranger than it did. By then we had moved to a Wimpy estate on the outskirts of town. My mother was by now a district nurse, and bringing us up largely on her own, my father having moved to France for work. A fish fingers and chips childhood, with a side order of chaos and fear. When my mother eventually married our hated stepfather, we were fifteen. It was a marriage doomed to failure.

The effect of this upbringing was that my brother and I quickly started making plans to escape the domestic situation and the prison of small-town life. We did this by forming a band and taking lots of drugs. I left school at sixteen and went to work in Iceland (the supermarket, not the country), while my brother stayed at school in order to keep a foot in the door of the house my father still kept in town, since living with our stepfather was intolerable. I ended up doing a couple of A-levels (one at home, one at Stevenage College), but any thought of university – the real ticket out – evaporated in the chaos. We'd had the customary brilliant English teacher who'd encouraged us to write fiction, and pushed us to apply for Cambridge, which we did. We passed the interview but deliberately flunked the entrance exam – I think my brother might have even been tripping.

Looking back, I can see this act of self-sabotage was a reaction to extreme mental disturbance. I was certainly deeply – if not clinically – depressed; spending days paralysed by a black lethargy; a stew of self-hate and anxiety churning in the pit of my stomach. It was only the promise of moving to London and starting afresh that pulled me out of the nosedive. I found a job in a steel-castings factory, rehearsed my band five nights a week, and moved out into a bedsit alone. Our friends had all flown the coop to university. My mother's second marriage had imploded, and she would soon return to Yorkshire. There was nothing to stay for, and only one thing to do: get out of town.

London was hard. To arrive at nineteen with no money or contacts was, in retrospect, suicidal. But we managed somehow – after five long years of bedsits and the dole – to break through. From working on building sites and as a cycle courier when I first arrived, I became a key-holder at a studio and learnt recording engineering. We found a drummer and a manager for our band, and wrote a set of songs that would take us to the next level. Writing was a constant and vital form of therapy at the time: poetry and lyrics, mainly, as I found I couldn't write fiction with the same ease as I had at fifteen. Our new songs confronted our years of trauma head-on – a lesson for later writing: don't shilly-shally, say what has to be said most urgently first. As Britpop raged around us, it felt cathartic to be singing these dark songs in front of increasingly large audiences. It was a form of primal screaming. Instead of internalising, I directed my anger outwards, and not just on stage (where I'd once skated a Fender telecaster into the monitors after a bad gig), but in the studio too. I could go there to record any time of day or night and express myself into a microphone. *Too bad we're not allowed to scream*, Prince once sang. But I could, and I did.

In the end, we made an album and four singles, toured the UK and Europe with Echobelly, and sold 20,000 records worldwide. We were reviewed by Charles Shaar Murray. Richey Manic was a fan, as was Brian Wilson, apparently. A modest achievement, by some standards, but I felt too much had been sacrificed to get there. My education, for a start. Looking back, I can see that the band was too important for us. It meant *everything*. We were never in it for the craic, for fame or groupies, or with an eye on future media careers. It was an artistic project that had to succeed – there was no safety net, financial or otherwise. When we split after a ragged European tour, with our manager deserting us to Australia to have kids with her partner, it felt like we'd failed. There was a pressing lack of money or any real measure of success. I medicated this perceived failure by getting married at twenty-seven, which turned out to be catastrophic. We were both too young, and my wife was physically abusive towards me. I'd recreated the domestic situation of my childhood in an adult relationship. We lasted three years, by which time I was pushing thirty and working on Camden Market to make ends meet. When I found myself living in the shared Crouch End flat, the intense depression of my adolescence returned, and I began walking every Tuesday night to the house of a strict Freudian in order to talk about it.

It's comforting to think that many of these experiences found their way, many years later, into my debut novel, which followed the adventures of a failed suicidal poet named Byron Easy (a novel which became one of the most unsuccessful and least talked-about books of the early twenty-first century). It was, by and large, a comic take on events. Art had performed its necessary alchemy; it had made order out of chaos, stylised it, smoothed down the rough edges. But, as Jeanette Winterson writes in her memoir, *Why Be Happy When You Can Be Normal?*, what *really happened* before art made its transformation was 'too painful. I could not survive it.' Art had provided the 'cover version', the story she could live with. By the time I started therapy, I was done with the primal scream method, of living daily with raw emotion, and wanted to investigate the past more cerebrally.

The problem was, the Freudian method requires you go back and experience that raw emotion again. It's clear now that fiction should always have been the way forward – in writerly terms, I should have been penning *Herzog* or *Ariel*, rather than trying to recreate the Plastic Ono Band album.

My therapist had different ideas, however. She told me I should stop writing altogether, and even throw away the notebooks in which I wrote copiously day after day. This self-absorption was unhealthy, a perpetuation of the pain, she said. The only place for self-confrontation was the safe space of her room. It's part of the persuasiveness of therapy that I even considered doing this. Maybe she was right, I thought. Maybe I was just extending the anguish by writing confessionally. I can see now this was part of her training, but her didacticism was infuriating. It seemed to demonstrate that she had no real understanding of me. Writing was (and is) as necessary as breathing. I could understand she had no real empathy with someone who'd spent years as a musician in an indie band, but it was infuriating and baffling that she had little conception of, or respect for, the artistic process.

Though her method wasn't ideal (in retrospect, I would have been better off having standard Psychodynamic therapy, or CBT), I never lost belief in the validity of the therapeutic process. Talking about my upbringing allowed me to come to terms with what I saw as my father's desertion of the family, and start talking to him again after fifteen years. I could see that my stepfather's aggression had been passed on to me – like all abusers bequeath their shit. Throwing guitars across stages and yelling into microphones had been a way of ridding myself of it. Now I needed the more nuanced method offered by fiction. While his physical abuse had been easy to cleanse, the emotional and sexual abuse was harder to confront. It took therapy to make me realise how profoundly damaging this had been; how undermining, how much of a violation. How it had resulted in years of self-disgust and suicidal impulses. When re-experiencing these emotions in the consultation room, I often wished I'd taken the chaise longue instead of the chair. My therapist made me realise I'd internalised more of the traumatic events than I'd previously thought, despite the emancipation provided by music.

The net result was that I became kinder on myself; drank less, stopped doing drugs, learnt to drive, and, later, gave up smoking (the hardest crutch to kick away). I also decided to go back into education. I was thirty-one before I went to university, and it required an Access course to get there. I spent three years at UCL reading English as a mature student in perhaps the best English department in the world at the time. I was doing it the hard way, perhaps, and it was certainly difficult doing acting gigs and playing bars to pay my way through. But it was a necessary step in my rehabilitation. And all the while, I was working hard on my first novel, the other wholly necessary thing.

By the time I took my last walk along the reservoir to my therapist's house I was almost thirty-three. She had agreed that our sessions were becoming less and less fruitful, and suggested I try someone else. The leave-taking is a moment all therapists are trained for, and they have to make the suggestion carefully. I was going out with a movement therapist at the time, so I knew how much thought, care and supervision goes into seeing each client. If the analysand is suicidal, the code of conduct prevents them making the suggestion of changing therapist at all. But I was no longer suicidal, just eager to start what I thought of as my new life. And anyway, I could barely afford to keep going. All her clients belonged to a different world. I often wondered whether these captains of industry, these millionaire actors, really needed three nights a week intensely reconstructing shattered childhoods for eighty quid a session. Or was it just a giant ego-trip for them; a chance to sound off at unlimited length on subjects their wives had long since vetoed as too raw or too boring? I was on a discount rate, something she never let me forget. When I complained about money, she would always say: 'If you're serious about our work, you should be doing everything in your power to pay for it. Have you considered getting another job? In a restaurant, maybe. You could do the washing up, or wait tables.' Part of this was deliberate provocation, I knew – one of her dexterous methods to make me reflect on how much I needed therapy. But I felt it had come to a natural conclusion. Writing fiction would be my therapy from now on.

In the end, I was glad I took the chair and not the couch. I can see that the decision allowed me to walk the middle ground I badly needed at time. Therapy was wholly necessary. I might not be here without it. But art was essential for dealing with trauma too. Its alchemy of chaos – its redemption of lost time – its creation of something beautiful where before there was only ugliness, violation and pain, made it eternally valid, whether it reached an audience or not. And yes, I've still got my notebooks.

UNRAVELLING THE SELF

Joseph Schreiber

One of my most precious possessions is a still from the classic 1919 film *The Cabinet of Dr Caligari*, created for me four decades ago by a besotted admirer, the oddly effete son of a burly local sportscaster. It is a close up from the final scene at the asylum, of Cesare, the mad doctor's imagined murderous somnambulist, peacefully examining a flower. It is my favourite moment in the film, a counterpoint to my own greatest childhood nightmare. Here, the monster is, in reality, a gentle soul. I had always feared the opposite, that someone would one day see the monster lurking inside me. But what I couldn't possibly know at the time I fell in love with that image was that, like Cesare, I too would one day be committed to a psychiatric unit.

I have always been a slow burner, capable of pretending to be normal for extended periods, even when I was aware of the subterfuge. So I went mad gradually, in my mid-thirties, over the course of months, even years, beginning with a bleak passage following the birth of my second child, and steadily ramping upward until eventually I tumbled into full-blown manic psychosis. In retrospect I can chart this progression only through the quality of my thought processes, by the amount of effort it took to stay grounded in the moment and not drift off into other possible spaces where a truer me might exist. I was spending more and more time disconnected, desperate to imagine a reality in which I could make sense of a self that was never an easy fit. I had been married almost ten years, had engaged in all manner of unequivocally feminine activities – I'd been a nanny, worked in a dress shop, given birth to two children, a son and a daughter – and yet I was unable to put to rest the feeling that no matter how much I longed to know what other girls and women seemed to understand naturally, I was never going to figure out how to *feel* female.

But at this point, I still lacked a vocabulary to name this persistent otherness, the intrinsic maleness I had carried for as long as I could remember. Even though it had never manifested itself in any obvious tomboyishness or an attraction to girls, I could never shake the fear that inside me there was a boy lurking. I was afraid he might be detected if I was not careful to monitor the way I spoke, walked or presented myself. Oddly, I experienced my own gender insecurity as an alienation from my body, but one that I imagined might be ameliorated if only I could push the internal masculine identity into the background for good. However, if even the most fundamentally female acts – pregnancy and childbirth twice over – could not a woman make, my distress and confusion escalated. What kind of creature was I? And, even worse, what kind of a mess had I gotten myself into now, sentenced to continue to affect an existence that felt increasingly performative with every passing day?

To complicate matters, somewhere in those early years of motherhood I had encountered, for the first time, an expression that stopped me cold: *Like a man trapped in a woman's body.* But I heard it wrongly ascribed to a lesbian novelist and I wondered if my instant, gut-level response meant that I too was a lesbian, even though I was inclined to think I didn't like women at all, let alone feel attractions to them. I had no idea what to do with this information and the only person in my life I could possibly share it with was my husband. Hardly an easy confession, but necessary, and all my fragile pretending to normalcy rapidly began to disintegrate from that point on.

With a strange mix of dread and excitement, I questioned whether it was some deeply repressed feelings that had fostered a lifetime of dis-ease with my own femaleness. Could my sexuality be the answer and, if so, what should I do? The possible answers threatened the very security of my home and family but I was simply unable to pull myself out of the vortex of an identity crisis that was spinning with an escalating intensity. Sleep became increasingly elusive and the world began to turn faster and faster until eventually I lost all my ability to reason, to rein in the racing thoughts that burst forth every time I opened my mouth. The entire month of May, 1997, was surrendered to Blakean angels in the backyard apple tree, voices that echoed in my head and a sudden conviction that knowledge of some great gay force in the universe had been bequeathed to me. The miracle is that I survived a month in that state – a month that culminated in a morning of violent confrontation and a call to the police.

In front of the entire neighbourhood on a beautiful June day I was carted off by ambulance and within hours had been committed to the psychiatric ward. When it finally came, the diagnosis of bipolar disorder was met with relief. My husband and I were calmed by the reassurance that all of my gender and sexuality confusion could be resolved with lithium, and life could regain some sense of order. But when I read in the brochure I was given that bipolar was also known as manic depression, I was sickened. That was something else altogether. I remembered the guy who used to pee in Coke bottles and leave them outside his apartment door. That couldn't possibly be me!

Upon my release following such a prolonged and spectacular breakdown, I was afforded one single meeting with a psychiatrist who warned me not to read up on my condition, avoid support groups and not talk to anyone else who was bipolar. He then passed me off to my family doctor. I returned home, determined to commit to recovery, take my medication religiously and become the parent, and the woman, I really wanted to be. For a while I was able to distract myself, against the doctor's orders, by reading everything about mood disorders I could get my hands on. But before long, questions about gender and sexuality resurfaced, clearer now without the haze of madness, and stronger than ever. Fortunately, I was also, after years of debating the idea that I'd misconstrued my sexuality, on the threshold of finally discovering that there was another, more accurate way to understand myself. As transgender. Not that that was a marriage builder either. After a few more years of painful soul searching, testing the limits of comfortable expression, and exploring the practicality of actually living as man, my husband and I agreed that I had to proceed with transition. He would support me, but could not stay with me. I was forty years old.

The years that followed were some of the best I've ever known. Testosterone offered an immediate sense of emotional grounding, an internal recalibration that felt so right. Over time, as my appearance changed, I was able to move forward into a new career, reinvent myself and feel a growing sense of completeness. It was, however, not without sacrifices. I lost friends, faced discrimination, and eventually had to slip into a closeted existence to ensure that I could maintain employment. I also had full-time care of the children, only receiving a twenty-four-hour respite once a week when they went to stay with their father. But I was stable – mentally and emotionally. I bought a house and a car and for the first, and only, time in my life held a rewarding, demanding professional position that I loved working as a service coordinator and advocate for adults with acquired brain injuries. Eventually I became so confident in my wellness that, with my doctor's support, I began to cut back my psychiatric medication.

Everything was good. Until it wasn't. Sometime in 2013, things began to fall apart. My son, who'd always had his own mental health challenges, was struggling with an addiction to alcohol. He'd spent time on the streets, and when he returned home, violent and disruptive episodes with friends were common. At the same time, the Executive Director at the agency where I worked began to demonstrate signs of dementia, and serious board management issues came to light. By this time I was the Program Manager and the most senior staff member in the office. As I tried to hold things together, the ground started to slip out from beneath my feet. And, of course, I was the last to notice how severely erratic and off track I had become until it was much too late.

Mental illness warps and distorts one's self conception. Prone to periodic ups and downs all my life, I was inclined to own my inconsistencies of mood, taking blame and assuming control when in reality I was riding a wave I could not see for being immersed in it. Having a diagnosis makes it no easier to actually recognise from within a tunnel of darkness or expanse of light that it is not actually you, but the illness at play. Ever the frog in the boiling water. By June 2014, with the Annual General Meeting approaching, and no one daring to intervene with my increasingly irrational behaviour, I was forced into sudden self-awareness when the psychologist on the board commented that I was speaking too fast. That was a clue I understood. I was manic. I checked and realised I hadn't taken my reduced dose of medication for weeks, maybe more. I just barely made it through the meeting, drove home keeping one eye on the centre line of the road, and collapsed. I never went back. I was banned from the office. Nothing I left behind – family photos, my diploma, my books – has ever been returned.

TRAUMA

In the aftermath of this second mania, barely functioning, dragging the entrails of my previous existence behind me, still in the whirling fog of denial, I believed I would be back at my desk in no time. The psychiatrist I had been seeing occasionally prescribed muscle relaxants instead of anti-psychotics and was unable to meet with me for a month. She never even ordered bloodwork. Meanwhile I was so unstable on my feet I could not even walk down the road. It was a summer of misery and madness, anger and frustration. And through it all I was hopelessly, recklessly alone. It would be another six months before my family doctor would finally be able to secure a place for me at the hospital's Mood Disorder Clinic, granting me an opportunity to obtain proper psychiatric support for the first time in the nearly eighteen years since my initial breakdown.

Of course, first I had to prove myself ill enough. By this point the manic residue had long faded into mild depression and I was forced to try to describe a period of time that I could only remember from my blurred and frantic internal unreality. I brought my daughter along as my witness. In addition, I had to educate the professionals about my gender history and try to sort the strains of madness from the dysphoria. I felt like I was on trial. My illness, as such a fundamental aspect of my emotional existence, was impossible to define, but I neither wanted to overplay it nor underestimate the devastation it had wrought. At the same time, I was trying my best to make positive changes in my life. Without the constraints of my job, I had 'come out' again, sought to create connections within the LGBTQ community and was starting to write. I was attempting to openly own the aspects of my identity I had been forced to keep buried. However, it was not a smooth process. I found the queer community an uneasy fit after so many years on my own, isolated and alone. I was healing, perhaps, but I was a long way from being well.

I was accepted into the clinic, but was always afraid that it was provisional. Oddly, it was a medical emergency – a pulmonary embolism and cardiac arrest – that helped secure the added support of a psychologist and an occupational therapist. It was a comfort to feel I was surrounded by well-rounded mental health care just as I was finally starting to unwrap a pervasive and troubling body dysmorphia, a profound sense of physical incompleteness heightened by the transphobia I encountered within LGBTQ spaces. A decade and a half after transition I was regularly reminded that hormones and surgeries could allow me to live as a man, but in the eyes of many people, they would never *make* me a man. As this bodied disaffection and an intense longing for affection began to weigh on my thoughts, it became a key focus of my psychotherapy, and seeped into my regular meetings with my psychiatrist and psych nurse as well. I couldn't avoid it.

And then came something I never expected. If my initial diagnosis as bipolar came as a shock, imagine my response when, nearly twenty years later, my doctor questioned that same diagnosis. She had tracked down my original hospital records and discovered they simply described me as delusional, nothing more. My reality crumbled. It set off a month of angry, impossible soul searching.

If I wasn't bipolar, what was I? Doubts rattled through my brain. Why had they given me handouts describing the condition? Prescribed lithium and warned me not to stop taking it? Had I not seen a record in a physician's office that indicated Bipolar I with psychotic tendencies? I wondered how, if I was not bipolar, going off my meds had led to such a devastating, career destroying manic episode.

Do we ever know who we really are? What does a diagnosis truly hold? How much does it form your identity, become something to cling to, define and explain the strange and uneven way your life has unfolded? Once you accept that you have a mood disorder, it can help frame a lifetime of ups and downs – relationships broken, bridges burned, inexplicable obsessions that rise and fall, strange U-turns in mid-stream. Take it away and you are left with no explanation for the failures of the past and little hope for the future. Recognising my bipolar tendencies was as critical to my sense of self as understanding my gender identity. I knew that neither fully defined who I was, but threaten to take one away and I was suddenly unbound.

I poured out my despair and confusion to my therapist, who assured me he saw no reason to question the diagnosis and offered to report my concerns to the doctor. At my next session with her, she apologised for causing me distress. An understatement. But in settling the validity of the bipolar designation, she set me a further challenge. She suggested that perhaps I was using the diagnosis as an excuse to avoid grieving the fact I was transgender and everything that had meant – everything it had cost me. That thought silenced me.

If asked, I would say that I have never regretted my decision to transition; it was, for me, after decades of unnamed gender insecurity, the only thing I could do. Once I realised testosterone would allow me shed my skin, metaphorically speaking, I could see no other path.

I had never thought about grief, or rather that grieving was something I would be allowed to do. To assert a transgender identity, to transition and leave one's birth gender behind, is supposed to be an act of affirmation. It's something for others to grieve. But, if I am completely honest, there are moments when I do wish I had never had to transition at all.

My psychiatrist's suggestion sat heavily with me. I knew what I did grieve: the fact that I had had to deprive my mother of her only daughter. When I was younger, my mother had confided that the only time the gender of one of her children mattered was when I was born. Her first child, a girl, had been stillborn. She had not wanted to get pregnant so early in her marriage and had not wanted the child. When the baby died she was consumed with guilt. She wanted another girl and that girl was me – a daughter to replace Catherine. I was followed by the births of two boys. This was a major reason why the boy I felt inside had seemed so monstrous. I was afraid of letting my mother down.

When I came out to her many years later, she asked for a little time to adjust but promised her unconditional love.

And never wavered in that. Or in her support. Yet still, it pains me that I struggled through so many of the mother–daughter moments she had cherished. When I got married, falling in love with a man was no problem, but I had no vision of a wedding or a white dress – it had never been part of my psyche. I conceded to the dress, but rejected the antique Irish lace she had saved to adorn it. Small things perhaps, but these things haunted me. To allow myself to grieve, I needed to recognise the possibility that she carried her own grief, to acknowledge her loss, and invite her to assure me it was okay. I wanted her absolution.

I never got it. I called my mother after that session with the doctor and she was strangely absent. She had been frail and physically declining for years, but on the phone she had always seemed ageless. I drove up to see her and found her disoriented and confused. The fridge was filled with an assortment of moulding leftovers. I did not know it at the time, but her lung capacity was now dramatically, irreparably reduced by osteoporosis. Within weeks she would be gone. My father would die less than two weeks after her. I was never able to have that conversation, to ask her how she truly felt about losing her daughter. I was left with a complicated, compounded grief.

Four years on, I'm still trying to untangle it all and figure out where I, my gender identity and my madness fit into this life lived, such as it is. The patterns are difficult to sort out, impossible to bring into any clear and lasting focus. The older one gets, the more we're inclined to try to make sense of where we are and how we got here. Looking back we see these lightning traces, these impossible threads that weave our lives together and give them meaning. Only in the bipolar unravelling of my gendered and anti-gendered realities can I begin to understand my very own strangeness and charm.

THE SHATTERING
Sam Mills

As a child, my father was a mystery to me. I once told friends at primary school that he had been kidnapped and was being held hostage by a gang of hostile tramps at the bottom of our garden, a macabre re-imagining of *Wurzel Gummidge.* There were the pills he took at night, the wardrobe where his work suits gathered dust, his absences, that strange white institution he sporadically stayed in, where we could only visit him every few days, and where he was guarded not by tramps but figures in uniforms. On one occasion, when he was home from the institution, we all went on a family outing by car. I was eight years old. I sat in the back with my brothers, reading a dog-eared copy of Roald Dahl's *Danny the Champion of the World,* which my mother had recently picked up for me at a jumble sale. My father was driving. I could see his face in the rear-view mirror. A frown knifing his forehead, a distance in his blue eyes, as if his inner tide was far out from the shoreline of reality. He was muttering to himself as though in conversation with a voice; I smiled, recognising that I mirrored his reflection, for I had the voice of Dahl running through my mind, and it was witty, rude, wry, and compassionate. Fiction can sometimes enrich us, leave us feeling full, but just as often a good book can leave us with a sense of wistful absence. In *Danny,* the eponymous hero has an amazing father who teaches him how to fish and takes him on secret poaching trips in the middle of the night. At the end of the book, there is a concluding message: 'A stodgy parent is no fun at all! What a child wants – and DESERVES – is a parent who is SPARKY.' It was hard not to stare at the picture of Dahl on the back cover, sitting in his Buckinghamshire garden, a tall man with a twinkle in his eye, and wish that through some absurd and contrived plot twist in my life I would discover he was my real father and he would whisk me away.

Back home, I flipped through a tattered dictionary. I wanted to discover a word for my dad's idiosyncrasies. If I could only find it, I thought, it would be like turning a key in a lock. Despite discovering new words I liked the sound of (*peevish, aberration, crasis*), nothing enlightened me.

Aged thirteen: I was sitting in my bedroom, the box room at the front of my house. My pen was scratching across a sheet of A4 paper; as I reached the bottom, I added it to the fat lever arch file which contained various novels-in-progress. I had become addicted to this experience, the joy of imagined worlds, the loss of self. Beyond my room, the house seemed full of shadows and sadness. My dad didn't work; my mother did a job she hated. Money was always lacking, a constant stress. My dad was mostly silent, did the housework, spent hours of each day asleep in his armchair, by which there was a sheet of paper with a scrawled list of things that his 'Voice' said to him.

I was hungry and it was nearly dinner-time. Dad was cooking. Downstairs, I watched him pull a tray of chips from the oven. He set them down on the surface. Stared at them gravely.

'You've burnt the chips, Dad,' I pointed out casually. I didn't really mind. I liked them that way, crispy and crunchy between my teeth.

He pulled off his oven gloves; I heard the pounding of his footsteps on the stairs. I looked at the chips for a while, watched them cool into a row of blackened fingers. As I ventured upstairs, I could hear weeping. I felt my heart thump, conscious that ignorance might be better than knowledge, that it might be safer to retreat. The bedroom door was ajar. I crept closer. Dad was sitting on the bed next to Mum, saying: 'I burnt the chips, I burnt the chips,' over and over. His face was red, as if the tears he was shedding had been wrenched from his gut; Mum was making shushing noises as though he was her child.

I crept back down the stairs. In the kitchen, I walked in circles and chewed nervously on an apple. When my mother eventually came down, she explained that my dad had 'schizophrenia' and that sometimes it was hard to get his medication right. The amazement on my face startled her. 'Didn't you notice all the pills he takes?' she asked. 'Don't you remember when he took off all his clothes and walked down the street and then none of the other children's parents let them come to play for a while...?' There was something oddly casual about her tone, as though we were exchanging gossip about someone else's family. Our discussion was brief; I was too shocked to summon any questions about my father's illness.

Later, after my parents had gone to bed, I sat in the bath and wept at this strange and sudden rewriting of our lives. Through the warped window glass, I could see the yellow lights of the house next door. I imagined the faint sounds of laughter as they sat and enjoyed dinner together: a conventional family, the one I'd fooled myself into thinking we were. At school I had been reading my nonsense poetry to my friends and they'd teased me for being 'mad'; did that mean his illness was weaving its way into my words? That night I was finally able to find the correct word in the dictionary. It informed me that schizophrenia came from Greek roots, *skhizein* meaning split/tear and *phren,* the mind. The key had turned.

Dementia Praecox: the original name for the illness. It was classified in 1899 by the German psychiatrist Emil Kraepelin, a contemporary of Freud's, who noted that many sufferers withdrew and sank to 'the life of a vagrant'. He thought that the defect at the basis of the illness was organic, that cortical neurons were destroyed by autointoxication. I visualise this concept – toxins produced in the sex glands, the intestines, the mouth, that poison the brain – seeing them as dark splashes leaking into the bloodstream like ink, deadly clouds drifting upwards. Kraepelin was wrong about toxins and the dementia element, however. Schizophrenia is quite different from Alzheimer's; though the mind is afflicted, but it does not necessarily degenerate. Indeed, some scientists have argued that the illness creates the reverse: a heightened consciousness, life experienced more vividly and sharply.

The Swiss doctor Eugen Bleuler grew up with a direct experience of psychosis: his elder sister was incarcerated at the Burghölzli Asylum at the University of Zurich. She was hospitalised there for life. For Bleuler, this trauma was a trigger, motivating him to help others. In 1908, when he gave a lecture at the German Psychiatric Association in Berlin, he renamed the illness. There he coined the term *schizophrenia*. This was a diagnosis that he gave his sister too: a name that captured the shattered quiddity of the illness, the internal tears between thought, emotion, behaviour, the fragmentation and disconnect.

My father became a spectre in our house, sporting a straggling beard, hours spent immersed in his Bible. He had been a playful parent when we were children. Upside down I remember being swung, when he picked me up and played Tick Tock, my ponytail whipping his shoes as I became a giggling pendulum. But now that I was a teenager, old enough to judge him, to seek worldly wisdom from him, I found myself lost, turning to my mother instead. She was his carer, the family breadwinner, acted as mother and father to us. Having been denied an education by her chauvinistic father, she attempted to do A levels in the evenings, followed by a psychology degree, but her daily grind as a secretary left her too tired, yawning over textbooks. Over the decades, I saw that tiredness set in deep, hollow her out. At the age of sixty-five, the diagnosis came. A year on, our dining room became her bedroom, my mother on a loaned hospital bed wheeled from ambulance to carpet, an oxygen machine with an undulating hiss keeping her alive during her last days with her family. I pictured the cancer as a poison ivy that spread over her lungs, digging in deep bitter green roots. I fed her soup and porridge and bought her a heap of presents that I wrapped in secret, ignoring the nurses' advice that we should celebrate Christmas early, unable to imagine life without her.

***

Autumn 2015: I know that something is wrong with my father, but I cannot pinpoint what the matter is. He is habitually not quite present, but he has been stable since our loss, anchored by his routine now that he lives alone as a widower: buying his newspaper, shopping, cooking simple meals, days bookended by the taking of medicines, anti-psychotics and more pills designed to counteract their side effects. He seems to be withdrawing, the daily retreat as subtle as the season, like the trees outside in our garden which are losing leaves, becoming stark, retreating into hibernation. Often it seems as though his life was playing out at a different speed to the rest of us, unspooling in slow motion.

I stay south with him for a few weeks. One day I cook lunch and set down the plates on the dining room table, my eyes skimming a stain on the carpet. My mother lived her last days in this room, and the stain was created by – a spilt drink? – a splash of urine? – now faded to watermark.

I go into the hallway and call for my dad once, then twice, and then again.

Two plates on the table. The empty place at the head where she once sat. Still standing, impatient with hunger, I spear a potato and chew it quickly. I call to Dad again. When there is no answer, I hurry up the stairs. 'Come in,' his quavery voice replies to my knock. He is sitting on the bed, looking at the clothes neatly laid out next to him – trousers, braces, shirt – as though he has been given a set of bad letters at a turn in Scrabble and can't make a word out of them.

'Why don't you have lunch in your pyjamas?' I suggest.

As he lumbers down the stairs, I think: *hang on, has he even taken his morning medicines?* One of our kitchen cupboards now functions as a medicine cabinet: I find a jumble of white boxes with scientific names and labels giving instructions for doses. Dad sits down before his plate of cooling chicken and vegetables. I pass him his pills. Silence; stasis. I pour him a glass of water and put the pills on a spoon. I raise them to his mouth. He opens it. I slip them in and pass him the water.

I cut up his food. A piece of chicken on the end of my fork meets his closed lips. He looks at me as though he can't hear the words I'm saying: *Dad, it's good to eat, you need to keep your strength up.* For one surreal moment, I feel as though

I'm an apparition he does not believe in. When I call 999 they ask if he is breathing, if he is in pain, and I have trouble explaining his state: he seems as though he is in a coma, yet he is awake. After I hang up, I take solace in the sound of him breathing in and out, but I cannot make his eyes connect with mine. The fading light in them chills me with a grief-flash: my mother lying in this room, on that makeshift hospital bed, the life seeping out of her. It is as though he is in a liminal state, body half-dead, mind in purgatory.

Bang! Bang! Bang!

My dad is in a hospital bed, on a ward for elderly men. His fists have a mind of their own. They fly up, crash down on the bed with a constant *bang! bang! bang!* I feel embarrassed by the noise, fret that he is disturbing the other patients and their visiting families. He looks like an incongruous white-haired baby; he needs to be fed, he cannot walk or move; and he barely speaks.

Tears are seeping from his eyes. I ask him if he's okay and with a rare moment of focus, he replies, 'I've got a cold.' Then the connection is lost and he drifts away again, catatonia pulling him under.

Fragments of memory, of Christmas morning 2011. My mum in the hospital bed, me showing her presents that she was too weak to unwrap. Her breathing was already shallow, but now it became desperate. It was like watching her being suffocated by an invisible being. I held her hand, called up the hospital, begged advice, woke my brother, who was sleeping next door, warned him that she was going. My brothers and I spent much of the day in tears. Our Christmas turkey burned black in the oven, setting off the smoke alarm; crackers sat unpulled; alcohol flowed. When I asked my dad if he was okay, his breezy 'Fine' sounded as though we were talking about the weather.

For three years, he had remained stable. In some ways, it had been more shocking than if he'd a breakdown. But now, now the shattering had occurred, and I had no idea when or if he would recover, if he would be able to speak again, or if he would be hospitalised forever.

Bang! Bang! Bang!

I stood up, leant over the bed and took hold of both his arms. Slowly, I began to lower them to the bed. I felt the physical strength of my dad in resistance; we began to struggle. I leaned in so close that my face was inches away from his. Our pupils reflected each other. I spoke to him through my eyes: *You're okay. I'm here. I'll always look after you.* I felt his fists pause. And then a change came over his face. The tension dissolved, and his expression summered into one of pure sweetness. Love shimmered between us. His eyes drifted shut. His hands twitched with the memory of compulsion, but lay still on the bed. As he drifted into sleep, I realised the pitch of his exhaustion, how hungry he had been for its release – his own desires thwarted by the peculiar perversions of his body.

I had always loved reading, gaining knowledge, the mind-fizz of new ideas, but schizophrenia was a subject I'd avoided all my life. My father and I had spent much of our lives virtually strangers, and perhaps I had avoided learning about his illness. Now I browsed the medical sections in bookshops, borrowed from the library, ordered second-hands online. Over and over, I read dry descriptions of the illness, of Kraepelin and Bleuler, of symptoms that were negative (apathy, lack of motivation, social withdrawal) and positive (hallucinations, delusions, hearing voices) (I thought they ought be classified negative and more negative). I learnt that it is a biological illness, but its onset can be linked to stress. It develops most frequently in late adolescence/early adulthood. A tragedy, such as divorce or a job loss, can act as a match that strikes against genetic potential, lighting the full flame of illness.

It wasn't until I discovered *When the Sun Bursts*, by psychoanalyst Christopher Bollas, that I found a book that made me tingle:

'Most people I know who have talked with schizophrenics have noticed that these feel like conversations not with someone whose ailment is derived from the fog of symptomatic preoccupation, or the dulling repetition of character patterns, but with a person who seems to be existing on the edge of human perception. Take LSD and you see things you would ordinarily never perceive. Become schizophrenic and you see these things without the aid of drugs.'

This is it, I thought, this is the book I've been searching for. Schizophrenia is an illness that is too idiosyncratic for the language of science; it needs poetry and imagination too.

Bollas was good at describing the slow onset of schizophrenia, the ways in which the self and body shifts and alters. 'Those on the verge of schizophrenia,' he writes, 'may experience profound changes in their way of seeing, hearing, and thinking. Early shocks may include an odd vividness of certain colors that can become eidetic or dreamlike in their intensity. This may be accompanied by an unusual sensitivity to sound.' Bollas describes the disorientation, the loneliness that comes with this strange metamorphosis: how sufferers feel afraid to tell their friends and family, at just the moment when they most need help. And he captures beautifully the sadness of this distancing: 'It as if he is gradually leaving our world; although still present, he has transported himself across some unseen line, crossing over into another reality that totally absorbs his attention.'

For the schizophrenic, a breakdown can entail a painful collapse of the self, that central 'I' that underpins our daily narrative and creates the illusory story of our past, present and future. The self is lost, it fractures into voices; fragments of self might even be put outside of the sufferer, into objects (a tape recorder, a vacuum cleaner), the landscape (a tree). This creates a deep dislocation in the schizophrenic's sense of time and space – which is why they might create a mythology ('I am being given instructions by an alien') as a desperate substitute for the 'real' world they have lost. This is also why there is a loss of desire in pursuing goals

– without an 'I' who is seeking achievement, and with the world around you not making sense anymore, perhaps they are no longer worth pursuing. The illness, then, is a vanishing act. For those left behind, families and friends and lovers, there is a grieving: 'Our type of mourning is unique as we are left holding the remnants of the person's former being.'

I read novels too, though I found it hard to find fiction that captured my father's condition. I devoured a well-reviewed novel that was written from a schizophrenic's viewpoint but seemed unconvincing to me. Given that the illness fractures the self, how can a coherent first-person voice narrating a classically structured story with a beginning, middle and end make any sense? For me, Will Self was a writer who knew how to write about madness. It was the surreal, nightmarish flavour of it that his stories captured, such as *The Quantity Theory of Insanity*, which plays with the theory that sanity is a fixed quotient in society: if you cure an asylum of schizophrenics in London, then a group of sane and rational people in New York will go crazy. Schizophrenia is the most surreal of mental illnesses. I once encountered a schizophrenic who related that, while lying in bed in hospital during a psychotic episode, he had received all his visitors without speaking, a blissful smile on his face; he was living out reality in a *Star Wars* film, and each person who visited appeared as a hallucinated character from the film.

Simplistic tales about schizophrenia failed to resonate with me. Art that captured its surreal, smashed psyche were the ones where I felt an intuitive response of 'Yes, that's it!

339

That's what it's like!' *Alice in Wonderland,* with its strange
dislocations of time and space and place – that was my dad's
illness. The modernist fragments of T. S. Eliot's *The Waste
Land* – 'These fragments I have shored against my ruins' –
that was my dad's illness. And Self, writing about a man who
seeks to find patterns of meaning in the graffiti on toilets
across London – that was my dad's illness. I remember as
a teenager sitting down and watching an episode of *Monty
Python*, my mum laughing with me, my dad silent. The
way it jumped from one mad scene to another, from a man
holding a dead parrot, to the chorus of 'The Lumberjack
Song', then back to something completely different – that
was my dad's illness.

And there was positive research surrounding the illness too:
I found consolation in this. I knew vaguely of the clichéd
relationship between depression and creativity. During
my teenage years I had shown symptoms of inheriting
my father's illness, though I had offset them by practising
Transcendental Meditation. But the studies that I discovered
were fascinating. Jon Löve Karlsson, based at the Institute of
Genetics in Reykjavik, conducted a study in Iceland which
examined the first-degree relatives of people with a history
of psychosis. They were 30 per cent more likely to be in
the Icelandic *Who's Who,* with many of them excelling
in academia, politics and the arts; they were 50 per cent
more likely to have published a book. Think of numerous
famous creatives who were on the knife edge between
genius and madness: Virginia Woolf, Sylvia Plath, Richard
Dadd, William Blake, Robert Schumann, Vincent van Gogh,
Herman Melville, to name but a few.

THE SHATTERING

The academic David Horrobin also cites studies showing that 'families with schizophrenic members seem to have a greater variety of skills and abilities, and a greater likelihood of producing high-achievers'. Einstein's son suffered from schizophrenia, as did Carl Jung's mother. When James Joyce's daughter Lucia developed schizophrenia, Joyce took her to see Jung, who said that they were like two people going to the bottom of a river, 'one falling and the other diving'. It sounded like an apt description of me and my father. My meditation and my writing felt so similar: dives into deep waters, a place of both silence and infinite possibility.

E. L. Doctorow, in the *Paris Review*, declared that 'Writing is a socially acceptable form of schizophrenia.' There are biological similarities between the brain chemistry of schizophrenics and creatives. Researchers at the Karolinska Institutet in Sweden cite that both healthy, highly creative people and schizophrenics have a lower density of dopamine D_2 receptors in the thalamus. The thalamus is a relay centre. It filters information before it reaches the cortex, which is responsible for decision-making; if less is filtered, more creative ideas can spark. As Professor Ullén, one of the researchers concluded: 'Thinking outside the box might be facilitated by having a somewhat less intact box.'

And this is why the gene perpetuates, it has been argued: in order for society to move forward, we need innovation, and with innovators there comes a little madness.

Of course, there is a danger of romanticising mental illness. For those with severe psychosis, there is no romance to their tragedy. But learning more about these genetic advantages did save me from an uneasy, lingering feeling that I had bad genes, that I was tainted in some way, that having children at some point in the future might not be a good idea. And, I hope, they might help us, as a society, to treasure the benefits of schizophrenia and psychosis, rather than seeing those who suffer from them as the Other.

After around five days in hospital, my father was sectioned and transferred to a psychiatric ward. There his illness was given a new label: *catatonia schizophrenia*. Of the schizophrenics group, his diagnosis had always been 'paranoid'.

Their theories for the cause of his catatonia were tentative, even strange. It might be severe constipation, they thought, a side effect of an anti-psychotic which could become lethal to elderly patients. Another cause might be the reduction in his medicines, something he had persuaded a doctor to do earlier in the year.

When I visited him on the ward, I took along a bottle of juice, and sat beside him, feeding him with a straw, having been warned that he might become dehydrated. The slurp of liquid, the sight of it moving up the straw, was a consolation, evoked a tenderness in me. A few weeks on, the day came when he was sitting upright at a table in his suit and greeted me with a 'Hello!' He followed this with several coherent sentences. I reacted to him like a parent thrilled by their child's first words.

I thought then that his strange attack was an anomaly, that he would be released and life would go back to normal. But

I found myself visiting him through the winter, and again in the spring when another catatonic attack had him sectioned; and again in the summer. The only good that came of these harrowing visits was the tenderness that blossomed between us, that a parent who had once been a stranger to me was now someone I felt close to. I saw more of his personality, which had been hidden behind the veil of illness: his sweet, introverted charm, his kindness. Whilst 'flatness and lack of emotion' is listed as a symptom of schizophrenia, I saw that, on the contrary, my father was highly sensitive, feeling everything so deeply, I thought, that his body seemed to have been unable to cope with such rarefied emotion and had shattered in response.

All through that year, and after he was finally released, I found myself haunted by the question of why the catatonia had occurred.

I thought back to my mother's death and his strange lack of tears. But then I considered how his illness had been treated over the years, the drugs and the sectioning and the incarcerations. If you spend years being told that you are crazy, and you become afraid to exhibit any sort of extreme emotion, because it is seen as an act of transgression, a possible prelude to incarceration, then how do you manage when you lose your wife? Maybe the urge to cry and scream is there, muffled by the meds. But perhaps there is a fear: are you allowed to express it? So the grief just sits there, a hard lump inside you, and there is no release, and one day it becomes too heavy, your body too tired of carrying it about, and so it just presses the off switch and caves in. After all, you might expect a widower to shut off or lose interest in food. These were the same symptoms that catatonia had inflicted on my father. Maybe it was the only way he was allowed to mourn. Maybe it felt dangerous to break down in a supposedly civilised world; maybe the psychiatric ward felt like a safe space, for all around him people were fighting and crying and screaming and he wasn't going to look any different.

And maybe it was also a test. A way of seeing if life *could* be sustained without his carer, the woman who had stood by his side all his life. Of seeing if there was a life that could be lived without her, if it was worth getting up in the mornings and taking pills and living a half-life, a quiet life, a life in the shadows. Of seeing whether other people would catch him and help him through his grief and back to reality.

PORNOGRAPHY AND ME

Tamim Sadikali

I remember exactly where I was, the first time I saw a pornographic image. I was thirteen, maybe fourteen, and away with the Scouts. Away from home, for the very first time. For one long weekend, the rules could be forgotten. There'd be no weepy Mum or shouting Dad – just the great outdoors and the company of boys, eager to be men. I wanted to be like the older ones – tall, strong and wearing my boots like they were a part of me. We made bivouacs under fading light while the Scoutmaster assembled logs for a fire. Night came and, exposed under stars, I had no fear. I was one of the gang. I knew it. I *felt* it. My stained, grubby hands looked like theirs. My boots were soiled, just like everyone else's.

As we prepared a meal, prising open tins and vacuum-packed chunks of protein, some older boys ducked away, returning with a bulging bag of goodies. A cheer rang round as cans of beer appeared, ring-pulls popping in stereo around the fire. The younger ones weren't allowed to drink, the Scoutmaster saw to that, but when a magazine started being passed around, he didn't stop them. A cluster formed around whoever held it, excitement rushing from a standing start. Lit only by flame against an ink-black canvas, I watched my friends morph. They were cooing, hooting, breaking out into shrills. A headiness filled the air, unrelated to alcohol, and it infected me. *What was this magazine?* When, finally, my turn came I still had no idea, but I recall feeling giddy with joy at being allowed in on the joke.

'Get a load of this, Tam,' jollied the biggest Scout in the pack, sitting down next to me like an elder brother. I've long since forgotten his name but that moment shaped my next twenty years.

***

I listen to a lot of radio. Exclusively talk; mostly 5 *Live*. And now and then there's a feature on addiction: alcohol, prescription meds, over-the-counter painkillers. Earnest phone-ins on gambling, steroids for the aspirational and cocaine for the chattering classes. Drugs for the successful, drugs for a crowd and others for splendid isolation. But no one ever talks about porn. More than thirty years later that still pinches, because a splinter from that camping trip had lodged in my flesh. For I'd returned with a secret. Lucy was now by my side: an imprint from that long weekend, like peaches and cream. Six pages – her complete spread. Tucked away behind my mattress. Now when Mum cried or Dad shouted, it was Lucy to whom I turned. She was uncomplicated. She didn't demand that I be special. And just like that, it didn't matter so much when girls I liked blanked me. Because Lucy would help me forget. Through my teenage years, this secret place was where I'd go to escape life's greyness. Suspend circuitous threads that my mind could not process. Administer salve on bruises that I seemed to pick up daily. Because Lucy and her playmates, they never lost their sparkle. They never said 'no'.

As much as I immersed myself, though, the real world could not be erased. By my late teenage years, a feeling had started growing – instead of being an answer, these magazines were a problem. But then I discovered hardcore porn and there was nothing else in God's good world to compete. By my twenties, I had become a boy-in-a-bubble. I loathed myself and hated porn even more, but I just couldn't look away. And then the Internet arrived.

As I neared thirty, I lost my virginity to a prostitute. One day I walked up a urine-soaked stairwell in Soho, handed over some notes to a woman whose accent I couldn't quite place, and came within seconds. The gulf between the sexual gymnastics I'd watched others enact and my own performance left me psychically comatose. I couldn't hold the thought – daren't dwell on it. But this pattern, of pain then salve, before pain returned and I applied more salve – a pattern put in place all those years ago on a camping trip – seemed unbreakable. And then one night, sitting alone in the kitchen of my parents' house, I began to write.

***

A question had been troubling me – how could one be human *and* sexual? I began making notes on paper but instead of jotting down thoughts, a bullet-pointed list, a dramatic scene surfaced in my mind. I could see this character, a man – me but not me – alone at night in his flat. And like David Kessler in *An American Werewolf in London*, he was suddenly hit – blindsided by a transformation. The man stands, paces, responding to sudden change. He strips, finds himself naked and boxes shadows. It was like watching a movie or rather, as author, being a director. I could zoom right in and slow down. Almost touch him. Hear his snatched breaths and see his eyes dart, looking for some way out. I was, for the first time, observing the acts of a passion-play in which I'd only ever starred.

With this man clear in my mind's eye, I scribbled furiously. I wanted to capture something – his desperation not to follow the script of his life – and yet still fail. Sitting at that kitchen table, I experienced the rarest of sensations: focus. Complete attention on a single point, concomitantly collapsing down all distractions. I went to sleep that night floating on a new high and come the next morning, I continued. Three days later, I had 10,000 words worth of scribbles. And for three full days, I hadn't even thought about porn.

So, would that be it? A three-day-long distraction? It was possible, and frankly odds-on, except that with the slowing of that initial burst, ideas continued surfacing. And then a thought... I could run with this. Continue the protagonist's story, even reach some sort of ending – whatever that might be. What if I could write 20,000 words, 30,000 – a book, even? *Me, write a book? A novel?* Surely not. Writing is what other people did. Plebs like me were born to sit in exposed-concrete buildings and stare at spreadsheets. Those three days should've remained a blip on my flatline but in writing that one scene, I'd begun to un-pack myself – strip back what had become compacted, hardened. And by continuing, I knew I wouldn't just be telling a story – I could pull up my own roots. How did pornography grip me so completely? Why me and not others? And, maybe… writing could help me break free. After all, in three days I had, unwittingly, disrupted myself. And beyond that – I'd unwrapped some personal truths. Surely by continuing, I could dig deeper.

With writing came a kind of transformation. Yes, there was catharsis in stepping out of one's own skin. But there was more. Because I wasn't writing just to document. Preserve record history. In wrapping truth in fiction, what mattered was reaching the reader emotionally. And for that, my words had to do more. They had to carry love and lust and hate. They had to sing. And when I found some stillness, dimmed the background hum, that became possible. I tuned in to an internal rhythm. A place from where sentences near wrote themselves. Instead of being constructed, words coalesced – were pulled together through some irregular, kinetic force. And from there, the process scaled out. Tone, timbre, rhythm and pacing – these were variables in an equation that could not be written down but which, in the right state of mind, I came to know by heart. There was mathematics behind 'impact' – but it was elusive. This writing game, it wasn't like making widgets in a factory. I had to do more than simply turn up and switch on the lights. That formula, the one I both knew by heart and then always instantly forgot – it only revealed itself when I dived deep – committed wholly to the moment. And for a person used to life in second gear, these were alien extremes.

I now had ambition. This character, this me-but-not-me... I was consumed with breathing life into him. I wanted to be published. I wanted to pass strangers on street corners, discussing my work. But for any of that to happen, I'd have to run with these new extremes. And so, after unintentionally breaking a circuit – one that had run riot over me for twenty years – I committed to a new direction. After all, what did I have to lose...?

I discovered a symbiotic relationship – the more I wrote, the more a sense of wellbeing returned. Achievement, excitement, anticipation for the next day... Stimuli that were foreign, were now driving me. And conversely, the greater my sense of wellbeing, the easier the creative process became. That immersion, that special place where the blank page was not something to dread – I could now find it at will. In truth, there was an obsessive quality to this new riff. From a certain angle, I'd swapped one compulsion for another. Except now I was centred within an act of creation. From seeding an idea to its nascent growth – it was me, controlling something amorphous to take shape and become beautiful.

I read voraciously, both fiction and non-fiction. I joined writing groups and attended workshops, seminars, masterclasses. I listened and learned. I wrote more and more, tore up my pages and started again. I'd lose myself for days in finding just the right groove. And through all this, and the dedication it demanded, I learnt a new truth – that I didn't need to follow the script of my life. That I was more than a hardwired set of responses to basic events. Of course, creative writing wasn't a panacea. Compulsive behaviours – ones that had settled into my marrow – could not be expunged so neatly. I needed more – other safeguards. I started swimming again and picked up my squash racket. I said a little prayer. So when I'd waver, I now had a stark choice: to return to old habits or run with the new. A simple, binary decision. No third way. The psychic energy needed to write – for my story to hit the notes I was reaching for – removed that option.

I finished the story of me-but-not-me. At some point along that journey, I discovered that I too could be charming. I found a partner and got married. My job morphed into a career. I became a father. I could've rejoined the rank-and-file and forgotten about storytelling, but I didn't let it go. Writing has stayed with me. For its own pleasure, as well as to act as a foil – to counter all those poisons available on tap. Twitter is my new weakness. It's how I now press 'Pause' and ignore what's really happening. Along with 300 million others. So maybe I'm not the only junkie but I don't want to go back. So when I'm alone and all options are on the table, I'll write. Because the act itself is revolutionary. From my privileged vantage point, the world is padded with distractions. Palliatives to tempt me, numb me; blunt me. The easiest thing would be to succumb. To ease off, kick back and let it all wash over me. But I want to be contrarian – it's good for the soul.

After the story of me-but-not-me was published, I stumbled upon a new experience. Literary criticism – book reviewing. Feeling spent in terms of fiction, this was a way for me to continue writing. I discovered my own style, a preference for indirect commentary. To say less about plot, character and other building-blocks, and focus instead on my journey as a reader. And from there, I'd spin a story about the story. A review as meta-story. Following my review of *A State of Freedom* by Neel Mukherjee, the Booker shortlisted author wrote to me:

> '...my heartfelt thanks, although "thank you2 seems too inadequate a response to your extraordinary review. I'm moved and honoured and delighted. The book has caused some bafflement among reviewers so it's extremely gratifying to read a rare review that "gets" the book.'

There's no money in reviewing – it is, in a literal sense, art for art's sake. The joy of discovery, the slow shaping of one's views. And through reviewing, I've discovered something else – short fiction. Because not everything in life is a novel. So I'm writing stories again. And beyond the joy in creativity, it's a kind of meditation. My way of staying human.

INHERITANCE IS SILENCE
Tomoé Hill

From a sea of silence emerges the message in its bottle, deafening in its simplicity. Closer to the end, my father's breathing tube was briefly removed; almost inaudibly came the words *help me*. The doctors said that he might not even realise what he was saying, the incoherent result of semi-consciousness. I wondered if it was the truth or an automatic response from professionals who knew that it made no difference anymore. It seemed absurd in its irrelevance as he was already long-shadowed by the inevitable night, but I could still imagine the stench of his words heavy and cloying in the room like the insistent false hope of flowers ill-matched to their receivers. It must only be at such times that you understand the extent of sickness: to read your future on the petals of lilies with their humid, metallic scent – harbingers of change and its indolic sweetness, a symbol of the flesh from rhizome to rot, yellow dust of pollen on your skin marking your acceleration back to the earth.

Like the doctors, I think he wasn't fully aware of what he whispered – although the guilt of those who know they will continue to live has a way of building impermeable and speculative structures around such things – nevertheless that phrase carried a lifetime of stoicism and rigidity, finally able to leave him, similar to the way mine also only untensed after his death. If the mind and body choose when to leave, then I think he chose his moment. There was no one in the room at the time he died, my mother and sister having just left. That, it could be said, was like him – we were always more adept at interrupted conversations, often speaking in books as if it were a better language: to speak in passages from another's voice was an implicit acknowledgement that the things we could not say would still find utterance. It was intimacy disguised in detachment, what I saw as the reconciliation of a man from a generation remote as another country, raised on unemotional silence: a natural way of speaking to a daughter he must have realised was bisexual early on; other voices to reassure my otherness. It was the natural progression from being read to when young – stories as safety, then later, when we could not summon our own voices, using others' in their place, no less familiar.

'Sorrow likes to give advance notice,' says the narrator of Fleur Jaeggy's story 'I Am the Brother of XX'. He explains the mistaken idea of death and grief being consequential – that they must necessarily, formally, be so. It is possible to grieve before death, without loneliness, for whether following a linear or non-linear chronology, we all have the same end. I grieved for my father at the age of ten though he was very much alive and well, waking one summer night from a nightmare, the one almost all children experience where a guardian, parent or parents die, then spending the time until morning sleepless over their first existential crisis – one neither they nor I could define beyond an uneasiness that what was in our lives could also be not there. Death was already no stranger to me, as we were abundant with well-aged relations who seemed to regularly and peacefully surrender to it in their sleep like gently falling dominoes; it had a small *d* and was mostly associated with roomfuls of other relatives only seen at such gatherings, a certain midnight-blue velvet dress being laid out again, the scent of brewing coffee and fondant icing on Danish pastry – death was sweet just as it was soft. But it could be said, until that night, that death was not personal.

There must exist books on the psyche that speak of solitude as having its beginnings in death; that one is more at home with it having gone through the shock of loss or grief, whether for others or the self. But that nightmare was none of those things. What I came to realise much later was that it was nothing more than reading a particular silence. To parse it as a child is to be an interpreter of a language one does not yet speak – the adult world. That I was able to at all was because I understood it from books, its thread guiding me through the labyrinth of relationships and their silences, then using those as templates against the mute emotions played out in front of me: a memory game without pleasure, a matching card whose revelation fills you with a knowledge that removes you from childhood.

'Being seems to me something more certain. Seeming more suitable to disappearing. And I felt apt to disappear.' How like an echo it is to read a thing like Jaeggy's passage, as if the words were a form of haruspicy: taken from your body, but until that moment unrevealed and unknown to you. Stranger still is to feel that in a certain instant they are shared with someone else, but then it is always the portents of death that are reliable, not the living. Even though he is gone, those words drift up from the page and into my head as if he spoke them unconsciously to me. *Help me.* To disappear, where you can be yourself and certain again – between worlds, between the lines, wherein lies consciousness and its not?

I remember there being more meaning in the way we communicated in times of crisis, because we were communicating with the presence of absence; a conversation made up of breaks and omissions that required an assumption that any person within it knew what was being spoken of as well as what could be said. If there was certainty in that method of communication it was predicated on the awareness that both speaker and listener could disappear, still leaving the conversation as intact as if it had been fully inlaid with real words. That awareness was also politeness, a way of allowing an exit should anyone wish to leave. There are other things I can also only see in hindsight: that I, too, was given sorrow's advance notice, a lesson I can trace back to a single line uttered when I was about eleven: *I don't wear my heart on my sleeve.* How I felt the strangeness even then of telling me he didn't want to be read, knowing I would find a way to read him nevertheless. I thought of it again when my mother recalled his twilight words. *Help me. Read me.*

The first time I heard it was in relation to some parental discord that I became the go-between of, trying to figure out what exactly its nature was and only knowing for some time that where there was one parent, the other was not. But then it was repeated, the second instance after a personal death, this time with a *D*, no amount of preparatory small deaths able to act as resistance against the destruction that it wrought for years, an entire family eroded from its coastal line – watching one person after another disappear, and not in silence. I think it was our reaction to become more silent, no one's heart on their sleeves bar my sister's, who did not quite understand this manner of coping, as if she were a changeling in the house. And in this way forms the division of family and the development of exactly how one views the world: the absorbers of grief versus the mourners. Sometimes it feels as if I am pliant with sorrow – bending with others' loss, a bent branch that bears the fruit of their silence. At other times I wish someone would bleed me and let that grief be absorbed by the ground, already rich with bodies releasing their memories back into the air like spores. *I don't wear my heart on my sleeve.* In the worst moments of my life I wanted to carve mine bloody into my arm, there for the world to see whether it wanted to or not. *Read me. Help me.*

When my father was sent to hospital, I called him from overseas. He could barely speak, long rasps of air swallowed before releasing a few words as if his body demanded a greater price for their expulsion. At regular intervals the phone would click and cut us off so that I would have to ring back, but it never occurred to me there was a fault. My preoccupied logic was that it must be something in place to discourage people from speaking to the sick for long periods and preventing their recovery. How like me – like us – it was, unable to read the obvious, that fault on the line so much like an exposed heart, a carved message. Because we distantly knew what that click and dial tone meant and continued as if we did not – until I stopped trying, both of us accepting the interruption as final, the final interruption. Fault as fatal, fatal as failure, failure as stoppage. To stop, to end, to cease to be, except in my head where it made sense to continue the peculiar normalcy of our communication. Disappearing in order to regain certainty in silence. Disappearing in order to read the other and to be read.

After that, I fully realised that admission meant no exit. There was no rationale for thinking it, and I kept this from everyone. But from then on, I regarded him in measurements: if he would still be here once my book was finished – and that, too, I read with his voice in my head, going back to my childhood and its safety – or if the newly lit candle on the table would extinguish itself first. In the end, it was a movie that marked it almost perfectly: the rolling credits, the ring of the phone, a nonsensically logical cause and effect. I simply knew when I heard it, and answered the phone with a sigh. The book was three-quarters read, the candle continued to burn. The scent of peppermint still pulls back a curtain on an afternoon laden with multiple finalities, the experience of a relief that seems clichéd, an invisible weight slipping from my shoulders and chest allowing a partial release of emotion. At night I would curl close to my edge of the bed – the pressure doubly returned, this time questioning why

I couldn't read my relationship as dead, false; one that even up until the moment he died, my father believed was true, the only thing he couldn't read in me. I curled closer, as if I could displace my guilt; the physics of grief.

To grieve is to realise that it is the outside world which exacerbates it and not ourselves, despite being enveloped in its solitude. There was a relief for us – I feel assured enough to say *us*, the entirety of our relationship based as it was on conversations that were not reliant on speech, or at least its completions – that it was a line that failed, for we could then say what we wanted to each other, in the way we were used to. Grief and death are almost impossible to understand even when the basic experiences are shared: we are so bound by their conventions that another's feels like exile from an already strange land – the alienation of alienation, so removed that even your existence feels merely theoretical. Can people truly communicate, severed? We were already adrift in our separate ways – but even at sea, there are signs. How else would we navigate the world, each other, ourselves, in and out of life and death but by reading?

What was my inheritance when he left? Solitude and temperament, even as the copper that was his fades from my hair, our only shared physical trait. But his most revealing bequest is the silence that remains behind my eyes: a disappearance where our thoughts and conversations are rhizomatic; beyond death.

What will I read when you are gone? I will read you.

THE ART OF LOST SLEEP
Venetia Welby

Some way in to my recent trip to Japan it occurred to me that I hadn't slept properly for twenty years. This hit me because for the first time since my teens, I actually was sleeping – despite the jet lag, despite the novelty and excitement of being in Okinawa, the place I'd dreamed about for a decade. It was a contrast to ill-fated 2005, when I took a job in China and realised I really might never sleep again.

There was a height to the white sky of Beijing in winter and both sun and moon were perpetually veiled in smog. I had left a liminal state – relationship dead, work a disaster, flat flooded – for a surreal one. Living in a dusty bedsit above Sanlitun, or 'Bar Street', I was being solitary and literary, determinedly. I was also not sleeping. Not at all, and I hadn't done so since arriving two weeks previously. Sleeplessness was, of course, no stranger to me. I was familiar with sleep's vagaries; I knew it as a capricious bastard that I lusted after, conscious all the while it was not to be trusted. Never, though, had it deserted me entirely before.

THE ART OF LOST SLEEP

I ate jellyfish and pigs' ears. I tutored small children who were also in limbo, staying in Beijing before being shipped off to Harrow School, speaking only what English I taught them. I wrote a bad novel about twenty-somethings escaping real life and starting again. I developed an affinity with panic and loss, walking for miles through the snow around the city, trying to physically exhaust myself. Every night my body would fizz into life, adrenalin surging through me, my mind sprinting to keep up. It seemed the beast was self-perpetuating. Each insomniac night piled one on the next, the cumulative unhinging jitterising effect making sleep the next night less and less possible. A white arrow of unbroken moon cycles, no breaks to recalibrate, recuperate, rejuvenate.

I feared I was becoming Esther Greenwood in *The Bell Jar*:

'I saw the days of the year stretching ahead like a series of bright, white boxes, and separating one box from another was sleep, like a black shade. Only for me, the long perspective of shades that set off one box from the next day had suddenly snapped up, and I could see day after day after day glaring ahead of me like a white, broad, infinitely desolate avenue.'*

I was an interdimensional being, exempt from the normal rhythms of humans. You might think that the upside of this is that it leads to some sort of unearthly wisdom. You would be wrong.

Far from the dreamlike state upon first waking where your imagination can fly into real life – the fertile marshland

* Sylvia Plath, *The Bell Jar*, 1966: p.135

where anything is possible and you can understand the multiverse – rolling sleeplessness diminishes creativity. It is impossible to make decisions, your flayed emotions are too raw, and the energy and optimism required to tell a story are replaced with self-doubt and despair. At no point did I fall in love with insomnia or give it credit for a single word written, as the Romanian writer E.M. Cioran seems to have done. A philosopher and (later regretful) supporter of the fascist Iron Guard in the 1930s, he wrote in *On the Heights of Despair*:

'Just as ecstasy purifies you of the particular and the contingent, leaving nothing except light and darkness, so insomnia kills off the multiplicity and diversity of the world, leaving you prey to your private obsessions. What strangely enchanted tunes gush forth during those sleepless nights!'*

Looking back on my strangely enchanted tunes, I can safely say they should have been stuffed, immediately, back in. 'What rich or strange idea was ever the work of a sleeper?' Cioran scoffed in *A Short History of Decay*†. I'd like to declare my interest in the sleeping camp for novel production – one foot in the real world must surely help.

In the end I presented my wraithlike self to a Beijing pharmacy and was sent away with zopiclone, a prescription-only sleeping pill in the UK. It allowed me to sleep for four hours at a time at the expense of a metal mouth, the taste

---

* E.M. Cioran, *On the Heights of Despair*, 1975: p.83
† E.M. Cioran, *A Short History of Decay*, 1992: p.147

of munching on nuts and bolts. A small price to pay. It was a far cry from my Chinese travels in 2000, my insomniac proclivities only marked by a short burst of narcolepsy and a sleepwalking episode that saw me jogging naked down a hotel corridor. At least I was asleep. In fact, on this trip I slept like Rip Van Winkle, even in a shack full of spiders the size of plates, trekking on the Burmese border.

When good sleep, assisted, finally returned to me at the age of thirty-five in Japan, I was staying in the rural district of Yomitan, Okinawa, researching a new novel. There was a savage sea to the front of my room and three great womb-shaped tombs at its back. It was the kind of place where I should, traditionally, not have slept at all, given the terrifying Japanese folklore I'd been looking into, given the coming typhoon. Below my window was an eerie green glow from the night fishermen. I tied my doors shut with a pair of tights, just in case the sleeping me decided to go for a wander.

Sleep began to be a problem for me at the age of fifteen. I had a lot of nightmares as a child – the intruder circling the house, the wolf outside the school, the old soldier who is really the devil. I was what people referred to without too much concern as 'a worrier'. In particular, I used to fret about bad things happening to those I loved, something I was able to soothe by telling myself that this was just my overactive imagination running wild. At fifteen, I experienced the will-she-won't-she die horror of cancerous decline. And then the all too real black grief, for the first time, as I mourned my adored, magical and too-young grandmother. I realised that bad things will happen to those I love. Imagination has nothing to do with it.

It was at this time that my little sister, aged eleven, stopped sleeping entirely. The school sent her, weirdly enough, to see a homeopath. She was given three different kinds of sugar pill to take in a precisely ordered and elaborate ritual. My sister never had problems sleeping ever again. I wish they'd tried that trick on me. My mother, by contrast, has struggled with insomnia ever since she had us.

There's good reason why the CIA uses sleep deprivation to torture its detainees. It can really fuck you up. One of the images that haunted me at night was from A.N. Wilson's *Stray*, the story of a cat who takes to the road and meets with the worst that humanity has to offer, spending a short, horrific stint in a laboratory. Until he escapes he has been unable to tell why the cat in the cage next to him cries out night and day, 'I cannot close my eyes! I cannot close my eyes.'* The scientists, it transpires, have cut off his eyelids and tied him to a treadmill, an experiment in sleeplessness.

Fernando Pessoa's erratic, disjointed and brilliant *The Book of Disquiet* mimics the state of the insomniac brain, capturing the vulnerability of the undefended mind at night. He, or Bernard Soares, Pessoa's, 'semi-heteronym who... always appears when I'm sleepy,'† speaks with a kind of venomous beauty of the 'catalogue of monsters' that come to those who cannot sleep:

---

* A.N. Wilson, *Stray*, 1992: p.125
† Fernando Pessoa, *The Selected Prose*, 2001: p.280

'They are the larvae of decline and waste, shadows filling the valley, the last vestiges of fate. Sometimes they are worms, repellent to the very soul that cossets and nourishes them; sometimes they are ghosts sinisterly haunting nothing at all; sometimes they emerge like cobras from the bizarre grottoes of lost emotions.'*

The feeling of aloneness in space and time is almost boundless. And then, of course, there's the gaping stupidity of the morning. The jangling overstretched unrested nervous system. The dread; the basic inability to function; the clumsiness. It won't stop, will it, until you're dead.

It's one of those things that's quite hard, I think, to explain to those who can sleep. It is a fundamental animal thing to do. The idea that you yourself are responsible is pervasive; if you could just get out of your own way. Lavender oil, mindfulness, a bedtime ritual. In the same way that some people think they understand clinical depression because they've felt down for a time and managed to snap out of it, so people who've had a bad night or two, experienced jet lag or stayed up all night partying think the deleterious effects they feel must be the same, just scaled down. But the complete unravelling of body and soul and the identity crisis that real insomnia entails exists in a different dimension.

GPs are wary of the unslept. In we stagger, glassy-eyed, primed to con them out of their limited quota of sleeping pills. I know, I know: they're addictive, they're bad for you, they're not a long-term solution. I tried other things. I

---

* Fernando Pessoa, *The Book of Disquiet*, 2010: p.37

attended a Sleep Clinic for eight weeks, the duration of which I spent madly awake: a restrictive 'sleep diet' had been imposed upon me, already starving. The rules of the diet meant that I was not allowed in my bedroom, still less bed, before midnight or after six in the morning. These were lenient terms I negotiated; it should have been worse. I'm not brilliant with rules and routines in general and these, at a time when I was on the floor, desperately sleepless, simply added anxiety.

I took a course in Autogenic Training instead, which is rather like a cult in that it has a number of trained initiates who may only pass on the wisdom in a prescribed series of private tutorials. Someone told me that all pilots underwent Autogenic Training and it meant they could fall asleep anywhere, in any position. This is for me, I said, the person who failed to sleep even on a cushy business class flight for work with a full actual bed on board and much of the free bar inside me. I took AT pretty seriously, clearing fifteen minutes three times a day to practise the ritual, which in a nutshell involved informing different anatomical parts of me that they were heavy and warm. And indeed they may have been, but this did not, sadly, pave the way to sleep.

What else? The list is long. In my time I have guzzled tinctures of hops, valerian root, passiflora and chamomile. I have resisted the guzzling of coffee and wine. I have practised yoga and meditation, performed visualisations and diaphragmatic breathing and progressive muscle relaxation and undergone counselling and CBT. I have bought sleep masks and blackout blinds and sampled over thirty different kinds of earplug. I have taken magnesium and 5HTP and melatonin, and a wide range of sedatives including one that rendered my husband insensible for two days but had no discernible effect whatsoever on me. Another gave me aural hallucinations in lieu of sleep. I have had the hypervigilant part of my psyche directly addressed and taken to task by a hypnotherapist and my dreams pulled apart by a Jungian analyst. Reader, I have lain in a gong bath.

The Sleep Clinic made it clear that every excessively wakeful person has this kind of list. The trick, they say, is to ditch all the aids and embrace insomnia, thereby short-circuiting the dependence on external crutches and the worry about not sleeping that perpetuates the cycle. Which would have been fine, if it had led to sleep.

Finally, I tried having a baby. I should make it clear that I got knocked up for better reasons than attempting to solve my insomnia. Nevertheless, I did have in the back of my mind the words of a GP from my youth, who said sagely that 'all these things' tend to sort themselves out when women get pregnant. A man, obviously. Anyway, it turned out to be true. For three months I could barely move or do anything other than sleep or throw up. I loved the sleeping part. Unfortunately, this was rapidly replaced with a kind of canine super hearing. I would wake – as if electrocuted – at the slightest rustle, no doubt nature's way of preparing me for the mandatory broken sleep of new motherhood. Thanks a bunch, nature.

Needless to say, my already fractured sleep did not cope well with the addition of night feeds and cripplingly early mornings. Soon I was back to the Beijing days of not sleeping at all, but also now having to be responsible for a whole new life. The latter in itself is pretty anxiety inducing, I found, but add in wobbly hormones and revolving sleeplessness and it feels nothing short of a catastrophe waiting to happen. I was like Voldemort, living a kind of twilight half-life, feeding from the energy of others – surviving, and little more.

Funnily enough, it was a trip to Thailand that saved me. I knew that here I would be able to buy Valium over the counter or something that might break the cycle and guarantee sleep. To my horror, a new law had just been passed and this was no longer an option. The pharmacist was able to give me something, though, something I'd never heard of. I figured that if it had survived the law it was probably akin to the Nytols of the UK and resigned myself to simply never sleeping.

But I did sleep and what is more, I started to feel better by day, too – a natural consequence of sleep, obviously, and also of being in Thailand, but perhaps more than these. When I came home to London, I could feel life in all its possibilities opening up once more. Imagine what you can do with a bank of sleep behind you. It is nothing short of transformative.

I went to my local GP and he laughed in my face. We don't do that here, he said. So I began the search for a new doctor and found one, at long last, who was open-minded and sympathetic to the plight of the unslept. He examined my dodgy Thai pills – trazodone, it turns out, an old-fashioned, atypical antidepressant that has been used at low doses, off-label, as a soporific. Different things work for different people, he said. Clearly these work for you. I've been sleeping better ever since.

I recently read an article that claims insomniacs can relax: the disorder is not the killer we all fear it must be in those dark wakeful hours. I disagree. It's certainly not much of a life when you stop sleeping. It's an issue that deserves to be taken more seriously and investigated with greater care. Doctors could (couldn't they?) be more open to trying different solutions and acknowledge that there are some things a milky drink ain't going to fix. There's a lot of media buzz about the risks of blue light emitted by our many devices, and about what is sacrificed by and for our twenty-four-hour culture. Increasing numbers of zombified problem sleepers are reported alongside the bizarre habits of willfully sleep-deprived Silicon Valley billionaires. We are unwitting initiates of that same cult of productivity that undermines the values inherent in technology itself: to save time and energy, and free up life for the things that really matter.

The phenomenon of cultural lag means we have little idea what the consequences of the tech revolution will be for humanity. I am not hugely optimistic that it will lead to better sleep for more people, but you never know. Maybe there's a robot for that, one that smashes you with a mallet if you move between midnight and dawn. It's probably worth bearing insomnia in mind now, though, just in case there's not.

STINGRAY

Rachel Genn

On her holidays, she dressed in fashions her oldest boy would soon detest her for: today – a sage-green slash neck, crepe too heavy for inland Spain, straight skirt, jade silk scarf around her bun. The afternoon had slowly doped her three children, so that she needed barely to nudge them from the pool up the stairs and to their beds where they lay, eyes closed, lids quivering, which she took to mean that she could nip to the bar.

It was a couple of hours, that's all, time enough for a good nap and on returning the air through the crack of the open door told her they weren't asleep. The door opened further and her knees hit the tiles with no noise and at the same time her hand clamped over her mouth.

The towel had dried in the short time between lunch and siesta: it hung down into the room from the marble sill, trembling to the smudge of their feet as they swapped places in the limited space, shoulders framed high in the open window, three small backs black against the straw light of the alley outside. *Do it*, they were saying to the middle boy because even the baby knew the middle boy was most likely to. The mother stayed on her knees to inch back out into the corridor, leaning forward to catch the underside of the doorknob and softly pull it closed. A recent convert, she blessed herself for each of the floors between here and the ground. They must have heard the click because there were thuds, then the slapping of their little soles in retreat on the tiles.

When she opened the door again she held her head high, as if it was the first time.

Back home, she's helping deliver from the abattoir to the shop; grudgingly letting go of the possibilities she felt were hers in Spain, but on occasion she still entertains how things could have turned out differently.

When she has a mind to, she uses the alternative endings she has in store to seduce whichever child is beside her. Knowing that even a paper cut-out for a toddler reveals her complex reasons, she adds a flower. How many *if onlys* she can avoid in a moment or two with the scissors! All she wants is time to listen out for whatever there is out there for her, but while she is listening out, the oldest girl with the dimples puts her fists in the fire, grasping for the cut-out with a flower.

Now she's a few streets from home and seeing smoke, she speeds up. With her fag in hand on the wheel and with one eye on the smoke, she cannot be sure it is from a house, let alone her house and she vows there will be no big surprises today by pressing out her cigarette in the ashtray. It springs back out like the others don't want it there.

The mother sees it is the new baby who is being hung out of the window.

Even in her brand new receptive form, this dangling baby can't possibly sense her Mummy pause at the bottom of the road before the weight of her indenture presses her foot to the accelerator again. Anyway, should a woman be chided for dawdling when she only suspects her house on fire from a street or two away? Anyway, nothing of what she saw on that journey up the road was going to make her, the stubborn little gypsy, increase her speed. But because both hearts have missed a beat at the very same time, and since regret is all about what we are lacking, an unwanted lesson about love has been learned.

When they fight, her loving husband who cannot drive hides her keys.

She fights in earnest but he is only performing, so in love is he.

There are no hiding places she cannot discover: she always finds them and then without a backward glance she abandons him and goes to her sister's house. If you had no choice you can't regret it, stop crying. Her sister had encouraged her to get rid of a fourth child because they had just got on their feet and started going abroad with them.

STINGRAY

Luckily, when driving her car she is still irresistible. The baby's woollen body, sturdy as a ham, appears whenever the wind clears the smoke. She approaches a turning circle beside which her house stands and sees that the baby is being held under the armpits – there are the straight arms belonging to the baby's oldest brother. The sight doesn't deter the mother from switching off the engine to slip silently down the last ten yards of the incline of the drive, the wave a stingray makes. What matters to her is the curve and dip together: the way pleasures sweep down through her head, entering at eye level, halving her brain; rippling her with the inevitability of coming to rest.

The stingray halts, plays dead.

Petite she may be but she reaches the landing in three ragged strides and drags the baby out of the brother's hands in through the bedroom window and onto the floor. One child shouts through the smoke. It's in the wardrobe! A bowl of water from under the spout of the spin dryer gets flung inside with one hand and there's a hiss of relief.

When the brothers talk about this in adulthood, they emphasise the baby's good nature throughout, but the eldest wants to crush his mother for the rendition she gave to his aunties. *He was holding her out like this* – she does a tottering impression that he curses as being nothing like him but it doesn't put her off – *like she was breakfast in bed he was bringing me.*

What in God's name did you take matches into a wardrobe for when she's three month old? Are you thick or crackers or what?

At thirteen, the big one is sure he's long since outwitted her so he doesn't bother replying. They share the same spirit: a tongue of fire split in two. Neither could see the similarities unless the other one wasn't there.

We didn't want her to breathe in the smoke.

So don't set fire to the wardrobe

She slaps the big one across the face before considering it the wrong thing to do.

Him I can forgive.

She wraps the middle boy's head in the crook of her elbow.

We didn't want anybody to see us.

In a matter of years, the baby who was saved that day had formed a habit of eating matches. Pica was suggested by a livestock merchant but the mother knew it was because of the fire and discounted Pica, even though she was well aware that to be drawn back to doing something you do not have to like it. By the time she was five, there was already a routine to this compulsion that was obscured from the mother. In the wardrobe, the child would soften the matchbox striking strip by repeatedly licking it. Then she'd soak the fat pink heads of the matches in a well of spit under her tongue, but she was so impatient to rid the matchsticks of their little sulphur helmets that she'd grind them between her back teeth too early and set a fire in her mouth. Eyes wide and mouth closed, she could absorb the pain and her lips closed to deny the wounds and no smoke emerged though there was a smell. If matches she liked were not available, she would leave the wardrobe to seek cigarette ash.

The mother had watched her pick up the square dish of the mosaic ashtray and lick the lines of the grout. After this, the mother had tried ash for herself and was upset at its dull, expected taste.

With the wardrobe closed behind her, she could breathe easily in the black space though it was never clear whether in here a person was trapped or hiding. It was a nest of sorts; her nest, rammed with her brothers' good jumpers worn to work, stiff with industrial paint, and walls that were lined with the corrugated pages of porn mags. Her cheeks brushed sheepskins that no one wanted but that were too dear to sling; further in the corners, she found half a dozen enamel ski badges by touch that she couldn't tell were green and white with a blazon of yellow: alpine. The child listened deep into the space and she took its commotion to mean something. What she sensed made her ready. A build-up made her make her mark on the walls. Her first efforts with the pin from a badge weren't enough to make the impression she'd imagined she would. With a pin, she struggled to carve a simple *m* of knees into the charred wooded walls, and she'd imagined those knees folded under her muse easily, perhaps to the left, a counterweight to the upsweep of her arm. Enjoyment came from involving herself in the risk of looking one way while moving in the other. When this child has her own daughters, whenever she kisses them a rude urge to embody them again will envelop her. In sittings, the woman on the wall grew, and perhaps in a way that limbs form in the womb, beckoned from who knows where, the energy of the figure was quietly drawn out of the saved child. In the dark she ignored the sense that concentrating wasn't considered appropriate for a girl and that what little girls should be like was also inappropriate for little girls to bother with, so she pressed herself into a silky pocket between the two, softening so as to be able to breathe and continue. This did not diminish her wants. And the wants tried to overcome an essence that had no form but that she protected, which later would solidify into her childhood as something stony and porous, a heavy lickable weight that could suck you back.

When she found a penknife, there was joy.

The first bold scores created a wrist: the figure had open wrists, no hands, because the child had no understanding of what she was doing, only that she must do it and this levitation needed her to ignore rules. The intention of the figure's arm was understood after it appeared to be in supplication, or was she nonchalant? The child may have been blessing the figure with that which she had never known and blending the curve and the dip into gesture, she could become what was promised behind that curved line, and in turn could withstand what was demanded of her later. She became able to stay very still in the face of what could be misunderstood about a simple line and looked again at the brittle magazines suffering the puzzlement over what was natural. Later she wondered if she had disabled the woman in the wardrobe to liken her to herself, for if she were whole, functional, she wouldn't stay in there, remains in the scrapings of someone else's blackness. The smell of the magazines whenever she opened the door made her imagine walking the plank. The way the stingray moves can make it difficult to tell its direction.

Minutes before they were expected to, both brothers say they won't carry her coffin, but it's too tiring for anyone to remember this for long and it's already boring, Oh God it's been said hasn't it that it's foolish to look for answers now, cruel – what kind of idiot believes in smoke signals? During the house clearance, two Albanian men turned up with a van and laughed at the wardrobe once they'd brought it out onto the drive and the sisters tried to laugh along because they knew it had always been a laughable piece of shit. Very soon the men left empty-handed and the sisters, one more injured than the other, had a bonfire made of wardrobe on their mother's back garden where not one joke was made or word spoken, and stared themselves into the grey eternity of embers. Who cared now whether the lick of the fire had mimicked the curl carved in the wood?

'Woah. Post-natal depression with all *thirty-four* litters?'

HOW TO WRITE ABOUT THINGS YOU CAN'T THINK ABOUT

Alex Pheby

So, let's say that something bad has happened. It's up to you what it is, but it's so bad that you, now, later, can't think about it. You won't think about it.

You don't have to think about it. It's the kind of thing that makes you want to kill and/or be dead. Don't be so dramatic.

It's bad.

So how do you write about it?

You don't.

Instead, put down a blank piece of paper and, while you distract yourself with something – it's up to you what it is – get to work. Work isn't pleasure, but it isn't pain either, not all the time, and the blank page fills up with words. What are they? It's up to you.

But is it? If you type and you've distracted yourself and you're not thinking about the thing that you can't/don't/ won't think about and you're working, then who is to say what it is that you're writing?

It's up to you.

So, the next day, you don't read what you did yesterday, but you get to work because work isn't pain. It's not pleasure, but the sound of keys clacking and pen/paper isn't thinking. If you catch yourself thinking, distract yourself. Look at the window – the curtains are closed – keep writing and the words will fill up the white space.

White space is a lot like the things you can't think about, a lot like the curtain pulled across the window that you don't want to pull aside – it's up to you: distract yourself with a sip of drink (what type? It's not important).

A full page of words that aren't to do with the thing that you can't deal with, that's the opposite of it, right? It must be to do with something else, so fill the page.

Once it's full it's one more layer between you and it, whatever it is – it's up to you.

The next day and the next day and the next day: now there's page after page after page of the stuff – can you see it? It's like...

...take a pencil, 6B, charcoal, black crayon, and while you're looking out of the curtained window, distracting yourself with an early drink, just rub across the page. Whatever's underneath comes through.

Don't look at it.

When kids draw they press too hard – don't press so hard, you'll ruin that table. So, without you looking, their pictures – younger than they are now, nothing like what they would draw now – are all there in negative space. All you have to do is a brass rubbing.

Have you ever been to a graveyard and, because you can't read the faded gravestone inscription, you put the thin tracing paper – not tracing paper because it would tear – not wax paper because it's too thick? Aren't crayons made of wax? It's up to you, but when you've finished you can read the words, the numbers, the dedication that was faded before, unrecognisable.

Negative space leaves a pattern in a block of static.

Turn the radio on, tune it out, turn the radio onto something with no content but some rhythm, and let your hands follow the beat. Look at them as they write. Don't look at the screen. Don't look at the page. Don't score your skin with a needle.

Keep doing it. Distract yourself. Look out of the closed window.

Next day do it again.

Next day do it again.

Some things just make you want to give up, but give up what? There's nothing to give up, because you aren't thinking about it. You aren't dealing with it.

It's not up to you, though; it deals with itself. It wants to be dealt with.

Ignore it. It isn't a thing – you are. Just be and do and act and work. What at? It's up to you.

So, it comes to the anniversary – what anniversary? There can't be an anniversary for things you can't think about. You don't want an anniversary. There won't be an anniversary. What's this obsession with the passage of time, anyway?

Retire to your room. Look up at the ceiling; tune the radio out. On the ceiling, in your thoughts, write all the things that aren't the thing that you can't think about.

The next day do the same.

Retreat inside. In there, where there's nothing except the loud static of an untuned radio, in *there*, get to work.

No. What is it that you're afraid of?

Whatever it is, it's terrible.

Write about something else – write about someone not you, doing things you don't do, to whom things have happened that you *can* think about. Think now; turn the radio off. Find this pleasurable since it isn't work and it isn't pain.

You enjoy daydreaming – you always have, which is why you like to write – and a person is doing whatever it is you want them to do, in the absence of the thing you can't think about. Onto this surface-static will come the outline, in negative, of the negative space of the drawings of your children that they have long grown out of. Their homework will come – quadratic equations pressed hard into the wood with the energy of someone who would rather be doing something else. These pictures will be visible under what you've written about the person you like to write about, over what they do, in absence.

Put it away. Try again.

Have you even been into the woods? The woods are full of all sorts of things: fungi, bicycle wheels, fallen branches, toads. Try not to cry, because... what are you crying about? You can't cry about things you can't think about.

Remember the things you've been writing? Go back to them. Without looking too closely, see if you can see a pattern. It's up to you, but don't worry – it's not that. The pattern is something else. It's bits of all sorts of things, but don't think too hard about it. It's up to you, and you won't/can't/don't make yourself think about it, so there's nothing to be scared of, but see what you recognise.

If you look down into the leaf dirt, the humus, and cross your eyes, you'll see something incongruous in the pattern. Incongruous things make you laugh. Don't laugh – laughing is just a prelude to tears – they open the door. Incongruous things can be scary – don't be scared, fear is a prelude to anger and anger is a prelude to tears. Instead, think of another incongruous thing, quietly, calmly, thoughtfully. It is up to you, but it's okay to think of incongruous things because incongruity and the thing you can't think about can't be the same thing, since that thing is very much at the centre of everything and incongruous things are off to the side.

Think of things that are off to the side.

Think of things that are just off to the side.

Stop thinking! – it's too close – take out the paper and pencil and write with a 4H those things that are off to the side enough so that they aren't just off to the side. Write about that person to whom the things you can think about have happened. Write the patterns of the things you see in the negative space.

The next day, do it again.

Tune in the radio.

And the next day. And the next day.

Every writer must edit their work, line by line, so on the next day look at what you've done.

HOW TO WRITE ABOUT THINGS YOU CAN'T THINK ABOUT

It's too dark.

Open the curtains, then, but only a little.

Return to the beginning and try again.

ENDURANCE: NARCOPOETICS (UNFINISHED)

Azad Ashim Sharma

'Sometimes it would be nice, I think – it would be a relief – to be so certain. To be so sure, to have such sharp edges. To know where one began and ended.'
– Katherine Angel

Between March 2018 and March 2019, I took a vow of sobriety to recover from drug addiction and alcoholism. Prior to that, I was a daily drinker and user of cocaine. I was never present, always skint, and beneath it all, in extreme emotional distress.

That distress was diagnosed by Dr Az H– at the Priory Hospital, Roehampton, as depression and anxiety. The cause of this co-morbid diagnosis was, in and of itself, something of a mystery. On the one hand, it could have been something I was dealing with, had been dealing with, all my life up to that moment when these two terms entered my lexicon. On the other, and this was Dr Az's suspicion, my status as a 'primary carer' for my severely autistic and bipolar brother Gyan had put me under duress, a duress I couldn't deal with alone or without some kind of exterior intervention. Dr Az noted that I used the words 'compressed', 'contained', 'restricted', and 'out of sync' many times during our one-to-one psychotherapy sessions. What Dr Az said was a mystery, or was always going to be mysterious, was whether the addiction had come first or whether the depression-anxiety came first. It was a matter of precession, before-ness, anticipation. Unlike the chicken or the egg scenario, it wasn't about what produced what but, rather, what was masking what.

Unlike my tired old GP, Dr Az got me on the right medication quite quickly, Venlafaxine 150mg extended release once daily. A drug that worked on both serotonin and norepinephrine: the first a happy transmitter pathway and the other one for energy. I was vapid; disoriented; prone to fits of extreme prodigious benders lasting up to seventy-two hours which left me physically, emotionally, financially crippled.

The drug really helped. I stopped crying myself to sleep around June 2018, ninety days into sobriety.

What I never thought was that the process of becoming an addict was so linked to feeling 'out of sync'; as if I couldn't seize or control my own experience of time.

Endurance: my capacity to endure drug use, to put my body through lines that, when totalled up, would go on for miles and miles. Often, when high off my face, I would go out for a cigarette and end up smoking two or three in a row. I imagined addiction as this never-ending cigarette. A cigarette you couldn't stop smoking. It would never end. Until, that is, you put it out. That 'duress', so perceptively thrown my way by Dr Az, shares etymology and meaning with endurance is of importance to me as I reflect on these twin processes of addiction and of recovery.

Addiction as endurance, then, impacts the very conception of time; a time that is lived without movement. I was suspended in time, buoyant, jubilant, quickly floating with anhedonia, vomit, blood. It's that kind of time that poet and philosopher Denise Riley wrote about when describing the death of her son in *Time Lies, "ithout its Flow*: 'You live inside a great circle with no rim'.* I was living a line of cocaine without end; a morning after that had no hope of reaching midday; enduring time in the duress of a continuous present; making the same choices, hoping for a different outcome.

***

In medias relapse means I am relapsing, which is a strange word that captures the immobilising thrill dovetailing with the shame and lack of self-care or even carelessness about the future.

Maybe even the present?

---

* Denise Riley, *Time Lived, Without its Flow* (London: Capsule Editions, 2012), p.10.

ENDURANCE: NARCOPOETICS (UNFINISHED)

Surely if I don't get away with this, the life I built for myself in the previous year, a year of sobriety/abstinence/all of that Go(o)d stuff, surely all of that is going up my nose? These thoughts pass before my eyes in neon cuneiform on the bedsheets. It's raining outside. The birds are chirping and the light is coming in. I'm blacking out and close to an overdose. I am in my grandmother's room. She died here in 2013 of too much life, old age and myocarditis. I'm on the edge here now, arrhythmia and vasoconstrictive palpitating. But the bugle/coke isn't working anymore. I'm conscious that, as that squatter in my head, Sisyphus, pushes more of the rocks up my nose, all I get is a feeling of wanting more.

A study about dopamine and drugs at the University of Michigan by Kent Berridge and Terry Robinson discovered that drugs are addictive primarily because the huge increase of dopamine produced by them creates 'an artificial inflated intensity' which drives the phenomenon of craving. They label this 'incentive salience', a theory of addiction where the brain begins to react to overindulgence by deconstructing desire so that the addict – me – is left wanting to do more without having the same results.* It's territory for brain damage; my brain is already broken. I'm re/collecting this experience into a piece of art that doesn't know what it wants from the process of its own re/creation.

Each line has the capacity to become 'a great experiential context', like Gregor Hens re-experiencing his first cigarette.†

---

* Maia Szalavitz, *Unbroken Brain* (New York: Picador, 2016), pp. 112–116.
† Gregor Hens, *Nicotine*, trans. Jen Calleja (London: Fitzcarraldo Editions, 2017), p.66.

For Hens, reminiscing, remembering, recollecting, this first cigarette 'offered [him] an experience that was narratable for the very first time'.* That's nice and everything, it sounds romantic, very *creatively non-fictional* but the sad reality is, for alcoholics and addicts, life passes in a blur. It's not until you approach the hard rock at the bottom that you jolt back into the world and give yourself and your behaviour the context you need for it to become narratable. That's the impetus behind the surrender; and I smash another line out.

***

I reached twelve months sober, attended regular 12-step meetings at Cocaine Anonymous, did other therapies, drank water and occasionally ginger beer (non-alcoholic), but there was a part of me that remained suspended in that moment just before sobriety, a part of me that maintained the addiction at a subconscious level, that waited like a subtle foe who sneaks up from behind to trip me over.

***

But the momentum of that fall is arrested; it suspends and delays the impact of the ground, the moment of grounding itself curtailed as the endurance that is addiction, which is recalled, repeated, relapsed into. This sense of time as without flow, is what Lisa Baraitser calls 'enduring time'.†
It is a sense of living in a point of viscosity, stillness, unbecoming, formlessness, present-tense-ness: 'this caesura

* Ibid., p.67.
† Lisa Baraitser, *Enduring Time* (London: Bloomsbury, 2017), p.20.

has duration. We differentially live it, are living in it, enduring it.'* Addiction has duration and it is also a caesura in the individual's experience of temporal duration.

Relapse is the embrace or re-embrace of endurance, it is a temporal experience without flow, with an excruciating duration. There is nothing to suggest that a relapse is a single episode; there is nothing to prevent it becoming a way of life; nothing to prevent the relapse turning into full-blown off your fucking face 24/7 active addiction. Why do addicts use a poison that they deep down know will fuck them up, like driving off a cliff? I don't have an answer, neither does the *Big Book of Alcoholics Anonymous.*

In Jeet Thayil's satirical rendering of the Bombay poets and artists of the 1950s, *The Book of Chocolate Saints*, his narrator, Dismas Bambai – a heroin addict and journalist/poet – provides a telling answer: '[It's] [a] way of killing time. Time is stretched or compressed depending on how much you're holding and how much you've done. You're never bored, not until you quit, then all the time you killed comes back.'† All that dead time rose in me like a zombified corpse of the person I used to know, the dead weight of that time just before sobriety, the dead labour of addiction.

In March 2019, what shouldn't have been inevitable, inevitably happened: I relapsed. But it wasn't a relapse in the sense of a singular event that derails recovery temporarily.

---

* Ibid., p.7.
† Jeet Thayil, *The Book of Chocolate Saints* (London: Faber and Faber, 2018) p.109.

This relapse is still ongoing.

It has prompted in me a querying into the experience of enduring addiction, the endurance of addicts, temporal as well as physiological, which I think only the letter on the page, the stillness of words against a great white indistinction, that may provide a way out for me.

I am writing to recover; I am writing to stay alive.

And in that I am not alone.

The 12-step programme is one that teaches the addict humility, self-knowledge, the ability and capacity to narrate their story and their recovery from the vantage point of a functioning member of society. I was a member of society, I was sober, I was happy to tell everyone what I was recovering from.

And then I wasn't.

By January 2019, the experience of enduring recovery became too much for me. Recovery contained for me, and still does even as a possibility now, a sense of what Sianne Ngai calls 'stuplimity': a sense of 'overwhelming excitement and stultifying boredom emanating from the same object'.* That object is, more accurately, an experience of time. I found recovery-time stuplimitous, should such a word begin to signify. I lacked perspective on what I'd managed to achieve. A year had passed and I was in the best shape of my life, but I was rapidly falling out of shape, lapsing,

---

* Quoted in Baraitser, *Enduring Time*, p.17.

blurring, enduring my own ingratitude, walking a long road into lines of discontent, restless lines of irritability. Although I was back at university, attempting to gain an MA in Creative-Critical Writing at Birkbeck, to compensate for not crossing the finishing line in 2017 when I was doing an MA in Critical Theory at the University of Sussex; although I had started a publishing company which was gaining recognition and respect amongst peers; although I was reading and publishing my poetry at a rate I'd never hitherto imagined nor achieved; although I was living instead of simply existing: none of that was enough.

I had yet to let go of the ravenous craving for more; more; more.

Where I used to greet the day with thoughts of affirmation and compassion, my mind started running on autopilot. I was meant to feel spiritually awakened, free, responsible, but all of this ended up compounding my already existing feelings of containment, restriction, out-of-sync with other peoples' time. I would walk into the rooms of 12-step meetings with an 'I'm doing sweet, mate' veneer, a smile that was so white it told the story of what would come next, a crook between the left corner of my lips and cheek, not quite sinister, but sick.

***

In medias relapse. What is different this time is that I am doing incredibly huge amounts of charlie/coke to try and get at something. I'm trying to get high, to escape the ennui of Greater London, to process the December 2019 election results.

I can pull excuses like white rabbits out my arse.

I can do this shit blind.

'Incentive salience' means wanting something but not liking it. It means desire escalates but pleasure doesn't. My lip quivers. The weird colours that penetrate me when I close my eyes form the faces of my mother and partner and their tears, when I eventually get honest with them.

I'll do it tomorrow.

They will berate me or be disappointed and I'll know I shouldn't be in this state but all I think about is the next line, the next sip of water, because I've heard you process the racket/coke through your kidneys and so if you want to lessen chances of death you should flush it out as soon as you put it in.

Incentive salience *in medias relapse* is a pathological overlearning of the process of insufflation. When will I put the straw down and stop inhaling? What kind of breathing is it?

There's a rattle in my chest.

Sisyphus has made it so far into my sinus that the rocks are trickling down my throat. I'm doing so much packet I'm post-nasal, poststructuralist, postcolonial, post-ideological but definitely not post/past cocaine. White noise, the sound of sniffing, the rumble of tolerance. I decide to crush up Valium into the snow on my bedside table and drink a bottle of camomile tincture and then a bottle of homeopathic drops that help with nausea and then I wait. I'm begging myself to sleep, wishing my heart would calm down and to be able to breathe through my nose again.

***

January–March 2019.

I ebbed and flowed around the streets of London, in and out of pubs progressing from lime sodas to 0% beers. The taste made me lust after the feeling I was denying myself. My first taste of a 0.5% beer turned me into a placebo pisshead. I imagined I was drunk, talking shit, shooting the breeze with other poets in the pub, forgetting to speak with an 'indoor voice'. And then the long lie-ins started up again, going to sleep exhausted and waking up as if my duvet was covered in weight plates with an alarm clock whinging at me like Shia LaBeouf quacking into camera one: just do it; just fucking do it.

I stopped attending 12-step meetings, stopped my gratitude lists, stopped doing the necessary work. I moved into the interval, unlearned the vow I took, un-spoke it, sucked the air back into my chest that made it sound like something real and necessary. Inertia as a state of mind. Unwillingness to care, staying with anticipation, and my subtle foe, myself, pulling at my ears, seeking my own destruction, unbecoming.

TRAUMA

On 13 March 2019 I was a year sober.

And then I wasn't.

I felt the click of a switch, a series of synapses blowing neural dust off themselves, as if a box had been ticked, as if suddenly I had decided or arrived at the decision that I was fixed, I was normal, I could enjoy the night, yes, the night, no longer keeping it in the day, just keeping it in the evening, like everyone else who wasn't an addict. I was about to experience life after sunset; I wanted to become the night; I was becoming the night. I hosted a poetry reading for my fledgling small press with unsure footing, leaning on the bar to ease myself into a 'normal' pint, none of that 0% or 0.5% shit, the normal stuff, for normal people, like me, being normal, doing normal things, leaning at the bar, drinking normally. And then another and another and another and another and another until I was spinning uncontrollably. Being drunk is feeling time move all around you but you, yourself, are still; a rock, an anchor; yes, I was grounded now, I felt my feet, felt them call my backside into a chair, felt my palms cradle my head, felt the warm embrace; and I endured; I persevered; and then the thought of getting cocaine was on me.

There must have been something else other than alcohol in the beer; there must be something else in alcohol other than alcohol. It was as if a seed had been swallowed with the first, sowed with the rest, and then it was germinating; flowering; quickening into an obsession. I felt liberated by this obsession, fixation, absolute seizure-by-cocaine-compulsion. I thought myself steadfast, strong, obstinate, stubborn, refusing to give up being myself, my true self, beneath all the water, a layer of stone, something concrete in me rising up through all the repression, suppression, digression, a huge slab of me, undying, unbecoming and then becoming true, regurgitating a desire, a drive, a monumental weight of discovery as if for the first time I was feeling this sensation to score drugs; I began sniffing in air, anticipation made me clam up, palms moistened, more light entered my peripherals, back straightened, I talked with more confidence, persuaded reluctant students (probably skint) to buy books, I sold other peoples' books with the same enthusiasm and passion I usually saved for the ones I published. I greeted everyone with a huge embrace, eagerly wanting their love and craving their attention.

The search for the subject of addiction is, contrary to Avital Ronell's assertion that 'Being-on-drugs' has 'everything to do with the bad conscience of our era', actually the *a priori* state of being-wanting-drugs.* Being-on-drugs always already implies the drop, the score, the exchange; it is a state of fractured interiority that requires the precession, the lapse into consumption of an illicit substance. Whilst Ronell is correct in underscoring that 'drugs are *libidinally invested*' what such investment necessitates as a precondition or proviso is the libidinal condition of want, need, desire pure and simple, a motivation to invest in the first instance.†

---

* Avital Ronell, *Crack Wars* (Chicago: University of Illinois Press, 2004), p.3.
† Ibid., p.25.

I was assured, cocksure, self-assured, quivering with a bristled, dangerous excitement on the shore between history and ontology. It was Nietzschean, this trembling, calling into question the very history of narcotics as he did in *The Gay Science*, wondering what links 'high-culture' with '*high*-culture', and I was asking people to consume-purchase-buy-sit-drink. I had spent so long living vicariously through them, this crowd of dear friends and associates, watching their breath turn to smatterings of ale-stained stupefaction, and now within myself I felt that surge into being, desire unchained, boundless and ready. This is precisely what Burroughs meant when he wrote about the 'algebra of need'; it is a strange equation of oneself with others through the substance, through the very decision to ingest a substance, as if filling oneself up with the substance gives one substance of an altogether different quality. Substance abuse qualifies the relationship between '*fractal interiorities*' or states of 'immanence' in which endurance is tested on the basis of its rooting out of connection.*

***

In medias relapse. It's not petrichor it's just the strange chemical sweat I'm exuding; it's not rain; it's just coke water on my forehead. I brush it away, I want to push the water out of my eyes and then they swell up and my nose is bleeding. The other varieties (shit the gear/coke is cut with) start doing labour. I have capacity again and my heart is returning to normal. I check the clock on my phone, it's 6 a.m. I started at 8 p.m. the evening before.

---
* Ibid., p.15.

ENDURANCE: NARCOPOETICS (UNFINISHED)

How has all this time elapsed? How did I end up lying here relapsing, sweating, moving lower and lower in search of dopaminergic wakefulness?

Sisyphus starts at the bottom again, slugging the rock up my nose, and I return to worse. The last thought I have before I fall asleep is: what if my gear is contaminated with coronavirus? And then a little white rock trickled out of my tear duct. I manage to scoop it off my cheek and rub it into my gums.

But I can't sleep. I want to know what is in this stuff; if the drugs stop working then there can't be enough drugs in the drugs.

What the fuck is going on?

I check my phone, licking the screen to see if there is any gear left on it. I type in 'what the fuck is going on with cocaine in the UK' to Google. This country is obsessed with white power/powder! In the last five years, cocaine use has doubled in the UK.* Purity is at a record high.† So all that bullshit about how cocaine is cut with rat poison, benzocaine, baby laxative, caffeine, amphetamine, lactose, or bloody magnesium oxide: all of that is a load of hot air.‡ Waste water analysis shows that 1/50 people use it every day in London.§

---

* Abby Young-Powell, 'Cocaine use doubles in Britain in five years...', *Independent* (May 2019).
† Ibid.
‡ Sharma, Unpublished (May 2020).
§ Young-Powell, *Independent* (May 2019).

In May 2019, King's College London and the University of Suffolk collaborated and found that 100 per cent of freshwater shrimp tested positive for traces of cocaine. Imagine that. Wired and absolutely fucking mad shrimp. At the University of Naples Federico II, they've looked into how cocaine traces are fucking with eels.* Yes, eels! The eels are high and under duress. Like the shrimp. Cocaine is in the water. They even make rehabs for eels now, giving them clean water for ten days to prevent muscle damage and lower their cortisol levels.† A rehab doesn't exist for shrimp.

I sit there fucked off my face and fucked off further at the ridiculousness of these statistics and facts. Who in their right fucking mind would contribute to this kind of bio- and eco-politics? I want to know right now what the statistic is for people who can peel a satsuma without the peel breaking, and so, coming off in one beautiful unified piece.

That's a statistic worth fighting for, I think as I lay out another line and inhale, feeling oddly comforted by the idea of the ghosts of eels and shrimps looking back at me on the black mirror.

***

In order to make my desire to score come to life in an actual, physical transaction, I had to overcome a troublesome and inconvenient obstacle: the public nature of my recovery.

---

* Frances Perraudin, 'Purity of cocaine in Europe at highest level in decade...', *Guardian* (June 2018).
† Ibid.

I had no doubt in my mind that everyone at the poetry reading knew of my condition, either because I had directly told them or because they had found out through friends-of-friends. It dawned on me that this was why so many askance looks had been directed at me leaning at the bar. I suddenly felt not-so-normal after all. I tried to reason with myself; I tried to steady myself. I was splitting myself apart, half of me stuck in the loop of obsessions and compulsions, the other enduring their procedure. The drunkenness lowered and I was less electric, clutching my chin, pulling at my beard for orientation and decision. No one would provide a link, no one in their right fucking mind, not here anyway, but do I really want to do this, of course I do I need to straighten up before I get home can't be staggering in the house; and I couldn't lie to myself I was drunk, proper drunk, I was concerned I was slurring so I silenced myself, communicating in gestures and head wiggles, descending into the fall, blowing in the wind, watching the weather as the sun set on my cheer. No; no. I needed an upper, I needed to rise up over the rut, reclaim my authority over myself, I needed to score as soon as possible.

Fortunately, I had some American poets in town. I wove a tale that they wanted some gear, no no not for me, I said on the phone to a woman I knew from *Tinder*, for fuck's sake the sign of desperation, no no not for me I am just trying to be a good host you know these Americans are so demanding and yes I know it's just like you know you're citizen ambassadors of the hegemony and here you are putting a recovering drug addict in harm's way and I know but I really need to stay in their good books you know it's just for the poetry connections. I am just trying to be the good host. Luckily this idiot didn't know too much about me and how much of a scheming con artist I could be when provided with the right motivation (cocaine), she provided the perfect code; the digits I quickly called and told the guy what I wanted and sent him the postcode of the pub. He offered me two grams for £100; I thought *quite reasonable* but I had to wait about thirty minutes.

I went outside, lit a cigarette, walking a little away from the pub, avoiding everyone who'd shown up for poetry. Then it came over me, the frustrating lack of immediate gratification (the primary psychosis of the internet age where everything is available at the click of a button or touch of a screen), the longing for the routine of getting into a really standard hatchback, a VW or a Toyota, sitting in the front seat with a stranger who shakes your hand to mask the drop, and in that moment of touch I pass the cash over.

Often no words are exchanged. I hated it when dealers would try to find out more about you. I wanted the gratifying anonymity of just collecting without talking.

The guy had slicked-back light brown hair, a face that looked like it had been chiselled from marble. He was classy and intimidating. I wondered if they sent him especially for me, to make me feel up-market, maybe I was up-market?, hosting poetry nights and drinking six-quid-pints in London.

I said thanks, leaving the car – I was right it was a Toyota Prius which I thought was clever as most people would think it was an Über – and lit up another cigarette. As I inhaled I felt the restlessness retrocede, quenched by the thrill of satiety.

***

In medias relapse: the term 'active addiction' is bad language; it does not perform the inactivity, the paralysing anhedonia. I'm alone in the duvet moistened with impurities and defects of character. It has been six months of continuous use, maybe not every day but at least thrice weekly; I am living a double life and as it unfurls I retreat back into my shell.

What is this alluring white substance? How insane is it that inhaling it into my deviant septum shrinks the world? All I want in this moment is to be here in bed, in darkness, in silence, going through the ritual of crushing up lumps into powder, using my bright orange Monzo bank card to cut the powder into lines and then using a straw (because you can contract Hepatitis from banknotes and ain't nobody got time for that fuckery) to hover strategically over the line and then become one with it in a breath's instance.

When you do cocaine you want to do more cocaine.

Incentive salience is the scientific way of labelling the reproduction of desire as it entangles with the illicit economy of white bricks.

It comes from the coca leaf which was reserved for Inca royalty and used by the Incas more widely as a medicine, to ward off fatigue, promote strength, says *The Independent* in 2006.*

I keep reading.

It was considered valuable like gold, it was considered a gift from the gods. That old Inca region, which extends across Peru, Bolivia and Colombia, still produces 75 per cent of the world's cocaine supply. They are doing the gods' work.

Shit gets weird when the conquistadors bring the leaves back to their homelands in Europe. Pope Leo XIII in the nineteenth century loved the stuff, gave it his gold medal seal of religious approval and was known to walk around carrying a hip flask of Vin Mariani (aka cocaine-wine). Loads of mugs through history loved the gear. Writers like Zola, Conan Doyle, Dumas, and royalty like Queen Vic, Shahs of Persia. It was once so easy to get you could just go to your local store and grab the gear.

Oh, the forgotten good days.

The lengths I have to go are extreme. Transferring money to a man I know as *Storm*, waiting for him to come and 'post me a letter' and then sneaking around the house so my poor mother doesn't see me at it. Coca-Cola once contained cocaine. I loved Coke as a kid, and now as a man-child I love the real stuff. Cocaine also becomes part of western medicine in the twentieth century due to the revolutionary

---

* Paul Vallely, 'Drug that spans the ages: The history of cocaine', *Independent* (March 2006).

process of isolating the cocaine alkaloid from the leaf (no one wants to be drinking cocaine fizz all day long, we want something less calorific, obviously). This process was pioneered by a German PhD student called Albert Niemann. So this is where the white powder and the injectable solution comes from. This sets in motion a whole load of contemporary experience, this one poor fella changed the fucking world with a chemistry set. Forget nuclear energy, this is the real revolution. Freud loved it and was raving about it in 1884 (if he could be a genius on it why can't I, that voice in my head starts, and I shut it up with another line). Then it becomes the trend amongst bohemians (me in the duvet). Fast forward to the late twentieth century and Pablo Escobar and all that stuff you can learn about from a Netflix binge. The world market for cocaine in 2006 was worth an estimated $400 billion. There are traces of it on 5 per cent of all UK banknotes.[*]

***

As I entered the pub I saw a friend of a friend, a gay-femme-guy called Jay and a couple of anarchists who lived in the abandoned church up the road from Borough station. I winked at Ray who was like me, an addict in denial, and we went to the toilet together and did a few bumps. I felt straightened, no longer drunk, pupils dilating and open to everything, an immense exteriority, confidence. Cole – an anarchist – and a Japanese art student who was living with the anarchists called Umi invited Ray and me back to the church to continue the night. So we left, saying our

[*] Ibid.

goodbyes, and after a quick pit stop to get more alcohol (Ray bought a bottle of vodka and I got some beers for the team) we were at the squat.

The squat had a distinct odour, musky, filigreed by mendicancy. It was welcoming. I do not remember much from this point. All the substances started to make the moment blur and I felt like the ground beneath me was made from sourdough. I endured conversation about the press, poetry, what I'd been doing, the Japanese art student went on a tirade about being a good person through art. I took that as a call to return home via cab. I just wanted them all to fuck off.

I called it on for two more grams before I left, timing it expertly and then I was in a silver Prius making my way south. To my home, to my room, my straws, my bank cards, my ritual.

***

March 2020. When I open my eyes it's 2 p.m. and life is happening to me.

'Have you been cheating?' Mum asks, hovering over me.

Sisyphus pushes mucus down my throat.

I've been caught. Thank fuck, it's over.

BIOGRAPHIES

Jenn Ashworth's first novel, *A Kind of Intimacy*, was published in 2009 and won a Betty Trask Award. On the publication of her second, *Cold Light* (Sceptre, 2011) she was featured on the BBC's *The Culture Show* as one of the UK's twelve best new writers. Her latest book is a memoir-in-essays, *Notes Made While Falling*. She lives in Lancashire and teaches Creative Writing at Lancaster University.

Marina Benjamin is a writer and editor who works in narrative non-fiction and memoir, producing books, essays and journalism. Her most recent books, *The Middlepause* (2016) and *Insomnia* (2018) have been published in the UK, US and Australia and translated into eight languages. She works as a senior editor at *Aeon Magazine*. In 2020 she edited *Garden Among Fires: A lockdown anthology* published by Dodo Ink.

Ian Boulton trained as an actor, then ended up playing the part of a community mobilisation consultant for over twenty-five years. This included significant spells living and working in Russia, Ukraine and Central Asia. A five-year project in the USA exploring how writing can help young students engage in community activism resulted in *Writing For A Change* (Jossey Bass 2006). All in all, Ian feels there has been far too much non-fiction in his life so now he tries to devote as much time as possible to made-up stuff.

Georgie Codd is the author of the fear-filled scuba diving memoir *We Swim To The Shark*, which was published in early 2020 and featured on BBC Radio 4 *Woman's Hour*. During the Covid-19 lockdown she founded the online 'antiviral' literary festival BookBound 2020, in aid of the mental health charities Mind (in the UK) and Changing Minds (in New Zealand). The festival archive remains accessible online for free. Watch and donate via www.bookbound2020.co.uk

Jude Cook lives in London and studied English literature at UCL after a career in music with his band Flamingoes. His first novel, *Byron Easy*, was published by Heinemann in 2013, and his second, *Jacob's Advice*, was published by Unbound in 2020. He has written for the *Guardian*, the *Spectator*, *Literary Review*, *New Statesman*, *TLS*, the *i-Paper*, *Review 31* and *3:AM Magazine*. His essays and short fiction have appeared in *The Stockholm Review*, *The Moth*, *The Tangerine*, *The Honest Ulsterman*, *The Mechanics' Institute Review*, the *Unthanks Anthology*, and *Structo*, amongst others. He is an editor for The Literary Consultancy, and teaches creative writing at the University of Westminster.

Yvonne Conza's writing has appeared in *Longreads*, *LARB*, *Electric Literature*, *Bomb Magazine*, *AGNI*, *The Millions*, *Catapult*, *Cosmonauts Avenue*, *The Rumpus*, *Joyland Magazine*, *Blue Mesa Review*, *The Adroit Journal* and elsewhere. She has been a finalist in many competitions, including the Barry Lopez Creative Nonfiction and the Raymond Carver Short Story awards.

Rhiannon Lucy Cosslett was born in Wales, has lived in France and Italy, and is now based in London. Her debut novel, *The Tyranny of Lost Things*, is an exploration of trauma and memory partly inspired by her own experience of post-traumatic stress disorder, and was published in 2018 by Sandstone Press. She is at work on her second, which is about the female gaze and is set on a Greek island, as well as various non-fiction projects. Before writing novels, she co-founded and authored the feminist blog and book

BIOGRAPHIES

The Vagenda, published by Vintage. She also writes and reviews for *The Guardian.*

Susanna Crossman is an award-winning Anglo-French fiction writer and essayist. Published internationally in print and online, she has recent work in *Neue Rundschau,* S. Fischer (translated into German) alongside John Berger and Anne Carson, *We'll Never Have Paris,* Repeater Books, *The Creative Review, 3:AM Journal, The Lonely Crowd, Litro* and more... Co-author of the French book *L'Hôpital Le Dessous des Cartes* (LEH), she regularly collaborates in international hybrid arts projects, currently the ecological fish cartoon *Arêtes.* Her debut novel *Dark Island* will be published in 2021. For more: @crossmansusanna
http://susannacrossman.squarespace.com.
Susanna Crossman is represented by Craig Literary, NY.

Thom Cuell is a senior editor at the literary journal *Minor Literature[s].* Their writing has appeared in anthologies including *We'll Never Have Paris* (Repeater Books) and *Manchester* (Dostoyevsky Wannabe). They live in Manchester.

Naomi Frisby is a writer, interviewer and educator. Her story 'The Time Is Now' was published in *The Book of Sheffield* (Comma Press); 'Role Play' was shortlisted for The White Review Short Story Prize, and 'The Bodies' was longlisted for the Manchester Fiction Prize. She is completing a PhD in Creative Writing at Sheffield Hallam University focusing on female freaks in circus novels.

Rachel Genn is a senior lecturer at Manchester Writing School/School of Digital Arts. Formerly a Neuroscientist, she has written two novels: *The Cure,* (2011) and *What You Could Have Won* (2020). She was Leverhulme Artist-in-Residence (2016) at University of Sheffield, creating *The National Facility For the Regulation of Regret* spanning installation art, VR, interactive and film (ASFF 2016) presented together at SXSW (2017). She has written for *Granta, 3:AM, MinorLits* and *The Real Story* and is currently working on immersive experiences exploring paranoia, a collection of non-fiction (*Blessed*) about fighting and addiction to regret and a collection on the neuroscience and poetry of intrinsic motivation (*Hurtling*).

Neil Griffiths is the author of three novels: *Betrayal in Naples*, winner of the Authors' Club First Novel Award 2005, *Saving Caravaggio*, shortlisted for the Costa Best Novel of the Year 2007, both published by Penguin, and in 2018, *As a God Might Be*, published by Dodo Ink. In 2017, he founded the Republic of Consciousness Prize for Small Presses. He is a director of Weatherglass Books. He lives in London.

Tomoé Hill lives in London and is a contributing editor at *Minor Literature[s]*. Some of her essays can be found at *3:AM Magazine*, *Numéro Cinq*, *Lapsus Lima*, and *Empty Mirror*. She also has pieces in the anthologies *We'll Never Have Paris* and *Azimuth*.

Juliet Jacques is a writer and filmmaker based in London. Her most recent book was *Trans: A Memoir* (Verso, 2015). Her short fiction, journalism, essays and criticism have appeared in *Frieze*, *Granta*, *Sight & Sound*, *London Review of Books* and many other publications. Her short films have screened in galleries and festivals worldwide.

Kirsty Logan's latest book is *Things We Say in the Dark*; she is the author of three short story collections, two novels, a flash fiction chapbook, a short memoir, and collaborative work including 'Lord Fox', a live show of spoken word, song and harp music, and *The Knife-Thrower's Wife*, an Angela Carter-inspired album. Her books have won the Lambda Literary Award, Polari Prize, Saboteur Award, Scott Prize and Gavin Wallace Fellowship. Her work has been optioned for TV, adapted for stage, recorded for radio and podcasts, exhibited in galleries and distributed from a vintage Wurlitzer cigarette machine.

BIOGRAPHIES

Rowena Macdonald has published two books: *Smoked Meat*, which was shortlisted for the 2012 Edge Hill Prize, and *The Threat Level Remains Severe*, which was shortlisted for the *Guardian*'s 2017 Not The Booker Prize. *Smoked Meat* is set in Montreal and *The Threat Level Remains Severe* is set in the House of Commons where Rowena has worked for the past twenty years. She was born on the Isle of Wight, grew up in the West Midlands and now lives in East London.

Anna Maconochie was born and raised in London, where she still lives. After several years in the film industry and the BBC she began writing short stories that touched on these settings as well as her home city. Her first stories appeared in the *Erotic Review* and then in several other print and online magazines, including the *Dublin Review* and the *Bitter Oleander*. She has also had a story in *Desire: 100 of Literature's Sexiest Stories*, compiled by Mariella Frostrup. Her first published short story collection is *Only the Visible Can Vanish*, with Cultured Llama Publishing.

Seraphina Madsen was born in San Rafael, California, and grew up on both the East and West Coasts of the United States. She taught English in France for four years and has lived in Germany, The Netherlands, and Sweden. She received an MA in Creative Writing from Kingston University, London. She resides in the UK. Her first novel *Dodge and Burn* (July 2016) launched a new independent UK publisher and received rave reviews.

Momina Masood is a Lecturer in the Department of English, Punjab University, Pakistan. She is a writer and her essays and creative nonfiction work has been published in several online and print magazines including *Minor Literature[s]*, *DAWN*, et al., and her academic work has been published and/or is forthcoming in *BioScope* and *Kohl*. She is currently researching Pakistani cult and exploitation cinemas with a focus on queer cinephilia and queer cult consumption, and will be beginning her PhD in Film and Media Studies at the University of Pittsburgh this fall. She tweets at @momina711

Paul McQuade is a writer and translator originally from Glasgow, Scotland. His work has been shortlisted for The White Review Prize and The Bridport Prize. He was the recipient of the Sceptre Prize for New Writing and the Austrian Cultural Forum Writing Prize. He is the author of *Hometown Tales: Glasgow*, with Kirsty Logan. His debut story collection, *Between Tongues*, is forthcoming from Cōnfingō.

James Miller is the author of the acclaimed novels *Lost Boys* (Little, Brown, 2008), *Sunshine State* (Little, Brown, 2010) and *UnAmerican Activities* (Dodo Ink, 2017) as well as numerous short stories. He is a founding member of the Extinction Rebellion group Writers Rebel. He has a PhD on American Literature and Civil Rights History and currently runs the MA and MFA in Creative Writing at Kingston University.

Sam Mills is the author of *The Quiddity of Will Self* (Corsair, 2012), which was described by *The Sunday Times* as an 'ingenious, energetic read' and *The Guardian* as 'so outrageous as to defy conventional review'. Her literary memoir about caring for her father, *The Fragments of My Father*, was recently published by 4th Estate; her next non-fiction title, *Chauvo-Feminsim*, will be published by the Indigo Press. She lives in London with her father and cat.

Alex Pheby's work concentrates on social exclusion and mental illness. He was shortlisted for the Wellcome Book Prize in 2016 and won the Republic of Consciousness Prize in 2019.

Monique Roffey is an award-winning Trinidadian-born British writer of novels, essays, a memoir and literary journalism. Her latest novel is *The Mermaid of Black Conch* (April 2020). Her novels have been translated into five languages and shortlisted for several major awards and, in 2013, *Archipelago* won the OCM BOCAS

BIOGRAPHIES

Award for Caribbean Literature. Her essays have appeared in *The New York Review of Books*, *Boundless* magazine, *The Independent*, *Wasafiri*, and *Caribbean Quarterly*. She is a founding member of XRWritersRebel, and an advocate for emerging writers in Trinidad, founding St James Writers Room in 2014. She is currently Lecturer on the MFA/MA in Creative Writing at Manchester Metropolitan University and a tutor at the Norwich Writers Centre.

Tamim Sadikali's reviews have appeared in *Open Pen*, *Bookmunch*, *Minor Literature[s]*, *Wasafiri*, *Critical Muslim* and *3A:M Magazine*. His story of 'me-but-not-me' became a sub-plot to *Dear Infidel* (Hansib, 2014). He has recently completed a short story collection.

Joseph Schreiber is a writer based in Calgary, Canada. He is the Criticism/Nonfiction Editor at *3:AM Magazine*. His reviews, essays and poems have been published in a variety of literary sites and publications including *Numéro Cinq*, *Minor Literature[s]*, *The Critical Flame*, *RIC Journal*, and *Poetry at Sangam*. He also maintains the literary site *Roughghosts*.

Azad Ashim Sharma is the director of the87press and the author of *Against the Frame* (Barque Press, 2017). He is currently studying for his MA Creative and Critical Writing at Birkbeck and has a collection of poetry entitled *Boiled Owls* forthcoming. His poems have also been published recently by *Stand Magazine*, the *Asian American Writers Workshop* and *Gutter Magazine*.

Christiana Spens is a writer, academic and artist based in Glasgow. She has written several books, including *The Portrayal and Punishment of Terrorists in Western Media* (Palgrave Macmillan, 2019) and *Shooting Hipsters: Rethinking Dissent in the Age of PR* (Repeater Books, 2016). She has a PhD from the University of St Andrews and is part of the Truth Tellers Collective, based at Kings College London, which creates and analyses artistic responses to political trauma. She also writes for publications such as *Studio International*, *Art Quarterly* and *Prospect* on art and politics.

Catherine Taylor is a freelance writer and editor and the former deputy director of English PEN. Her criticism, features, and essays appear in *Guardian Review, New Statesman, FT Life & Arts, The Economist, TLS, Independent, Irish Times* and *Aeon + Psyche* magazine. She is editor of *The Book of Sheffield: A City in Short Fiction* (Comma Press, 2019) and is currently at work on *The Stirrings*, a cultural memoir of Sheffield in the 1970s and '80s.

Tom Tomaszewski is a psychotherapist based in London. He published a novel, *The Eleventh Letter*, in 2016, and performs pieces at occasional events. Most recently he published a paper, *Noticing the Effects of Narcissism*, in *EMDR Therapy Quarterly*, the journal of the British EMDR Association. He enjoys mysteries, cinema, and practising EMDR and psychoanalysis.

Emma Jane Unsworth is an award-winning novelist and screenwriter. Her latest novel, *Adults*, was a *Sunday Times* Bestseller and is being adapted for television, with Unsworth writing the script. Her previous novel, *Animals*, was adapted into a film, for which Unsworth wrote the screenplay. The film premiered at Sundance Film Festival 2019 and Unsworth won the award for Best Debut Screenwriter at the British Independent Film Awards 2019. She also writes for various magazines and is a columnist for *Grazia*.

Saskia Vogel is from Los Angeles and lives in Berlin, where she works as a writer and Swedish-to-English literary translator. Her 2019 debut novel, *Permission*, has been translated into four languages. She has written on themes of sexuality, power and the art of translation for publications such as *Granta, The White Review, The Offing, The Skirt Chronicles*, and *The Paris Review Daily*. Her translations include work by Lina Wolff, Katrine Marçal, Karolina Ramqvist, Johannes Anyuru and the modernist eroticist Rut Hillarp.

Anna Vaught is a novelist, poet, essayist, short fiction writer, reviewer and editor; she is also a secondary English teacher, tutor